THE
Language
OF
Argument

THE
Language
OF
Argument

TWELFTH EDITION

Larry W. Burton
GEORGIA SOUTHERN UNIVERSITY

Daniel McDonald
UNIVERSITY OF SOUTH ALABAMA

Houghton Mifflin Company
Boston New York

Printed in the U.S.A.
Library of Congress Catalog Card Number 2006035873
Instructor's examination edition: ISBN 978-0-618-91771-6
Student edition: ISBN 978-0-618-91755-6

2 3 4 5 6 7 8 9—CRS—10 09 08 07

To Haley Spencer Burton

Contents

PART ONE

FORMS OF ARGUMENT   1

Persuasive Writing   3

Induction   25

Deduction   46

Semantic Argument   123

Statistics   149

PART TWO

ARGUMENT FOR ANALYSIS 177

PART THREE

LITERARY ARGUMENT   249

PART FOUR

EIGHT RULES FOR GOOD WRITING   287

Rule 1: Find a Subject You Can Work With   289

Rule 2: Get Your Facts   292

Rule 3: Limit Your Topic to Manageable Size   300

Rule 4: Organize Your Material   302

Rule 5: Make Your Writing Interesting   307

Rule 6: Make Your Writing Emphatic   312

Rule 7: Avoid Language That Draws Attention to Itself   317

Rule 8: Avoid Mechanical Errors   322

Final Reminders — 342

Appendixes — 349

Thematic Contents

◼ DIVERSITY

◼ EDUCATION

▓ LANGUAGE

▓ LAW

▧ SPORTS

▧ TOBACCO

▧ WOMEN'S ISSUES

Preface

The purpose of this edition remains the same: to teach students to read argument and provide material around which they can write their own argumentative essays. The selections cover a range of provocative issues. Some are notably persuasive; some are not. Most of today's hot topics are represented.

This edition is no longer than the previous one, but much of it has changed. In Part Two, "Argument for Analysis," we have added many readings to introduce new areas of argument:

- The cost of high school proms
- The death of Pope John Paul II
- Barry Bonds
- Intelligent design
- Nudity in the Bible
- Stem cell research (pro and con arguments)
- The usefulness of the SAT
- Terri Schiavo
- Airline regulations for "wide-bodied" passengers
- Workplace productivity
- Problems with male voters
- Physical appearance as a hiring factor

All of the arguments in the book are intended to create excitement and controversy in the classroom. Students can be asked to write on any of these, either analyzing the argument or responding to it. Teachers could conceivably assign a different title to each member of the class.

With two or three carefully chosen exceptions, the arguments illustrate good writing; they are models a student can learn from. The badly written pieces stand out. The writer lacks a purpose or gets lost in metaphor or obscure language or long sentences. When students complain that an essay is hard to read, ask them what features make it that way. They can learn from this.

As in the past, we have had to avoid areas that are too topical. This book won't appear until some months after we send in the manuscript. And the arguments must be relevant two or three years after that. Therefore, we have few titles on political subjects. These become old news quickly. Students today don't know about Vietnam or Iran/Contra. Those two years from now may have little interest in Saddam Hussein or Hurricane Katrina.

The short selections should produce a good result. We are not concerned that students know all the facts about some area of controversy (health-care reform or stem cell research, for example). We'll be happy if they can read an argument and say, "That's an unrepresentative sample" or "Where did those statistics come from?" or "Post hoc rides again!"

In the same way, the ninety brief arguments in the "Exercises for Review" sections should be useful. A teacher could divide a class into teams of four or five and give each team a dozen examples to work on.

In Part Three, "Literary Argument," we offer short selections by William Shakespeare, Andrew Marvell, John Donne, John Milton, Mary Wollstonecraft, Jonathan Swift, Jane Austen, Robert Browning, W. S. Gilbert, Irene B. McDonald, and Cardinal Newman. We hope teachers and students will have productive discussions about the ways in which imaginative literature illustrates principles of persuasive writing.

In Part Four, readers will find a new section on using the latest technology (see Rule 2: "Get Your Facts") and the Appendix includes examples of documenting material from electronic sources.

An instructor's manual with answers to exercises and discussion questions in the text is available at *college.hmco.com/pic/burton/12e.*

We are indebted to a number of people. We owe a great deal of thanks to Patricia Byrd for helping with the details that cropped up as this edition was rounding its way into final form.

We are grateful for the suggestions of the following reviewers, who provided useful guidance for this revision: Ashley Bonds, Copiah-Lincoln Community College; Brenda D. Boudreau, McKendree College; Cheryl Cobb, Tidewater Community College; Fawcett Dunstan, Community College Baltimore County; Gwyn Enright, San Diego City College; Geraldine Gutwein, Harrisburg Area Community College; Beth A. Klaisner, Wright State University; James R. Sodon, St. Louis Community College; Abby Spero, Montgomery College. Irene B. McDonald, Nicholas J. McDonald, Linda Burton, and Jim Clark offered materials that found their way into the book. They were—and happily still are—a sustaining intellectual resource.

Larry W. Burton
Daniel McDonald

THE
Language
OF
Argument

PART ONE

Forms of Argument

Japonica
Glistens like coral in all of the neighbouring gardens,
And today we have naming of parts.
—HENRY REED

Persuasive Writing

"We can never expect to prove anything upon such a point. It is a difference of opinion which does not admit of proof."

—JANE AUSTEN, *PERSUASION*

Most writing is persuasive writing.

When you write, you want something. You want people to be more informed and to accept your point of view. You want them to do something. You want them to see you in a positive way. Good writing is writing that gets the effect you want.

A study of the techniques of persuasion will make you more concerned about your audience and about forms of writing that have a good or bad effect on them. It will keep you from speculating vaguely on some topic that cannot be proven with evidence. It will help you know when you're making sense.

■ WIN YOUR AUDIENCE

To make a persuasive case, you have to know your audience. This will help you choose your words and shape your style.

One body of readers—say, a group of fraternity men—may respond to a direct appeal in strong language; another group—say, members of a Methodist congregation—may reject your whole argument if you use a word like "crap." One group will respond to wit, another to biblical quotations, and still another to a spread of statistics. Some readers will be offended if you write "ain't," "black," "symbiotic," "Dear Sir," or "and/or." Most audiences will be bored if you write vaguely about "Civic Responsibility" or "Tomorrow's Promise," but some audiences and occasions may call for rhetorical generalities. A detailed analysis of a social problem would be out of place at a political rally. The writing that would produce a great letter or advertisement might be unsuccessful in a sociology term paper. Some people will be impressed by "symbiotic relationships" and "a thousand points of light"; some won't. You have to know your audience.

3

A central feature in argument is creating a personal voice to express your views. Too often individuals with a strong case fail to be persuasive because their writing style makes them sound like a computer, a demanding top sergeant, a condescending aristocrat, or a stubborn child.

Let your writing sound like a human voice. Most readers respond favorably to a concerned and courteous tone. When addressing a committee, refer to the members in your presentation. ("I'm sure you ladies and gentlemen recognize how complex this question is.") When writing a business letter, try to use a direct, personal style. ("I'm sorry about your problem, Mr. Baker, and I hope we can do more for you next time.") Routinely, work to avoid a hostile tone. Don't write, "You must do this," when you can say, "We would like you to do this promptly" or "I need this by Wednesday." Never write, "I will not do this," when you can say, "For these reasons, I cannot do this now." Don't protest, "You're too ignorant to understand my point"; say, "I am sorry I did not make myself clear."

This tone can be difficult to maintain. At times you will want to rage out with righteous indignation or ego-gratifying scorn. Don't do it. Remember that anger never persuaded anyone. In argument, nice guys finish first.

The point deserves repetition. An Alabama attorney looking back on a lifetime of courtroom experience said, "When I was young, I thought that lawyers won cases. Later I believed that facts won cases. Now I think that clients win cases. When the facts aren't overwhelmingly against him, the jury will find for the person they like best." The celebrated trials of Jean Harris, Larry Flynt, John DeLorean, Bernhard Goetz, Jeffrey Dahmer, Martha Stewart, and Michael Jackson seemed to work on that principle.

The persuasive force of sweet good-nature can hardly be overstated. Occasionally, lawyers have to press a personal injury suit against Disneyland or Walt Disney World. The attempts fail because Disney is too fixed in the public mind as sweet, clean, and moral. One frustrated lawyer said, "You might as well try to sue Mother Teresa."

■ DEFINE THE ISSUE

A study of logic shows the importance of defining your issue. Some topics are flatly unarguable. They would produce vague speeches and incoherent essays.

Some issues rely more on a definition of terms than on evidence. When two people argue about whether George W. Bush is handsome, for example, they are not disagreeing about his hair, teeth, or clothes, but about a definition of *handsomeness.* If they can agree on a definition, they will probably agree about George W. Bush as well. Similarly, the question of whether capital punishment is wrong hinges not so much on the character of the act (the pain, the possibility of error, the protection afforded society) as on the definition of *wrongness.*

Aesthetic and moral questions are often unarguable because individuals cannot agree on the terms involved. The meaning of any word is what a body of people say it is. (A telephone is called a *telephone* because English speakers regularly use that word to denote it.) But in these special areas, people do not agree. What is handsomeness? What is beauty? Theoreticians have sought objective standards, but the quest seems fruitless. Is a Greek temple more beautiful than a Gothic cathedral? Is Bach's music better than Mary J. Blige's? Who can say? The decision rests on a subjective judgment that does not lend itself to evidence. When friends tell you they prefer U-2's music and the taste of Miller Lite, you can't argue with them. It's a good time to change the subject.

Like beauty, the idea of goodness is not easy to define. Seeking an objective basis for calling actions right and wrong, authorities have cited scriptural precedents; they have based systems on the inalienable rights of each human being; they have insisted that nature provides a moral example. But these definitions have not been universally accepted. If two individuals could agree that morality resides, say, in a natural law, they might then *begin* to talk about capital punishment. In general usage, however, moral terms remain so ill-defined that such issues cannot be argued meaningfully at all. (If you have to write on beauty or morality, focus your essay on some concrete example—say, arson or pop art or Vanna White—and work in as many "for example" and "for instance" references as you can.)

Moral and aesthetic questions are further removed from argument because they often produce emotional responses. Two individuals who agree in defining *handsomeness* might, for example, still disagree about George W. Bush because one objects to his conservative politics or his personal style. It is, of course, unreasonable to let emotions color such a judgment, but it happens all the time. You might be completely persuaded that capital punishment is cruel and barbaric yet, at a given moment, argue that hanging is too good for a child murderer or a political terrorist.

Vague definitions make argument impossible in many areas. Saab has been proclaimed "the most *intelligent* car ever built," and Royal Copenhagen "the only *elegant* musk oil cologne." The advertisement insists "Only Tareyton has the *best* filter!" Are these claims true? Until the key words are defined, the statements are no more subject to being proved with evidence than is "Razzle dragons, popple stix." Nonsense is neither true nor false.

Many areas of modern controversy hinge on definitions of terms. Do animals "talk"? Can children "sin"? Is running a "religious" experience? Is prostitution a "victimless" crime? Do computers "think"? Was Terry Schiavo "alive"? It depends on how you define the words.

Only when terms are defined and mutually accepted can you begin gathering evidence to prove something. You can, for example, argue whether Tiger Woods or Jack Nicklaus was the better golfer because their records in all tournaments, their total number of wins in major tournaments, and the qualities of a good golfer are generally agreed on. Is it true that smoking causes lung cancer, that Iraq had weapons of mass destruction, that Gordon's is the largest-selling gin in the world? These questions can at least be argued.

■ MAKE YOUR CASE

Finally, the study of argument will let you know when you are making sense. It will tell you if your sample is sufficient to support an inductive conclusion, if the expert you want to quote is a reliable authority, if your words express the meanings you want, and if your statistics are relevant.

A survey of logic will make you a more perceptive reader. You will be better able to recognize strengths and weaknesses in particular arguments. It will be harder for people to lie to you.

The essays in this book will show you writing patterns to imitate and to avoid. You can't become a good writer simply by knowing how words are spelled and where commas go. You need a clearly defined topic, a body of information, and a concern for the interests of your reader. *What you have to say is of the essence in good writing.* The study of logic should make what you have to say more meaningful.

And knowing how to write will make your ideas more persuasive. Of the arguments that follow, some are convincing and some are not. None is helped or hurt much by the facts defining the issue. Invariably, the successful arguments have a focus and a voice; they use language and layout that make them easy to read. The unsuccessful ones use techniques that turn off the reader.

Observe these techniques and learn to avoid them. An argument can't be persuasive if it isn't read.

EXERCISES

Can you argue the truth of these statements?

1. Basis—"At last, skin care for people with real skin."
2. Mexico City's Copper Dome is higher than the Empire State Building.
3. Beer drinkers make better lovers.
4. It is wrong to say "between you and I."
5. Every student should read *Hamlet*.
6. Time is a trapezoid.
7. Vacation in Florida—"The Rules Are Different Here."
8. "Blessed are the pure in heart, for they shall see God."
9. All prisoners eligible for parole should be tested for the AIDS virus.
10. "Only Armorall works like Armorall."
11. A diamond is forever.
12. No woman is happy with the way she looks.
13. Immorality is corrupting every area of our nation. Only a moral renaissance can save America now.
14. One way to relieve the gasoline shortage is to legalize marijuana.
15. L'Oreal—"Why be gray when you can be yourself?"
16. Pregnancy questionnaire—"Do you have any unusual-looking family members?"
17. Body tattooing is a form of art.

Restoring Perspective: $1,000 for the Prom Is Immoral

Peter A. Brown

My new hero is the principal who canceled his school's senior prom, not just to prevent underage drinking and sex at post-event parties, but to make the kids and parents consider how they spend their money.

It is the best recent example of an authority figure standing up to both the culture of conspicuous consumption and of rights without responsibilities.

When teenagers, or for that matter adults, think it is the norm to spend $200 on tennis shoes, $250 on blue jeans and $5 on a cup of coffee, it's no wonder our society has lost its sense of perspective.

What Kenneth Hoagland, the principal at Kellenberg Memorial High School in Uniondale, N.Y., did in refusing to accept the excesses of the prom, which he rightly labeled "an exaggerated rite of passage that verges on decadence," was demonstrate common sense.

His willingness to uphold his Roman Catholic school's values, even at the cost of alienating students and their parents, is an example for not just other educators, but for everyone in this society.

After all, you have to break some eggs to make an omelet, and in making his decision he certainly went against the accepted norm in one of the nation's most affluent counties.

But the lavishness of the prom culture to which he said "no," unfortunately, is the norm in most middle-class communities, too.

Here in Orlando, for instance, I know a parent who this month spent $500 for her daughter's homecoming dance, a much lower-key event than the prom.

"No" is a word that parents, educators and public officials across the country ought to learn to pronounce.

Hoagland rightly thought that there is something innately wrong with students spending $1,000 or more on their prom outfit, flowers, limousines and the rest. And that didn't count the cost of the post-prom parties—at beach houses or "booze cruises"—that students attended, where the use of alcohol and the lack of supervision created "a time of heightened sexuality in a culture of anything goes," as he put it. Kellenberg High School, he said, "Is willing to sponsor a prom, but not an orgy."

SOURCE: *Orlando Sentinel*, Oct. 21, 2005. Reprinted with permission.

And, not backing down, Hoagland put the blame squarely where it belongs.

"Over the years parents have become more active in creating the 'prom experience,' from personally signing for houses for a three-day drug/sex/alcohol bash, to mothers making motel reservations for their sons and daughters for the after-prom-get-togethers."

One group of students, obviously with parental help, had contracted to rent a house in the Hamptons, a swanky summer playground for the jet set, for 36 unsupervised hours at a cost of $20,000.

Last March, Hoagland warned the students and parents who organize the post-prom bashes to clean up their act. It did no good; the spring prom for the class of 2005 was just more of the same.

Immediately afterward, school administrators decided to scrap next spring's prom, but did not tell anyone until September, when they made their decision public.

Now, it is easy to applaud Hoagland for trying to stop those activities that are blatantly illegal—underage drinking and drug use. Discouraging, or at least making more difficult, teenage sex is also high on the public-acceptance meter, even in places like Long Island.

But, here is what Hoagland did that made me admire him so much: He took on the culture of affluence that is part of the environment, not just there but in most of this country.

In Uniondale, where Hoagland estimates the average income of his students' families to be $100,000 or more, at least the people have the money. Unfortunately, the mentality he refused to tolerate also shows its head in many less affluent areas, too.

"There is a root problem for all this, and it is affluence. Affluence changes people. Too much money is not good for the soul. Our young people have too much money," said Hoagland.

"Most people think of sex and murder when they hear the word morality. But here is a morality of money. The bad use of money or wealth in any form is immoral," he told the parents in announcing the prom cancellation.

Later, in an interview, he got to the heart of the matter: "We don't discuss often enough how money changes you. Now, even if you are in a situation where you can afford certain things, the question we should ask ourselves is, should I spend my money on that? We don't ask that question enough."

"Is it appropriate for a 17-year-old graduating from high school to spend that much" on a dance?

Brother Hoagland didn't think so, and neither do I.

How about you?

DISCUSSION QUESTIONS

1. How long did it take the author to get to his point? Do you think this helps the persuasive process?
2. Whom is the author addressing? Is he talking to high school students?
3. Does it make a difference that the principal was running a Roman Catholic school?
4. "Kellenberg is willing to sponsor a prom, but not an orgy." Is the "orgy" feature an essential part of his argument?
5. Does the author strengthen his case by not emphasizing the alcohol-drugs-sex excesses?
6. The principal cancelled the spring prom but didn't announce the fact until September. Why did he delay making the announcement?
7. "Too much money is not good for the soul." Do you think this is true?
8. Do you spend for $200 for tennis shoes and $250 for blue jeans? Would you if you could? Are you better off not doing that?

HELP WANTED IMMEDIATELY!

WOULD YOU STUFF ENVELOPES FOR
$300 TO $500
WEEKLY
$2 FOR EACH ENVELOPE YOU STUFF!

HELP SOLVE YOUR MONEY PROBLEMS. No more worries over inflation, recession, bills, and other costs. If you are looking for easy, extra income to relieve financial pressures, then you owe it to yourself to investigate our offer.

HERE IS YOUR CHANCE to earn extra money working at home by becoming an active participant in our successful mailing association. You receive cash daily for the envelopes you stuff and there is no limit. You stuff as many as you desire.

NO EXPERIENCE OR SPECIAL SKILLS ARE REQUIRED. Our HOME MAILER'S PROGRAM is designed especially for people with little or no business experience and provides step by step instructions.

$$

You may work in the comfort of your own home, choose your own hours, and set your own pace. So there is no need to leave your present job, you can do both. This kind of program is also ideal for students. The financial possibilities are unlimited — get the whole family to join in, or form workshops with your co-workers or friends. Beyond mailing our sales letter, you will reap huge profits from manufacturers anxious to utilize your services. Furthermore we will show you how to expand your operation and boost your new income as high as you wish to go.

HOW IS THIS POSSIBLE?

There are several mail order companies who want to expand their business, but do not want to hire more people. If they hired more employees, they would have to be supervised, rent more office space, and it would increase their insurance rates. It would be just as efficient for them to make an arrangement with an independent company to perform the same task.

This program is designed to help people cash in with a company that needs home workers. Each member is an independent home worker. You work for a company that renders an excellent commission to have their circulars mailed.

We invite you to take part in our success. The money you earn is up to you. There is no requirement on the number of pieces you mail each week. You can take on whatever amount you want and quit whenever you like. There are absolutely NO obligations.

All business can be done through the mail and we give you complete assistance on every step to insure your success. You can START THE SAME DAY YOU RECEIVE THE INSTRUCTIONS and begin RECEIVING MONEY WITHIN TWO WEEKS. You will be supplied with all the necessary materials to be stuffed.

OUR GUARANTEE

We welcome you to this program and extend to you our unconditional guarantee that everything we have said about this program is true and that you will be delighted with the money you make. Our goals and continued success depends upon your 100% satisfaction with the **HOME MAILER'S PROGRAM.**

TO GET YOU STARTED IMMEDIATELY, we must require a one time only fee of $12. This covers our expense in showing you what to do and guarantees you can work with us as long as you please. You will NOT be required or asked to pay for any additional information, manuals, or instructions. Inasmuch as we would like to send you these materials free of charge, we must protect ourselves from those who are not serious and have no intention but to satisfy their own curiosity. Naturally, no business can afford to send out costly material to everyone who writes in for it. This small charge insures that you will be sent the necessary material to start our program.

YOUR REGISTRATION FEE REFUNDED
when you submit your first 100 envelopes

DO NOT DELAY — START IMMEDIATELY!!!!
Do not let this extraordinary
opportunity pass you by!

DISCUSSION QUESTIONS

1. This circular appeared on a university bulletin board. What do you see in the text to suggest it's aimed at a specific audience?
2. Does the ad have an argument? What is it? At what point in the document did you know it?
3. Discuss these features of the ad:
   a. voice
   b. vocabulary
   c. use of white space
   d. type size
   e. subheadings
4. Are there any turnoffs to the ad? Why wouldn't you send $12 to the Home Mailer's Program?
5. How is this ad different from most help wanted ads? Does it do anything differently from a typical magazine ad for a product?
6. Ask your classmates if they want to participate in the Home Mailer's Program. Why wouldn't they want to? How many people do you know who make $300 to $500 weekly stuffing envelopes?
7. If you're going to "reap huge profits," why would you have to work two jobs? After all, the circular says you can "boost your new income as high as you wish to go."

Even Terri Schiavo's Death Won't Stop the Politicians

Carl Hiaasen

As this is being written, Terri Schiavo is still barely alive, and still easy prey for the politicians who have so despicably exploited her tragedy. They will exploit her in death, too. You can bet on it.

Rebuffed again by the courts, Gov. Jeb Bush hit a new personal low last week. He called a press conference to declare that a "renowned neurologist" had raised doubts about whether Schiavo was really in a "persistent vegetative state."

The doctor, William Cheshire, turns out to be a conservative evangelical who is renowned mainly to close friends and immediate family.

In addition to working at the Jacksonville branch of the Mayo Clinic, Cheshire is "director of biotech ethics" for an outfit called the Center of Bioethics and Human Dignity. He has expounded against stem cell research and other issues of interest dear to the Christian right.

Cheshire offered up his wisdom about Schiavo's condition after spending 90 minutes at her bedside and watching tapes provided by her parents, who've opposed removing her feeding tube. He did not perform a medical examination of Schiavo, which makes his report all the more suspect.

Dr. Ronald Cranford is a University of Minnesota neurologist who did examine Terri for the State of Florida. Here's what he told The New York Times: "You'll not find any credible neurogist or neurosurgeon to get involved at this point and say she's not vegetative. Her CAT scan shows massive shrinking of the brain. Her EEG is flat-flat. There's no electrical activity coming from her brain."

That's consistently been the medical finding, and one reason the courts have ruled repeatedly in favor of Michael Schiavo's efforts to remove his wife's feeding tube.

Even if Gov. Bush sincerely believes all those judges were wrong, it's reprehensible that he would at the 11th-hour scrounge up a sympathetic physician and try to pass him off as an expert on the vegetative condition.

SOURCE: *Mobile Register,* March 29, 2005. Reproduced with permission of *Miami Herald* in the format Textbook via Copyright Clearance Center.

Cheshire hasn't published a single paper on the subject in any known medical journal. Most of his articles focus on headache pain, which was never Terri Schiavo's problem.

But the governor wasn't finished posturing. He said the state Department of Children & Families might physically take custody of Schiavo because of anonymous allegations of abuse in the hospice.

Pinellas Circuit Judge George Greer promptly said he would tolerate no such theatrics. Still, Floridians had to marvel at the absurdity of Jeb seeking DCF "protection" for Schiavo. Under his watch the agency has been a disaster, marked by contract scandals, ineptitude and horror stories of children left to die or even disappear while under state supervision. Given a choice between DCF care and a hospice, take the hospice. At least you won't get misplaced there.

Speaking of lost, that's where some sober-minded Republicans find themselves after this debacle. The party that preaches state's rights and individual freedom has now given us the biggest, most intrusive federal government of all time.

That the Congress basically climbed into Terri Schiavo's private deathbed is not only disgraceful, it's scary. This was a family matter and nobody else's business. Five years ago, in the midst of their guardianship battle with her husband, Schiavo's parents conceded that their daughter was in a persistent vegetative state.

Then they went national, and that's when the circus started—the waling Bible-thumpers, the goofballs with their homemade crucifixes, the pious anti-abortion lobby and their rabidly misinformed bloggers. Close behind were politicians on the scent of votes and money.

"This is an important moral issue and the pro-life base will be excited that the Senate is debating (it)," said a memo sent last weekend to Senate Republicans, who then passed the bill that recycled the Schiavo case once more through the courts.

Topping the list of shameless exploiters is House Speaker and shake-down king Tom DeLay, who's already touting the Schiavo crusade to raise legal funds in advance of a possible unrelated indictment by Texas prosecutors.

Delay is highly selective with his compassion. He recently voted to slash Medicaid by $15 billion, which would adversely affect millions of needy patients who, unlike Schiavo, actually have a chance to recover.

Next among the hypocrites is Senate Majority Leader Bill Frist, a doctor who knows better. But he so badly wants to be president that he couldn't pass up a chance to ingratiate himself with evangelical church leaders.

As a lawyer, our own freshman Senator Mel Martinez also knew the inevitable outcome. Yet he had no qualms about floating false hope for Schiavo's parents in exchange for scoring a few brownie points with the right-to-lifers.

All this was staged with blithe disdain for the judicial process, which isn't surprising. The Bush administration loves to bad-mouth judges. How fitting that some of those who ruled in Michael Schiavo's favor were appointed by the president's own father.

The whole thing was one of the most cynical charades in memory. From the Congress to the White House to the statehouse, they all got their piece of Terri Schiavo.

By the time this columns appears, she might be gone, but you can be sure that the politicians and the zealots they're courting will never let this poor woman die.

Even when she's dead.

DISCUSSION QUESTIONS

1. Did the introduction to this essay catch your attention? How soon?
2. What does the information about Governor Bush and Dr. Cheshire tell you about argument by authority?
3. Compare the medical credentials of Dr. Cheshire and Dr. Cornford. Were their investigations thorough?
4. Do you admire the husband for wanting to remove his wife's feeding tube? Does this seem callous?
5. Why does Governor Bush get involved in the medical issue at all?
6. The governor is concerned about anonymous allegations about abuse in the hospice. If there were such allegations, why didn't he mention this?
7. How long would you like to be kept alive after your brain is dead?

Dr. Durant Demonstrates Psychokinesis

Dr. James Durant, Professor of Psychology at Millburn University, demonstrates to a companion his celebrated powers of psychokinesis. The photograph was taken at the Faculty Club before a dozen professors. The event was supervised by Dr. Xavier Crosert, Dean of the College of Arts and Sciences.

Courtesy of Redstone Wire Service.

DISCUSSION QUESTIONS

1. To establish the credibility of this argument, you must consider the photograph itself as well as the many references and sources involved. How reliable as authorities are each of the following?
   a. Dr. James Durant
   b. Professor of Psychology
   c. Millburn University
   d. a dozen professors at the Faculty Club

   e. Dr. Xavier Crosert

   f. Dean

   g. College of Arts and Sciences

   h. *The Language of Argument*

   i. Daniel McDonald and Larry W. Burton

   j. University of South Alabama

   k. Georgia Southern University

   l. Houghton Mifflin

2. If your investigation found all these sources to be reliable, might you still have reason to doubt the existence of psychokinesis?

Color Me Pro-Choice

Mitchell Farnum

I don't spend a lot of time with homosexuals, chain-smokers, feminists, porn-buyers, atheists, vegetarians, or problem drinkers—but when the issues get legal, I am with them. I am pro-choice.

I think adults should have options.

I want options. I want my Marriott room to have a Gideon Bible and porn movies. Let me decide if I want to buckle my seat-belt, or drive to 11:00 Mass, or swing out to the dog-track. Let me send my kids to public school or to Holiness Tabernacle Academy. I may invite Jews and blacks to join my private club, but don't tell me I have to accept orientals or women or somebody's cousin. It's *my* club.

I don't like people with oppressive theories. They come around telling everybody what to do. Local 7–11's shouldn't sell *Playboy*. Poor women can't have abortions. Nancy Cruzan should stay hooked to that machine for another seven years. Consenting adults must go into their bedrooms and behave sensibly. Who needs this crap?

I want to make choices, even dumb ones. If I buy my Big Mac with the large order of fries (and extra salt), that's OK. If I don't buckle my seat-belt, so what? If I smoke a pack or two a day, leave me alone! I've got my rights. And among them is the right to take the consequences of what I do. Man, it's *my* life!

Also, let me believe what I want to. You're hearing from a man who sub-scribes to the *National Enquirer* and the *Sun*. So the evidence is shaky about UFOs and the Shroud of Turin and vitamin E and the Kennedy assassination? So what? If I want to believe dramatic theories, that's fine. (Tomorrow I may send off $15.95 for a talisman containing Lourdes water.) And you're free to believe your theories. If you want to think Elvis is dead, that's your business.

All this freedom is for adults who can take care of themselves. With people who can't, OK, let's pass laws. I don't mind rules that protect kids and AIDS victims and neurotics and wheelchair people and the homeless. I want laws in areas where we're all helpless—those protecting the environment and the purity of foods. I can live with traffic regulations and *some* antigun laws. I want ex-cons and psychopaths to have trouble buying a gun, but don't tell me *I* can't buy one.

SOURCE: Reprinted by permission of the author.

Summing it up, I don't like meddling people. Spare me from censors and pro-lifers and gay-baiters and temperance advocates and anti-smoking Nazis and anybody who would enforce prayer or "political correctness" in the schools.

But don't get me wrong—I'm not some antagonistic nut. I love a lot of things—babies, Heineken beer, golden retrievers, Willie Nelson, my wife, the Atlanta Braves (with all their faults), and the Roman Catholic Church (with all its faults). And if you want to be Baptist or agnostic or gay or vegetarian, great! If you turn on to *All My Children* or Guns N' Roses, hey, that's fine with me. It's a big world, friend. Enjoy yourself.

Just stay off my back.

DISCUSSION QUESTIONS

1. Whether you agree with it or not, is this argument easy to read? What problems attend an argument that is not easy to read?
2. Specify the features that make this easy to read.
3. What is the author like? Do you find him appealing or unappealing?
4. How intelligent is the author? Is he just mindlessly angry, or is he well informed on the issues involved?
5. Do his extreme positions hurt his case? Do you think he really smokes two packs a day, refuses to wear his seat-belt, and believes that Elvis is alive?
6. Were you offended when he said he might not want women or orientals at his private club? Or when he said, "Who needs this crap?"
7. What is implicit in his complaints that "poor" women can't get abortions? That Nancy Cruzan should stay on her life-support machine "another" seven years?
8. Does the author just want to be left alone? Has he no compassion for the sufferings of people around him?
9. What is the purpose of the last paragraph, in which he affirms babies, golden retrievers, and Willie Nelson?
10. Does this argument sound like writing or talking? How does the author's "voice" help the case he's making?

Of Paul De Man and Deconstruction

Alice Kracke

SHROUD
By John Banville
Knopf, $25

The Irish author John Banville's "Shroud" is itself a shroud, a roman à clef concerning the life of Paul de Man (1919–1983) teacher at Cornell (1960–66) and Johns Hopkins (1967–1970), and distinguished Yale professor (1970–1983). Paul de Man is the father of American deconstruction or, more precisely, rhetorical reading: a theory of language which focuses on figurality—metaphor personification, symbol, etc.—and the production of meaning in a text. The amazing thing about Banville's novelization of this theory that confounds many is the irony behind "Shroud's" conception: Banville himself never attended university but is, rather, an autodidact. At once brilliant in its pastiche and clever in its construction, "Shroud" ends as uncertainly as it begins, which is appropriate considering that, within the realm of deconstruction, there is no *logos* and no *telos*. Suffice it to say, "Shroud" narratively performs the very theory it allegorizes. The effect for the reader of such a performance is that, when you finish "Shroud," you return to the book's beginning for some guidance or clue as to its meaning only to confront, once again, the book's first line: "Who speaks?"

"Shroud" does not answer that question nor does it mean to. The story engages quite suspensefully at times but ultimately resists, true to deconstruction, easy answers. Enshrouded in mystery the novel operates as a poststructural "Pilgrim's Progress"—replete with secular allegories—possessing a "tell-tale heart." As in the Edgar Allan Poe story, we have here a most unreliable narrator in the character of Axel Vander, internationally esteemed scholar, writer, teacher and intellectual. Poe's "The Purloined Letter," favorite of deconstructionists, also figures prominently in "Shroud" but is refigured in Banville's hands. That is, what has been stolen and hidden—in this case the nature of Vander's identity—has been right under one's nose all along. Or has it?

SOURCE: *Mobile Press.* Reprinted with permission.

The questions linger long after one finishes "Shroud," the central one being: Just who is Axel Vander? The real-life Vander, Paul de Man, was born in Antwerp, Belgium. From 1940 to 1942, during the Nazi occupation, de Man published 180 book reviews and articles in two Belgian newspapers, Le Soir and Het Vlaamsche Land, that had been taken over by collaborators. This fact did not surface, however, until 1987, four years after de Man's death. The revelation caused a seismic upheaval in academia and the aftershocks are still being felt. Scholars continue to discourse concerning it, in a sense perpetually resurrecting the figure of de Man.

Banville performs a similar reanimation of de Man through Vander, who meets a young woman he suspects is about to upset his life, and who does, but not in ways Vander anticipates. Vander the Pilgrim of this story, wanders throughout "Shroud" seeking some "other" to validate his existence, experiencing along the way "negative faith" as Banville puts it. When we meet Vander, blind in one eye, crippled in one leg and drunk, he is well ensconced in academic privilege on the U.S. West Coast in the fictional city of Arcady, presumably Stanford.

After receiving a letter from Antwerp from the young woman, Catherine Cleave, Vander grows increasingly paranoid regarding what she knows of his past. He decides to accept an invitation to speak at an academic conference in Turin, Italy, in order to meet Cleave and discover the extent of her knowledge. She meets him there, where we get glimpses of both their pasts.

Although Vander's past is ambiguous, we do know two things about our narrator: He lies and he drinks, heavily on both counts. Early in the novel, Vander says, "All my life I have lied. I lied to escape, I lied to be loved, I lied for placement and power; I lied to lie." Throughout the novel, between gulps of coffee and booze, Vander also tells us that he is starting to forget things. As if swilling repeatedly from the river Lethe, the more Vander drinks, the less he remembers. The result is a vexing conundrum regarding Vander's identity. The more you read, the more Vander seems to recede from your grasp until, at the end of the book, you ask yourself what Vander asks himself twice on the last page, "What am I to think?"

Indeed what is one to think of Vander? Vander speculates on just this question at the beginning of "Shroud" as he prepares to meet Cleave in Turin. Apostrophizing her, he says, "Perhaps . . . someday soon a publication will pop up from the presses in an obscure corner of academe with a posthumous essay in it, by you, on me, and I shall be disgraced, laughed at, hooted out of the lecture hall. Well, no matter."

A posthumous publication concerning de Man did "pop up" in 1989 with the publication of "Responses: On Paul de Man's Wartime Journalism," a tome containing essays by roughly 40 international intellects, Jacques Derrida, the French father of deconstruction, among them. Banville's response in "Shroud" is to offer de Man redemption. Again apostrophizing Cleave, Vander says, "I am going to explain myself, to myself, and to you, my dear. . . . The notion haunts me that I am being given one last chance to redeem something of myself . . . It occurs to me to wonder if that might have been your real purpose, not to expose me and make a name for yourself at all, but rather to offer me the possibility of redemption."

Banville made a name for himself before "Shroud." His novel, "The Book of Evidence," was shortlisted for the Booker Prize in 1989, and critics concur regarding his linguistic facility. Although his diction and command of language throughout "Shroud" are nothing short of genius, Banville lays down the authorial mask, aligning himself with Vander and de Man in a moment of sacrificial vulnerability. Vander says, "Though they might question my grasp of theory and even doubt my scholarship, all were united in acclaiming my mastery of the language, the tone and pitch of my singular voice; even my critics, and there were more than a few of them, could only stand back and watch in frustration as their best barbs skidded off the high gloss of my prose style. This surprised as much as it pleased me; how could they not see, in hiding behind the brashness and the bravado of what I wrote, the trembling autodidact hunched over his Webster's, his Chicago Manual, his Grammar for Foreign Students?"

As Banville shows in "Shroud," we all always already perform our identities, wearing masks that hinder us in seeing each other as well as ourselves. As in the altar call at a successful revival, Banville knows that his own response to the invitation puts the rest of us on the spot. Can we similarly respond and voluntarily remove our own masks? Significantly, neither Vander nor Cleave succeed in seeing the Shroud of Turin while they are there. As Banville's novel so deftly demonstrates, though, what's important is not the veil but the man behind it with whom, upon death, we will all finally come face to face.

DISCUSSION QUESTIONS

1. What is the author's point in writing this essay? What is she trying to convey?
2. How far did you read before you saw her purpose?
3. Is her case helped by the use of specialized vocabulary: roman à clef, figurality, autodidact, pastiche, logos, telos, etc.? How many of these words did you look up?

4. ". . . when you finish *Shroud*, you return to the book's beginning for some guidance or clue as to its meaning . . .": Does this sound like a book you're anxious to read?

5. "As Banville shows in *Shroud* we all always already perform our identities, wearing masks that hinder us in seeing each other as well as ourselves." Is it clear to you what this means?

6. After reading this essay, do you know more about Paul De Man than you did before you read the essay?

Induction

Ivan: I think my wife is having an affair with a florist.

Peter: Why?

Ivan: I came home and found a rose on the dinner table.

Peter: I think my wife is having an affair with a railroad man.

Ivan: Why?

Peter: I came home and found her in bed with a railroad man.

—RUSSIAN JOKE

Induction is the process of drawing a general conclusion from incomplete evidence. Most of the things you know, you know by induction.

You believe, for example, that polar bears are white. But because you haven't seen all polar bears, your judgment is based on limited evidence. The two or three polar bears you have seen were white. Those shown in *National Geographic* or on the Discovery Channel were white. Everyone you know agrees they are white. From this information, you reasonably decide that all polar bears are white.

This process is induction. You consider evidence you have seen or heard to draw a conclusion about things you haven't seen or heard. The intellectual movement from limited facts—called a *sample*—to a general conviction is called an *inductive leap.*

Most conclusions regarding past, present, and future events are based on this kind of leap. You believe, for example, that Balboa discovered the Pacific Ocean, that taking Tylenol eases a headache, and that the Republicans will win the next presidential election. Because you can never secure all the evidence relating to these questions, you reasonably make judgments from the evidence you have.

It is equally reasonable, when you hear induced conclusions, to inquire about the number and kinds of facts that went into making them. For a claim to be credible, its sample must be (1) known, (2) sufficient, and (3) representative. If you are told simply that the FBI is directed by Jewish conspirators, you can withhold belief on the grounds that the sample is not known. No evidence is given to support the accusation. If you hear a famous athlete's low IQ cited to demonstrate that athletes (or members of the athlete's race or nationality) are generally ignorant, you can respond that the sample is not sufficient. One example proves nothing about a large group. And if you hear the cruelties of the Spanish Inquisition used as evidence of the repressive views of Catholics in general, you can insist that the sample is not representative. Spanish practice in the fifteenth century is hardly typical of worldwide Catholicism today.

You should recognize such unsupported claims when you see them. Try to keep them out of your own writing.

■ IS THE SAMPLE KNOWN?

You frequently hear statements that lack evidence. An advertisement announces that "Ban is preferred by seven out of ten American women." A *Globe* headline reports "Seven Out of Ten Husbands Are Cheating." Rumors whisper that green M&Ms are aphrodisiacs, that McDonald's hamburgers contain worms, and that Procter & Gamble is involved in Satan worship. Such claims can be dismissed if no evidence is offered to support them.

A variation popular with exposé writers is to make an extravagant claim and then point to conclusive evidence—which happens to be unavailable. They argue that superbeings from outer space built Stonehenge and that President Warren Harding was murdered by his wife—then they regret that evidence is lost in the past. They talk confidently about Bigfoot, Atlantis, and the Loch Ness monster—and then lament that proof remains out of reach. For years, tabloids reported arthritis cures, sacred statues that talk, and other wonders that occurred "behind the Iron Curtain." Popular writers insist that UFOs are extraterrestrial spaceships and that a massive conspiracy led to the attempted assassinations of President Reagan and Pope John Paul II—then they protest that government officials and law enforcement agencies are withholding crucial evidence.

When you become familiar with such stories, you begin to see a pattern. The tabloids and the talk shows tell you about the audio tapes of intimate conversations between President Kennedy and Marilyn Monroe. They mention a dog who can read and an 87-year-old woman who is pregnant. Where are these amazing wonders? You know where they are. They're elsewhere, in some distant place. You can't get there from here.

All these are inductions with an absent or unknown sample.

An immediate and notably disturbing example occurred not long ago. The United States invaded Iraq because of its threatening weapons of mass destruction. Billions of dollars and thousands of casualties later, we learned there were no weapons of mass destruction. Some examples are obviously insufficient.

IS THE SAMPLE SUFFICIENT?

Induction with an insufficient sample is also common. You regularly hear charges like these:

> Most labor leaders are crooks. Look at Tony Boyle, Frank Brewster, Jimmy Hoffa, and Roy Williams.
> Running is dangerous. You saw what happened to Jim Fixx.
> Don't talk to me about Puerto Ricans. I lived next to a Puerto Rican family for two years.

Clearly, the indicated samples—*four* labor leaders, *one* runner, and *one* family—are inadequate evidence on which to base any broad conclusion.

Insufficient samples lead to stereotyping. They underlie the simplistic descriptions you hear about college professors, Republicans, epileptics, Southern Baptists, African Americans, Jews, Swedish stewardesses, athletes, and cab drivers.

Persuaders commonly try to enhance the effect of an insufficient sample by insisting their examples are "typical" or "average." In argument, the words "typical" and "average" deserve immediate suspicion.

IS THE SAMPLE REPRESENTATIVE?

A sample is *unrepresentative* when it is not typical of the whole class of things being studied. It is easy to see that you cannot gauge your town's attitude toward a proposed liquor tax by polling only the citizens at a corner tavern or only members of a local fundamentalist church.

Nevertheless, conclusions based on an unrepresentative sample can sound persuasive on first hearing; for example, "Women are better drivers than men; they have fewer accidents." Here the sample is large enough—a substantial body of accident statistics—but it is not broad enough to be meaningful. The conclusion concerns *all drivers*, but the sample group includes only *drivers who have had accidents*. To be representative (that is, typical of the whole area under discussion), the sample must include all four groups involved:

1. Men
2. Women
3. Drivers who had accidents
4. Drivers who had no accidents

This broad sample would show that there are fewer women in automobile accidents because there are fewer women driving. The isolated accident statistics are meaningless if they are not compared to those for all drivers.

Similarly, if you hear that 80 percent of all San Quentin convicts came from homes that served liquor, you can't draw much of a conclusion. The implied judgments describe *everyone,* but the sample includes only *convicts;* there are no general statistics with which to make comparison. Perhaps 80 percent of *all* homes serve liquor. Then, of course, the narrow statistics become meaningless.

Photographic evidence is usually induction with an unrepresentative sample. A candidate's campaign photographs show him and his loving wife walking on the beach with their children. They show him late at night reading important books and thinking deeply about the problems of the day. The pictures you see are chosen from dozens taken by professional photographers and media people who arranged settings, chose clothes, and told the candidate how to stand and what to do. When you see such photos, ask yourself, "What would this candidate look like if I saw him right now?"

You must remember too that photos can be faked. The cover of *TV Guide* (August 25, 1990) carried a glamorous picture of Oprah Winfrey. Later it was revealed that her head had been superimposed on the body of Ann-Margaret. Recent literature celebrating multiple UFO sightings at Gulf Breeze, Florida, offered sensational prose and doctored photographs.

Any induced conclusion is open to question, then, if its sample is too small or unduly weighted in some way. *The Hite Report* on female sexuality was based on responses to questionnaires mailed to chapters of the National Organization for Women, abortion-rights groups, and university women's centers; on information from women who saw notices in newspapers, the *Village Voice, Mademoiselle, Bride,* and *Ms.* magazines, and who wrote in for the questionnaires; and on responses from female readers of *Oui* magazine, which ran the questionnaire in its entirety. Clearly, the sample does not represent all American women.

Polling can produce interesting aberrations. Currently ESPN invites audience members to vote on the Web on who is going to win the NCAA football championship and who is going to win the Heisman Trophy this year. This will produce results that are (1) statistical and (2) meaningless.

Any poll with a selective sample—that is, where some individuals choose to respond to it and others do not—is unrepresentative. Those who choose to respond cannot represent those who don't.

■ POLLING

People can misuse a poll to make it support a favored opinion. They can announce the results of surveys that were never taken. (Politicians have for years made good use of "private polls" to enhance the prestige of a lagging candidate.) They can phrase a poll question to draw the response they seek. (Evangelist Jerry Falwell asked, "Do you approve of the present laws legalizing Abortion-on-Demand that resulted in the murder of more than one million babies last year? Yes _____. No _____.")). Or they can inflate others' polls. A memorable example occurred in 1972, when Washington television station WTTG asked viewers to write in their opinion of President Richard Nixon's decision to mine North Vietnamese harbors. The final poll result showed 5157 supporting the president and a much smaller number opposing him. Later investigation showed that some 4000 of the votes favorable to Nixon came directly from the Committee for the Reelection of the President.

What is an adequate sample on which to base a reliable judgment? There is no easy answer. It varies with both the character of the question and the degree of probability you want.

You should remember, however, that a small sample—if genuinely representative—can sustain a broad conclusion. George Gallup assesses the opinions of the American public by polling 1500 individuals. But because his sample is chosen so that every adult American has an equal chance of being interviewed, the Gallup poll, like similar polls, is a reliable source of information. The mathematical probability is that, 95 times out of 100, a selection of 1500 anonymous people will give results no more than 3 percentage points off the figures that would be obtained by interviewing the whole population. In the past 23 national elections, the Gallup predictions were an average of 2.3 percentage points off the exact results.

In the 1980 presidential election, however, both the Gallup and the Harris polls were 4 percentage points off the final total. Apparently many voters made up their minds at the last minute, after these polls had been completed. Both Carter's and Reagan's personal pollsters, who surveyed opinion right up to election eve, predicted the final results exactly.

In later contests, the polls were impressively accurate. In 1984, Gallup predicted Ronald Reagan would win 59 percent of the vote; he won 59.1 percent. In 1988, it said George Bush would win 56 percent of the vote; he won 54 percent. In 1992, Gallup said Bill Clinton would win 43 percent of the vote; he won exactly 43 percent. In 1996, Gallup predicted President Clinton would win reelection with 50 percent of all registered voters; he won 49.9 percent. In 2000 Gallup described the election as a virtual tie, and the popular vote supported this prediction. George W. Bush had 48 percent, while Gore captured 48.3 percent of the vote. In 2004, Gallup said George W. Bush had 49 percent support for the presidency. He received 50.7 percent of the vote.

Burns Roper, head of the Roper Organization, said, "When I see a poll result and it's opposite to my personal feelings, my first instinct is to reexamine my personal feelings."

■ OCCAM'S RAZOR

Even in everyday experience, you commonly use very limited information to draw a tentative conclusion. This is not unreasonable. If you see that a friend is not wearing her engagement ring and is behaving despondently, you may speculate that she has broken her engagement. The evidence is not sufficient for you to offer condolences, but it will keep you from making jokes about marriage.

If you hear from a friend that a new restaurant is disappointing, you will probably choose not to eat there—at least until you hear a contrary report. Your conclusion is based on a tiny sample, but it is all the sample you have. As your sample grows, so will your degree of conviction.

With induction, you should remember *Occam's razor,* the maxim that when a body of evidence exists, the simplest conclusion that expresses all of it is probably the best. A classic illustration occurred in 1967, when New Orleans District Attorney James Garrison sought to prove that Clay Shaw, a local businessman, was involved in the assassination of President Kennedy. He submitted that Shaw's address book carried the entry "Lee Odom, P.O. Box 19106, Dallas, Texas," and that the number "PO 19106," when properly decoded, became "WH 15601," the unlisted phone number of Jack Ruby, slayer of Kennedy's assassin Lee Harvey Oswald. (The process involved "unscrambling" the numerals and—since P and O equal 7 and 6 on a telephone dial—subtracting 1300.) Thus Garrison used the entry in Shaw's address book as inductive evidence leading to a sensational conclusion. But Occam's razor suggests a simpler explanation, one that proved to be true: Shaw was acquainted with a businessman named Lee Odom, whose Dallas address was P.O. Box 19106.

You should remember Occam's razor when you read the many books and articles that "reexamine" famous crimes. Routinely, they conclude that people like Lee Harvey Oswald, Alger Hiss, Lizzie Borden, Bruno Hauptmann, Carl Coppolino, James Earl Ray, the Rosenbergs, Alice Crimmins, Jeffrey MacDonald, the Atlanta child murderer, and Sacco and Vanzetti were really innocent. The true criminal was either a shadowy figure whom nobody saw or members of some complex and incredible conspiracy. Occam's razor says that the person with the motive and the opportunity and the gun is probably guilty. It submits that the 16-year-old Greek girl who had an illegitimate baby probably was not captured and impregnated by space aliens.

As you read, carefully examine the facts underlying conclusions. Are they given? Are they sufficient and representative? As you write, support your generalizations as much as you can.

EXERCISES

How reliable are these inductive arguments?

1. In a study of a possible relationship between pornography and antisocial behavior, questionnaires were sent to 7500 psychiatrists and psychoanalysts, whose listings in the directory of the American Psychological Association indicated clinical experience. Over 3400 of these professionals responded. The result: 7.4 percent of the psychiatrists and psychologists had cases in which they were convinced that pornography was a causal factor in antisocial behavior; an additional 9.4 percent were suspicious of such a connection; 3.2 percent did not commit themselves; and 80 percent said they had no cases in which a causal connection was suspected.

2. Do you prefer your hamburger flame-broiled or fried?

3. In an article warning of the dangers of cholesterol, *Time* showed the clogged arteries in the heart of an 85-year-old woman.

4. How can you argue that large families frustrate the individual child? Benjamin Franklin was the eighth child of his parents. There were six in the Washington family, and Abraham Lincoln had seven brothers and sisters. The Jeffersons numbered 10; the Madisons, 12; the Longfellows, 8; and the Beethovens, 12.

5. Do you prefer a hamburger that is grilled on a hot stainless steel grill or one cooked by passing the raw meat through an open gas flame?

6. *Psychology Today* asked its readers to answer questions about paranormal activity. The responses showed that 85 percent of the women and 78 percent of the men believe ESP exists. Wow!

7. I don't care what you say about stereotypes. Most of the blondes I know are dumb.

8. In August 1994, immediately after Michael Jackson married Lisa-Marie Presley, a Time/CNN poll was conducted by the Yankelovich Partners. They polled 600 people, a carefully chosen, representative sample, and produced a result in which the margin for error is ±4 percent. The result: the largest group of respondents—41 percent—believe the marriage won't last a year.

9. Cola drinkers were asked to compare glasses of Coke and Pepsi for taste. The Coke was in a glass marked Q and the Pepsi in a glass marked M. A majority of those tested said they preferred the taste of Pepsi.

10. Certainly it's obvious from the newspaper reports that rich and famous people have a higher proportion of divorces than the general public.

11. A study of 3400 New York citizens who had had a recent heart attack showed that 70 percent of them were 10 to 50 pounds overweight. Clearly, obesity is the cause of heart disease.

12. Arguing that eighteenth-century English poetry was essentially prosaic, Matthew Arnold offered a passage from "Pope's verse, take it almost where you will":

    To Hounslow Heath I point and Banstead Down:
    Thence comes your mutton and these chicks my own.

13. Don't tell me that homosexuals aren't sick. I'm a psychiatrist with a large number of homosexual patients, and all are deeply disturbed. Every one of them.

ESSAY ASSIGNMENTS

Write an essay either affirming or opposing one of these claims. The arguments you encounter in your background reading will probably be inductive, and so will your essay.

1. This school needs an honor system.
2. Prisoners should be brainwashed.
3. ESP has been proven to exist.
4. Opera is a waste of time.
5. Rock music is a national danger.
6. Jogging is a perfect exercise.
7. Gays and lesbians should not be allowed in the Boy Scouts and Girl Scouts.
8. The drinking age should be raised to 24.
9. X is worth saving. (Fill in the X.)

Cast Men Out of Polling Places

Matthew Miller

Tired of timid bromides offered by both parties that can't make a difference? Well, here's an idea so far outside the box it may not get the hearing it deserves. It's time to disenfranchise men and allow only women to vote.

This isn't pandering to the fairer sex; it's practical. And I'm not talking about forever. If we could deny men the vote for, say, five years—which strikes me as modest payback for the centuries women were kept suppressed and voteless—we could create a better, saner America.

Why do I say this? Suppose that you want an America in which everyone has basic health coverage, every full-time worker earns a living wage, and every poor child has a great teacher in a fixed-up school. I'm with you; in fact, I want these things so much I wrote a book about how both parties might come together on this agenda in ways that blend the best of liberal and conservative approaches—and while still leaving government as small as it was when Ronald Reagan was president. After asking some top political consultants how to make the ideas more actionable, I commissioned a poll for the book as well.

That's when I found out: Men are the problem. "Welcome to my world," said my pollster, Guy Molyneux of Peter Hart Research, who knew what was coming.

At first glance, as I read the poll results, I thought his prediction would prove wrong. Health care was the first area we tested. The proposal was to give low-income workers who don't get insurance from their employers a federal grant that allows them to purchase basic health coverage.

After hearing brief arguments for and against the idea, 57 percent of women favored it; only 29 percent opposed.

Men supported it 51–43—not a resounding margin, but one still suggesting they view health care as ripe for action.

(Interestingly, Republican women favored the health care proposal by 52–32, while GOP men opposed it, 38–52. If those ladies would just have a word with their husbands, I thought, we'd have this thing sold.)

But that was the high-water mark for men, who plainly tune out and begin brooding about their guns once you get past health coverage.

The next proposal we tested aimed to do something about the tens of millions of people living in or near poverty despite living in homes headed by full-time workers. We asked voters about greatly increasing the federal tax credit for low-wage workers, so that full-time workers would have an income of at least $9 an hour, lifting most above the poverty line.

This federal living wage supplement won by 51–39 among women; among men it lost by 40–52.

Finally, we tested a proposal to dramatically raise salaries for the best teachers in order to recruit higher-caliber college graduates, especially for the poor kids who need better teachers the most. The plan would also make it easier to fire the poorest-performing teachers. Women supported the concept 46–40 men opposed it 35–56.

Each of the proposals we polled had to be oversimplified to fit into a short survey, but the message came through loud and clear: This kind of agenda could pass on Venus; it's an uphill battle on Mars.

Everyone has a theory purporting to explain why this is so. Women are nurturing types who cherish health care and education; men think about battleships and nukes. Makes sense, I suppose, but I don't pretend to know the full answer, and I'd just as soon skip the pscyhoanalysis.

I'm not saying men are irredeemable. They can learn. They can be educated. But look what we're working with. Who knows how long it will take men to get wise to what makes for a decent society? If we're looking for results in that can-do American spirit, why wait?

I say, deal men out of the vote for five years. Put the right sports on TV and they'll hardly notice. When the dust clears we'll have one heck of a country. Can't Oprah, Dr. Phil and the other megahosts who reach women get this debate going?

DISCUSSION QUESTIONS

1. Do you feel this is a serious argument? Does the author really want men to be denied the vote? If the answer is no, what does the author want?
2. The argument is built around three poll questions. Does the poll seem reliable? How does the author show this?
3. Is this written in scientific language? Comment on the terms used: "timid bromides that can't make a difference," "a fixed-up school," "brooding about their guns," and "time it takes for men to get wise." Is this good writing?
4. Is it significant that Republican men are more likely to oppose health care changes than women? Who makes the laws in Congress?
5. One suggestion is that better teachers are paid more than inferior ones. How can inferior teachers be identified?
6. Do you think Oprah could, in fact, "get this debate going"?

Praying for Pope John Paul II's Death May Be More Appropriate

William F. Buckley, Jr.

At church on Sunday the congregation was asked to pray for the recovery of the pope. I have abstained from doing so. I hope that he will not recover.

The seizure brought on by his dramatic trip to the hospital a week ago suggests the international sense of his indispensability. Pope John Paul is a graphic figure in the lives of Catholics and many non-Catholics. He is, of course, a towering theological figure who has presided over the development of Catholic thought and practice for the 26 years of his papacy. He is a major historical figure, who began as a Catholic seminarian in a Poland subservient first to a Nazi overlord (they hanged him in Nuremberg), then to a communist overlord (nothing happened to him—the communists are never prosecuted).

I remember him as he was leaving Havana to return to Rome. Fidel Castro was there to recite the diplomatic amenities. The pope was standing on the gangway of his airplane and suddenly rain fell. As John Paul spoke under an improvised parasol, his three-minute farewell address evolved, in near-perfect Spanish, into a homily on water's purifying mission. All of Cuba watched on television, no doubt hoping, for an exhilarating moment, that Castro would melt away, Cuba shriven from the antipodal reign of a tyrant who came to power even before the pope did, and will outlast him.

Unless it were to happen that Castro died tomorrow, and the pope a week later; but we must see through the blur of the rain to realities of the day, which are that the pope almost died the day that he was taken to the hospital. "We got him by a breath," one medico leaked the news, and another said, "If he had come in 10 minutes later, he would have been gone."

The temptation is, always, to pray for the continuation of the life of anyone who wants to keep on living. The pope is one of these. In the past, he recorded that he did not plan ever to abdicate, that he would die on the papal throne. It is presumptuous, in thinking about John Paul, to suppose that in arriving at that decision he was motivated by vainglory. What exactly he had in mind we do not know, but can reasonably assume that he was asserting pride in physical fortitude, consistent with his days as a mountain climber and a skier. Perhaps there is a element of vanity there. Not many sovereigns leave the throne, except at the hands of embalmers.

There is the further question, distinctive to the throne of St. Peter. To leave it before death can be construed as forsaking a mission charged by God almighty. That isn't the consensus of theologians.

Cardinal Angelo Sodano, the Vatican's secretary of state, said simply, "If there is a man who loves the Church more than anybody else, who is guided by the Holy Spirit . . . that's him. We must have great faith in the pope. He knows what to do."

What to do includes clinging to the papacy as a full-time cripple, if medicine, which arrested death by only 10 minutes, can arrest death again for weeks and even months. But the progressive deterioration in the pope's health over the last several years confirms that there are yet things medical science can't do, and these include giving the pope the physical strength to coordinate and to use his voice intelligibly.

So, what is wrong with praying for his death? For relief from his manifest sufferings? And for the opportunity to pay honor to his legacy by turning to the responsibility of electing a successor to get on with John Paul's work? Muriel Spark commented in "Memento Mori": "When a noble life has prepared old age, it is not decline that it reveals, but the first days of immortality." That cannot be effected by the hospital in which the pope struggles.

DISCUSSION QUESTIONS

1. Does the author genuinely want Pope John Paul II to die? Is this a cruel attitude?
2. What is the author's attitude toward Pope John Paul II? Is he in any way critical?
3. Buckley is sometimes mocked for using pompous and erudite language. Does the language here seem pompous or erudite?
4. Comment on the use of argument by authority in this article.
5. Does the attack on Fidel Castro help this argument? Why or why not?

We Don't Need Immigrants

Dan Stein

America needs a "time out" or pause in immigration. The reason is simple: We are in the middle of the largest sustained flow of immigration in American history. We need a time out to ask ourselves "Why?"

Why do we need more immigration? Why add 100 million more people?

- Do we need more people? Are we underpopulated? Not likely.
- Is there an acute labor shortage now in the United States? No one believes that.
- Not enough traffic? C'mon!
- Too much prime farmland or wetlands to pave over, water tables too high in California and Florida, too much wildlife in what's left of our national parks? What do you think?
- Too much beachfront property going undeveloped? You find it.
- Do we need immigration to improve public education? Been to L. A. or Miami public schools lately?
- Does immigration reduce the U.S. crime rate? Not a chance.
- How about to improve medical care? Give me a break.
- Do we need immigration for our national security? Obviously not.
- Are we too homogeneous to be a legitimate nation? We're pretty diverse now. How would you say things are going?

Bottom line: We don't need immigration now, so why have it? We once needed immigration to settle a wilderness, and later to fuel the labor needs of the early industrial revolution. That ended with the Model T. For 20 years, we've had a high immigration rate without asking this basic question: Why have it at all?

America's great strength has been the American people and our innovative spirit, and our self-reliance. We once had abundant resources and favorable geography that enabled our people to prosper as we developed the nation.

The cultural inheritance and commercial foundation laid down by the Framers and early settlers proved a durable template to absorb periodic groups of immigrants as they were needed.

Today, we don't need immigrants, but they come anyway.

Current law runs an immigration system that lets immigrants in because a relative came earlier—very nepotistic. This process, called pyramiding chain migration, works like a chain letter, multiplying numbers and creating huge backlogs.

Other evidence is emerging as well: Nepotism means immigrants come because of who they know, not what they know. Result? Immigrants are more likely than natives to be less skilled, less educated, rely more on welfare, be in jail and cost more than they contribute.

A moratorium or pause in immigration would stop an endless flow of newcomers long enough to peer into the future, catch our breath and change course.

We need this national debate. We owe it to our children and grandchildren, if not ourselves.

DISCUSSION QUESTIONS

1. Who is the intended audience of this argument? Discuss these possibilities:
   a. senators and representatives
   b. all U.S. citizens
   c. naturalized U.S. citizens
   d. immigrants
2. The author says, "We are in the middle of the largest sustained flow of immigration in American history." How many immigrants is he talking about? Where does the figure of 100 million come from? Does it matter?
3. The author uses ten bullets, all in the form of question and answer, to address various issues. Are the questions provocative? Where's the evidence for his claims?
4. What evidence is offered for "Immigrants are more likely than natives to be less skilled, less educated, rely more on welfare, be in jail and cost more than they contribute"? Is he working with a known sample? A representative sample of immigrants? A sufficient sample? Is he stereotyping?
5. The author says that "immigrants come because of who they know, not what they know." Discuss the consequences of admitting immigrants because of "what they know."
6. Is the writing interesting? Provocative? How do the bullets affect the way you read the argument?
7. One feature of good writing is real names. Why doesn't Stein mention the names of famous immigrants?
8. Why is this essay less persuasive than it could have been?

Ban Boxing

Robert E. McAfee

As a practicing physician, I am convinced that boxing should be banned.

First, boxing is a very visible example that violence is accepted behavior in our society—outside the ring as well as inside. This sends the wrong message to America's youth, and at a time when so many kinds of violence are on the rise, it is a message we should stop.

Second, boxing is the only sport where the sole object is to injure the opponent. Think about what a knockout really is: It is a cerebral concussion that knocks the victim senseless! Boxing, then, is morally offensive because its intent is to inflict brain injuries on another person. And it is medically indefensible because these injuries so often lead to irreversible medical consequences, such as subdural hematoma, nonfatal acute intracranial hemorrhages, "punch drunk syndrome," progressive neurological disorder and serious eye conditions.

Third, medical science can't take someone who has suffered repeated blows to the head and restore that person to normal function. Many physicians, with new methods of brain scanning, have seen an otherwise young and healthy individual sustain serious and permanently disabling injuries due to boxing, sometimes in just one fight. This causes many physicians to conclude that our society should ban boxing. And sadly—slowly but surely—as many of our nationally known veteran boxers can no longer hide the long-term effects of brain injury, the public is beginning to understand what only doctors and family members previously knew.

What about the argument that injuries occur in other sports? Quite simply, in those sports, injuring the opponent is not the accepted method of scoring or winning. And in those sports, there is an attempt to wear protective equipment that will minimize injury. But scientific evidence shows there is no really effective way to prevent boxing injuries that may have a lifetime effect—even from one fight.

And finally, to those who say boxing "gives poor kids an opportunity to get out of the ghetto," I have a better suggestion. Let's take each young person with that precious, undamaged brain and combine some education with that same commitment to excellence he has for boxing. I guarantee that

SOURCE: Reprinted from *USA Today*. Reprinted by permission of the author.

youngster better success over a lifetime—and perhaps a longer and healthier life, too.

Boxing is morally and medically offensive. So as a physician, I believe boxing should be banned.

DISCUSSION QUESTIONS

1. How effective are the author's introduction and conclusion? Is it clear what he is talking about?
2. The author makes three arguments against boxing. What are they? Is one of them more compelling and persuasive than the others? Why?
3. The author challenges two arguments made by people who defend boxing. What problems arise when such challenges are made?

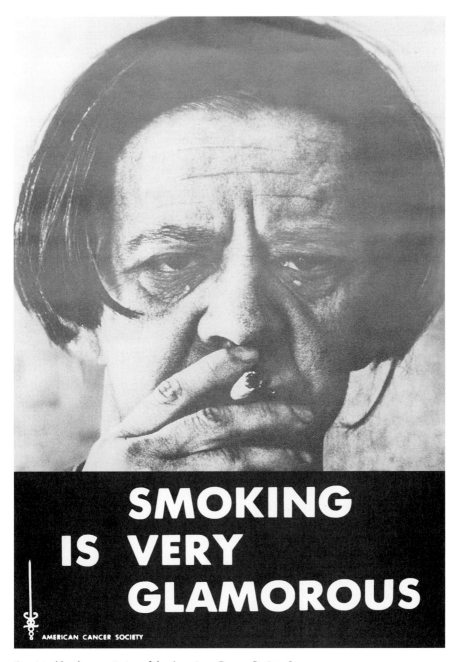

Reprinted by the permission of the American Cancer Society, Inc.

DISCUSSION QUESTIONS

1. The author uses irony. What is really meant by the claim that "Smoking is very glamorous"?
2. If the author is making a statement about how smokers look, what is the evidence?
3. Where do you think the Cancer Society people and their photographer found this woman? Give reasons for your answer.
4. Put in terms of inductive argument, is the sample known, sufficient, and representative?
5. What does this argument tell you about photographic evidence in general?

Fast Food Terror: A Tale of Two Cities

Timothy Wheeler, M. D.

By now it is an all too familiar nightmare. Violent armed robbers take over a restaurant, terrorizing employees and customers. The predators herd the hapless victims into a refrigerator with the intention of killing them. Shots are fired, and the gruesome disaster ends.

Wait. This isn't the story of a Wendy's restaurant in New York City last week. It is the eerily similar drama played out in a Shoney's restaurant in Anniston, Alabama in 1991. But this story had a just, if not exactly happy ending. That time, it was the criminals, not the good guys, who were shot.

In nearly identical scenarios—the violent takeover of a restaurant by armed criminals—one outcome was a hideous tragedy, and the other a triumph of courage. The difference in results was no accident. It was the logical conclusion of deliberate and widely divergent public policy in the two states where the crimes occurred.

New York doesn't trust its citizens to arm themselves for self-defense. Alabama does. Thomas Terry, the hero of Anniston, was discreetly but legally carrying a .45 caliber handgun when the robbers took over the restaurant. Facing two armed thugs, Terry shot one dead and severely wounded the other. None of the other patrons was harmed, other than Terry, who sustained a grazing wound to the hip.

Alabama law allows broad discretion for local law enforcement officers to grant handgun carry licenses to "suitable person[s]." Thomas Terry amply proved himself such a suitable person by risking his own life to save the lives of nearly two dozen customers. What an incalculably precious gift he gave them! Affirming Alabama's statutory recognition of the right to carry a gun, the state constitution proclaims "that every citizen has a right to bear arms in defense of himself and the state."

By contrast, the New York gunmen faced no opposition to their unspeakable cruelty. In fact, under New York's strict gun control laws, any restaurant employee or patron who had armed himself would be considered as guilty as the murderers. Only the wealthy and the politically connected can lawfully carry a handgun.

SOURCE: This article appeared in the May 31, 2000 edition of the *San Diego Union-Tribune*. Reprinted with permission of the author.

And so it was by this dictate of law that the New York killers enjoyed the unfettered opportunity to force six men and one woman into a walk-in refrigerator, bind and gag them, and shoot each one in the head. Five died and two were gravely injured.

Civilized people recoil from such vile acts. Those who would ban firearms seek comfort in the vain hope that if we pass laws to get rid of guns, such horrors would cease. Against all experience, against all that science tells us about the protective value of guns in responsible hands, the gun banners babble on.

The most recent spectacle of babblers was the Million Mom March. According to a *Washington Times* report, fewer than 500,000 gun-control advocates gathered on the Mall in Washington, D.C., to call for more gun laws. They believe, apparently, that the 20,000 or more gun control laws we already have are not enough.

The chief babbler was daytime TV "Queen of Nice" Rosie O'Donnell. But O'Donnell wasn't so nice last year, when she savaged guest Tom Selleck on the air for being a spokesman for the NRA, a charge he denied. In another pronouncement, she recommended the imprisonment of all gun owners.

This year, O'Donnell has relaxed her stringent anti-gun stance—for herself, anyway—by employing a private security guard. It seems the guard has applied for a permit to carry a gun. But Rosie insists her security measures are for the safety of her child, so her flip-flopping really isn't rank hypocrisy.

Such elitism is an undercurrent of all laws prohibiting citizen self-defense. In the post-Civil War South, that elitism was directed against blacks. In New York at the beginning of the 20th century, it was directed at people marked as foreign-born anarchists and revolutionaries.

Today the elitism is more egalitarian. In those states without "shall issue" carry laws, police chiefs practice the elitism of local politics. Under discretionary firearm carry laws, affluent celebrities and politicians are often deemed "suitable persons," but everyday people—Wendy's employees, for example—are not.

The November elections will be in part a referendum on gun ownership. To vote intelligently, we must consider that firearms are used to save lives far more often than they are used to take them. As decades of criminology research has shown, it is the career criminal, not the regular citizen, who misuses guns most.

Let us remember the life-saving utility of firearms in good hands. At the polls, let us vote to preserve that right of self-defense in memory of five innocent souls.

DISCUSSION QUESTIONS

1. This essay offers an inductive conclusion about "deliberate and widely divergent public policies in two states." How large is the author's sample?
2. This kind of analysis calls for statistics, not anecdotes. How many murders per capita were committed in each state in 1991? (You can find this information in your library or on the Internet.)
3. Would it weaken the author's argument if there were more per-capita murders in Alabama than in New York?
4. What is the evidence of Rosie O'Donnell's "hypocrisy"? Is her need for protection greater than an average citizen's?
5. "Firearms are used to save lives far more often than they are to take them." How could anyone document this? How does one count the number of saved lives?
6. The author is listed as "Timothy Wheeler, M.D." Does the "M.D." give special authority to his argument?

Deduction

"You have an M.B.A. from Harvard.
Of course I believe you."

—WENDY WASSERSTEIN, *ISN'T IT ROMANTIC?*

Deduction is the opposite of induction. Where induction moves from specific facts to a general conclusion, deduction moves from a general truth to a specific application. Because there are many kinds of deduction—some quite complicated—this discussion aims to be little more than a useful simplification.

The vehicle of deduction is the syllogism. This is an argument that takes two existing truths and puts them together to create a new truth. Here is the classic example:

> MAJOR PREMISE: All men are mortal.
> MINOR PREMISE: Socrates is a man.
> CONCLUSION: Socrates is mortal.

In everyday life, you'll find many examples of deductive thinking. The syllogism is often abbreviated, with one of the parts implied rather than stated.

> You haven't registered, so you can't vote. (IMPLICIT MAJOR PREMISE: Anyone who does not register cannot vote.)
> No man lives forever. Even old Tom Beck will die someday. (IMPLICIT MINOR PREMISE: Tom Beck is a man.)
> Anyone can make a mistake. After all, Roger is only human. (IMPLICIT CONCLUSION: Roger can make a mistake.)

Many informal arguments can be resolved into syllogistic form. You do this so you can analyze them more systematically.

A deductive argument is considered reliable if it fulfills three conditions: (1) the premises must be true, (2) the terms must be unambiguous, and (3) the syllogistic form must be valid. These requirements will be considered in turn.

■ ARE THE PREMISES TRUE?

First, the premises must be true. Because the major premise of a syllogism is usually derived by induction (that is, it is a general statement drawn from specific facts), you can judge its reliability by asking whether the facts that produced it are known to be sufficient and representative. Here is a vulnerable example:

> Gentlemen prefer blondes.
> Senator Wilson is a gentleman.
> Senator Wilson prefers blondes.

This syllogism reaches an unreliable conclusion because the major premise is unproven. The generalization about blondes exists only as a cliché (and as a title by Anita Loos); it was not induced from any known sample. You have heard the common argument for lowering the drinking age:

> Anyone old enough to fight is old enough to drink.
> Eighteen-year-olds are old enough to fight.
> They should be old enough to drink.

This syllogism will be persuasive to anyone who accepts the major premise. Many people find the premise vulnerable.

Political partisans regularly use dubious major premises (a war hero would make a good president, a woman would make a poor one, etc.) to produce the conclusions they want.

■ IS THE LANGUAGE UNAMBIGUOUS?

The terms of deductive argument must be clear and consistent. If definitions change within a syllogism, arguments can be amusingly fallacious:

> All cats chase mice.
> My wife is a cat.
> Therefore . . .

> All men are created equal.
> Women are not men.
> Therefore . . .

This kind of argument can be genuinely misleading. The advertisement "See *The Lord of the Rings: The Two Towers*, the Academy Award Winner" was based on this syllogism:

> The Academy Award-winning movie is worth seeing.
> *The Lord of the Rings: The Two Towers* is this year's Academy Award-winning movie.
> *The Lord of the Rings: The Two Towers* is worth seeing.

Here the phrase "Academy Award-winning movie" is ambiguous. In the major premise, it refers to the movie voted Best Picture of the year; in the minor premise, to a movie winning one or more of the dozens of lesser awards given annually. *Lord of the Rings: The Two Towers* won awards for sound editing and visual effects.

Ambiguous examples are not always frivolous. Consider these syllogisms:

> Killing an innocent human being is murder.
> Abortion kills an innocent human being.
> Abortion is murder.

> A private club should have the legal right to accept or exclude anyone it wants.
> The Junior Chamber of Commerce is a private club.
> The JCs should have the legal right to accept or exclude anyone they want (translation: they shouldn't have to admit women).

These syllogisms went all the way to the U.S. Supreme Court, where the terms "human being" and "private club" were analyzed carefully.

A provocative advertisement is based on this syllogism:

> You should be anxious to buy a genuine diamond ring for only $5.
> We are offering a genuine diamond ring for $5.
> You should be anxious to buy this ring.

The advertisers offer a ring containing a 0.25-carat diamond chip. This isn't a diamond in the sense you usually think of one.

■ IS THE SYLLOGISM VALID?

A reliable syllogism must have valid form. This requirement introduces a complex area of discussion, because there are many types of syllogisms, each with its own test of validity. Commonly, "valid form" means that the general subject or condition of the major premise must appear in the minor premise as well. It is easy to see that this argument is false:

> All murderers have ears.
> All Methodists have ears.
> All murderers are Methodists.

What makes the argument unreliable syllogistically is the fact that the term "murderers" does not recur in the minor premise. A major premise about "all murderers" can only lead to a conclusion about murderers. Similarly, the premises "If Taylor loses his job, his wife will leave him" and "Taylor does not lose his job" produce no necessary conclusion. The condition "lose his job" does not occur in the minor premise.

When an invalid syllogism appears as argument, it usually maintains that things with one quality in common share a kind of identity. Such argument takes extreme forms:

> The father of Miss Smith's baby has blood type O.
> Billy Garrington has blood type O.
> Therefore . . .

> The American Civil Liberties Union opposes capital punishment.
> Mike Bradshaw opposes capital punishment.
> Therefore . . .

Because the crucial term does not appear in both premises of these syllogisms, their conclusions are no more valid than the claim that all murderers are Methodists.

These three tests, then, permit you to judge the reliability of a deductive argument.

Some deductive arguments combine several syllogisms. Consider this example:

> When a man becomes emotionally disturbed, there is a recognizable change in his voice patterns.
> When a man tells a lie, he becomes emotionally disturbed.
> When a man tells a lie, there is a recognizable change in his voice patterns.

> When a man tells a lie, there is a recognizable change in his voice patterns.
> Senator Ted Kennedy is a man.
> When Senator Ted Kennedy tells a lie, there is a recognizable change in his voice patterns.

> When Senator Ted Kennedy tells a lie, there is a recognizable change in his voice patterns.
> There was a recognizable change in the Senator's voice patterns (as recorded on a PSE device) during his interview on the *Today* show.
> Senator Kennedy lied during his interview on the *Today* show.

This kind of reasoning produced the *National Enquirer* headline: "Senator Kennedy Lied about Rape Case." Notice that all three syllogisms have doubtful premises, and the last has an invalid form.

You can construct sequence syllogisms to analyze the advertising claims "For all you do, this Bud's for you" and "Why be gray when you can be yourself?"

■ INDUCTION OR DEDUCTION?

Because most syllogisms begin with an induced major premise, certain arguments can be analyzed as either induction or deduction. Consider this example: "Jamie Herubin doesn't drink; he'll make a fine husband." You can read this as a syllogism and attack the implicit major premise "Anyone who doesn't drink will make a fine husband." Or you can treat it as induction and argue that the sample (the fact that Jamie Herubin doesn't drink) is insufficient to sustain a conclusion about his prospects as a husband. With such arguments, it is best not to quibble over terms; either approach is satisfactory.

When you evaluate a syllogism, don't judge it as true or false, but as reliable or unreliable. An unreliable conclusion may nevertheless be true. From the doubtful major premise ("Anyone who doesn't drink . . .") you cannot reasonably deduce that Jamie Herubin will make a fine husband. But he might, in fact, make a very fine husband. In rejecting the syllogism as unreliable, you simply say that the claim is not proven by this argument.

You can recognize the distinction between truth and a reasonable conclusion by recalling a passage from Eugene Ionesco's *Rhinoceros*. In the play, the logician argues, "All cats die. Socrates is dead. Therefore Socrates is a cat." And his student responds, "That's true. I've got a cat named Socrates."

Recognizing the syllogistic form of an argument will help you analyze its reliability. It will also help you to structure an argumentative essay. In deductive writing, the first paragraph offers the major premise, and the last paragraph, the conclusion. The body of the theme tries to demonstrate the minor premise. This is, for example, the structure of the Declaration of Independence. (The Declaration of Independence can be found on page 275).

EXERCISES

How reliable are these deductive arguments?

1. Of course Susan is a poor driver. She's a woman.
2. A medical procedure that preserves life and health should be legal. Abortion preserves life and health that would be endangered in a clandestine operation. Abortion should be legal.
3. Professor Costello's new book on marriage should be pretty informed. After all, he's been married four times.
4. Both Catholics and Protestants are Christians. No one can be both Catholic and Protestant. Therefore, no one can be a Christian.
5. The Easter Island statues could not have been carved, moved, and erected by mere humans. The work must have been done by superhuman agents.
6. The Easter Island statues were carved, moved, and erected by superhuman agents. Space travelers who could visit the earth must be superhuman agents. So the Easter Island statues must be the work of space travelers.
7. Genuinely oppressed people (like African Americans) have lower academic scores and shorter life spans. Women do not have these. Women are not oppressed.
8. The Book of Revelation says the Antichrist who will introduce the last days is identified by the number 666. Count the letters in the name R-o-n-a-l-d W-i-l-s-o-n R-e-a-g-a-n. What do you get?
9. I know I'm not supposed to lust after my neighbor's wife. But Mary Davis lives way over in Biloxi, and she and Billy Miller aren't married.
10. My condition is beyond the help of medical science. Fortunately, Dr. Harris is a quack.
11. "Any public school curriculum on sex education should meet a four-point test: It should be true, healthy, legal, and constitutional. The only classroom teaching that satisfies all four is to teach children sexual abstinence until marriage."—Phyllis Schlafly
12. "If you don't like fast driving, why don't you go to Russia?"—Charles Bowden
13. The Declaration of Independence says I have a God-given right to "life, liberty, and the pursuit of happiness." This means I have a God-given right to protect my life. I have a right to own a gun.
14. "If God didn't believe in the death penalty, why are the graveyards so full?"—Ed Anger

ESSAY ASSIGNMENTS

Write an essay either affirming or opposing one of these statements. The arguments you encounter in your background reading will probably be deductive, and so will your essay.

1. There's nothing wrong with buying a term paper.
2. Evolution is a foolish theory.
3. Cable TV should not be permitted to show uncut R-rated movies.
4. Baseball players have no right to strike.
5. America needs stronger libel laws.
6. There should be no required courses in college.
7. The miracles of Jesus prove he was God.
8. X is a disease; it should not be punished but cured. (Fill in the X.)

Ebonics Be a Complex Issue

Bill Cosby

I remember one day 15 years ago, a friend of mine told me a racist joke.

Question: Do you know what Toys "R" Us is called in Harlem?
Answer: We Be Toys.

So, before the city of Oakland, Calif., starts to teach its teachers Ebonics, or what I call "Igno-Ebonics," I think the school board should study all the ramifications of endorsing an urbanized version of the English language.

After all, Ebonics be a complex issue.

If teachers are going to legitimitize Ebonics, then all authority figures who interact with children—such as law-enforcement officers—will have to learn it as well. In fact, the consequences of a grammatical accident could be disastrous during a roadside encounter with a policeman.

The first thing people ask when they are pulled over is: "Why did you stop me, officer?" Imagine an Ebonics-speaking Oakland teenager being stopped on the freeway by a non-Ebonics speaking California Highway Patrol officer. The teenager, posing that same question Ebonically, would begin by saying: "Lemme ax you . . ." The patrolman, fearing he is about to be hacked to death, could charge the kid with threatening a police officer. Thus, to avoid misunderstandings, notices would have to be added to driver's licenses warning: "This driver speaks Ebonics only."

Since people with driver's licenses tend to drive, what happens when an Ebonics-speaking youth drives into another state? Kids who speak Oakland Ebonics would find it difficult to converse with someone fluent in Pennsylvania Ebonics. And Tennessee Ebonics would be impossible to decipher.

Consider the following phrase: "I am getting ready to go." Even before Ebonics, Southern people changed the way they announced their imminent departure by saying: "I am fixing to go." Ebonically schooled Tennessee kids, however, would declare: "Ima fi'n nah go." Meanwhile, depending on your geographic locale, that same idea would be expressed in a variety of ways, such as: "Ima go now," or "I be goin' now," or the future imperfect "Ima be goin' now."

If Ebonics is allowed to evolve without any national standard, the only language the next generation would have in common would be body language. At the moment—if there are any current rules to Ebonics—one of them seems to be that any consonant at the end of a word must be dropped, particularly the letter G. This allows certain words to be strung together into one larger word. Ergo, the Ebonically posed question "Where was you workinlas?" translates into English as "Where were you working last?"

Of course, this query is most likely to be found on a job application, which means that Ebonics-speaking youths will not get a job unless they are aware that "working" and "last" are two words instead of one. Therefore, companies interested in recruiting Ebonics-speaking workers would need to hire Ebonics-speaking assistants to provide translations. That would open up employment opportunity by creating the new job of "Ebonics specialist." But even a staff of Ebonics specialists could cause chaos.

Suppose an Ebonics-speaking nurse hands a patient some eye drops and says, "Put'em in an ear fur near." (Translation: "an hour from now.") A non-Ebonics-speaking patient might fill his ear with Visine.

Then there's the tourist problem. Until now, foreign visitors only had to learn a modicum of English to get by in America. A quick Berlitz course and they could haltingly say: "How are you?" With Ebonics an official language, tourists also would need to learn an Ebonics greeting such as: "Sapnin'?"

Another factor inherent in the widespread acceptance of Ebonics would be its cultural impact. In Hollywood, for instance, film studios would be delighted to have two categories instead of one in which to group African-American actors. While there always would be parts for "non-Ebonics black people," casting agents also would be asking: "Can you act Ebonics?" Naturally there would have to be English subtitles for Ebonics movies. (Maybe Ebonics is actually a conspiracy to resurrect the old "Amos & Andy" show.)

A lot of kids make the argument for Ebonics by insisting: "But this is the way I talk on the street!" In London, I guess Cockney would be the equivalent of Ebonics. And though they may study Cockney at Oxford as part of literature, I doubt they teach it. Granted, if you don't teach Ebonics, the children will find it anyway. But legitimizing the street in the classroom is backwards. We should be working hard to legitimize the classroom—and English—in the street. On the other hand, we could jes letem do wha ever they wanna. Either way, Ima go over heanh an learn some maffa matics an then ge-sum 'n tee an' then I'll be witchya.

DISCUSSION QUESTIONS

1. Bill Cosby is famous. How would you react to the argument if the author were unknown? What kind of questions would you ask? Why?
2. How do jokes affect the argument? Do they make it interesting? Do they make it persuasive?
3. Are the situations described by Cosby beyond the realm of possibility? Discuss them as evidence supporting or not supporting this syllogism:

   Major: All teachers who legitimize Ebonics are making a mistake.
   Minor: Oakland teachers are legitimizing Ebonics.
   Conclusion: Therefore, Oakland teachers are making a mistake.

   What evidence supports the "Major" premise?
4. Cosby argues "We should be working hard to legitimize the classroom—and English—in the street." What does he mean?
5. Can you find another syllogism in Cosby's argument against teaching Ebonics? What's the major premise? Minor premise? Are the terms clear?

Death Penalty Deters Violent Crime

Senator Strom Thurmond

Does the death penalty have a legitimate role in our efforts to punish vicious criminals? I believe that it does.

I am convinced that the death penalty is an effective deterrent. The threat of capital punishment does deter violent crime. Not only does it deter individual behavior, it has value in terms of general deterrence as well.

By associating the penalty with the crimes for which it is inflicted, society is made more aware of the horror of those crimes, and there is instilled in the citizens a need to avoid such conduct and appropriately punish those who do not.

In addition, capital punishment serves the society's legitimate interest in retribution. Justice requires that criminals get what they deserve. Justice demands that such inhuman action not be tolerated. The death penalty recognizes society's belief that there are some crimes which are so vicious, heinous and brutal that no penalty lesser than death will suffice.

The American people agree with me. A recent Gallup Poll shows that public support for the death penalty is at the highest point recorded in more than half a century, with 79 percent favoring the death penalty for murder. The public opinion on the issue of capital punishment must not be ignored.

Briefly, I want to discuss a few specific cases where the death penalty is clearly warranted. I believe a discussion of these cases will help my colleagues to understand why we need a federal death penalty.

In Ogden, Utah, Pierre Selby and William Andrews robbed a hi-fi shop and in the course of their armed robbery, forced five bound victims—three of whom were teen-agers—to drink cups of poisonous liquid drain cleaner.

Selby also tried to force Orren Walker, the father of one of the teenagers, to pour the drain cleaner down his own son's throat. When Walker refused, Selby attempted to strangle him to death with an electrical cord and then repeatedly kicked a ballpoint pen deep into his ear. Selby then proceeded to shoot each one of his victims in the head.

Another case which was truly heinous and depraved occurred in January of 1988 in a Landover, Md., apartment. Kirk Bruce and two alleged accomplices, in an orchestrated plan, shot and killed four men and a woman.

SOURCE: Reprinted from the *Mobile Press Register,* July 18, 1990. Reprinted by permission.

Bruce's victims were shot execution style with close-range shots to the head. Some were shot as many as eight times. Others were chased into rooms of the apartment and gunned down.

One victim, who survived to testify at Bruce's trial, was hiding beneath a bed but was discovered and also shot in the head. She lay there critically wounded when one of the murderers came back into the room, told her he knew she was still alive, and shot her again.

Finally, the case of Robert Alton Harris should be mentioned. We must not forget the heinous crime Harris committed. On July 5, 1978, just six months after he completed a $2\frac{1}{2}$-year prison term for beating a man to death, Harris decided to rob a bank in San Diego.

Looking first for a getaway car, he spotted two teenage boys parked at a fast-food restaurant. Harris forced the youths at gunpoint to drive to a nearby reservoir, where he shot and killed them as they begged God to save them. Later, he ate their unfinished hamburgers.

These cases truly provide examples of individuals who should face imposition of the death penalty. In all of these cases, the defendants received the death penalty.

However, under current federal law, were these cases to occur on federal land, the death penalty could not even be considered. The law-abiding citizens of this nation demand action on federal death penalty legislation, not life imprisonment legislation. They deserve to have a death penalty which will deter violent action against them and will provide swift, appropriate punishment for individuals who choose to commit heinous crimes.

DISCUSSION QUESTIONS

1. The author expresses a number of syllogisms. One is this:

   > Any law that deters crime and protects the public is just.
   > The death penalty deters crime and protects the public.
   > The death penalty is just.

   What evidence supports the minor premise?
2. Do the three stories of cruel murderers support the claim that the death penalty deters crime?
3. Another syllogism:

   > Justice demands that murderers be executed.
   > The death penalty executes murderers.
   > Justice demands the death penalty.

   What evidence supports the major premise?

4. Syllogism:

> When the public supports a law, it is just.
> The American public supports the death penalty.
> The death penalty is just.

What evidence supports the major premise?

5. Are the stories of the three horrible murders intended to make a rational argument? To produce a rational response?
6. Is this an example of good writing? Consider the first paragraph, the language, the sentence length, and the paragraph divisions. Did you find this easy to read?

Justice Department Detects Discrimination Against Native Americans

John Leo

Asheville, N.C., is the site of a brand-new legal question, never raised before in the annals of political correctness: Should the federal government be involved in determining the mascot or nickname of your local high school sports teams?

Erwin High School in Asheville is being investigated by the Justice Department's Civil Rights Division for using the nicknames "Warriors" and "Squaws" and for having students dressed as Indians at games and pep rallies. The investigation will center on whether the Indian theme creates a racially hostile environment that violates the civil rights of Indian students, according to a letter sent to the school system by Bill Lann Lee, acting head of the Civil Rights Division, and Lawrence Baca, a department attorney. The letter was a response to a complaint from an Asheville nurse, Pat Merzlak, a Lakota Sioux Indian.

Some Indian activists and their allies have campaigned against Indian nicknames for years. Some 600 schools have dropped these names. More than 2500 have not. But so far, the Justice Department has never tried to intervene. This is a first. It is also a fresh example of how broad concepts like "hostile environment" and "racial harassment" are constantly being extended from serious issues to minor and symbolic ones.

On the nickname issue, a reasonable case can be made on either side. Indian activists say that it's wrong to use living people as mascots. But on the college level alone, teams are named for Gaels, Scots, Norsemen, Dutch and the Fighting Irish, as well as Seminoles, Chippewa, Aztecs and the Fighting Sioux. Some nicknames certainly sound like slurs—Redskins and Redmen—but most Americans don't think that Braves, Chiefs, Warriors or famous tribal names fit into this category.

Most Indian names were adopted to indicate that the teams using them have a fierce fighting spirit. This may help promote a stereotype of Indians as savage or hopelessly primitive, particularly when war whoops and tomahawk chops are part of the act at sports events. But many nicknames seem harmless or positive. Some were clearly intended to honor Indian nations or heroes—the Chicago Blackhawks celebrate the Sauk chief Blackhawk, and the Cleveland Indians were named, by a vote of fans, to honor the first Native American major-league star, Lou Sockalexis. And if Indian nicknames are inherently oppressive, why do many Indian and Indian-dominated schools use them?

Debatable issues like this are the proper concern of schools and local communities. When the feds intervened, Asheville had already spent two years and a good deal of money to prepare students at Erwin to make their own decision on a possible change of nicknames and mascots. Students had many discussions and met with the chief of the large Cherokee community in western North Carolina. Student support for a name change, which had reached 44 percent, dropped to 24 percent after the federal intervention.

The Civil Rights Division says it was bound to act after receiving the Merzlak letter, but Asheville was an odd choice for its first nickname intervention. The local community was already addressing the issue. The school usually has only one or two Indian students at a time, and local Indian opinion at the Cherokee community seemed indifferent. The damage claimed in the case was allegedly inflicted on a single Indian student, Rayne Merzlak—Pat's son—who never filed a complaint with the school district and had long since graduated when the feds moved in.

A letter such as the one sent by the Justice Department carries the implied threat of spending the school board into submission. The board chairman says it might cost $500,000 in legal fees to fight back. About $8 million in federal school funding is also at risk, but the Justice Department lacks jurisdiction and would have to go to the Department of Education to cut funds. Or it could go to civil court, seeking damages and an injunction against the school board.

The Civil Rights Division has a reputation of using the threat of costly litigation to get what it wants. In 1993 the division targeted the city of Torrance, Calif., for allegedly discriminating against minorities in written tests for police and firefighting jobs. The city said the tests were fair and widely used, so it dared the division to sue. It did, and last year federal judge Mariana Pfaelzer found the suit so unfounded and frivolous that she ordered the government to cover Torrance's legal costs, about $2 million.

In the Asheville case, the Justice Department asked for so much paperwork that the school district says it will take staff 12 full working days to provide it. One of the requests is for the names and racial identifications of all students who have performed as Indian mascots. This wretched excess seems to ask the board to violate the federal Family Education Rights and Privacy Act. Lawyers for the board say they will refuse to comply.

The division has short-circuited normal democratic debate, intervened clumsily, and attempted to manufacture a grave civil rights violation out of a nickname. Apart from that, it's behaved professionally.

DISCUSSION QUESTIONS

1. The Government's argument is deductive:

   MAJOR PREMISE: A public school should not be allowed to create a racially hostile environment which violates the civil rights of minority students.

   MINOR PREMISE: Erwin High School's use of Native American names for sports teams and mascots creates a racially hostile environment.

   CONCLUSION: Erwin High School should not be allowed to do this.

   Is there a weakness in this syllogism?
2. How many people do you know who cannot be called minorities in one way or another?
3. Do you feel that names like "Braves," "Indians," "Redskins," "Blackhawks," and "Warriors" have negative associations?
4. Could a person argue that sport names like "Cowboys," "Razorbacks," "Broncos," "Raiders," and "Rebels" have negative implications? What about "the Fighting Irish"?
5. Given a large enough population, couldn't someone be found who feels oppressed by any of these names? When should the Civil Rights Division respond to complaints?
6. What qualities of the essay make it clear that Leo is a fine writer?

All in Favor of "Gun Control", Raise Your Right Hand

DISCUSSION QUESTIONS

1. What argument is being made here?
2. Some authorities favor gun control laws. Adolf Hitler favored gun control laws. Some of the anti-gun people are like Hitler. How valid is this as a syllogism?
3. What is the effect of the argument appearing in a cartoon rather than in written language?

A Broader Approach to Respect for Life

Jerry Darring

A. Russell Smith, discussing abortion in the September 2 issue of *The Catholic Week,* proposes that we 1) pray and fast; 2) promote the adoption alternative; 3) hold an annual gigantic Rally for Life; 4) pray and sing around abortion clinics; 5) delink abortion from other life issues. I will let others comment on Smith's proposals; I will focus on what Smith apparently does not know, what he definitely does not care about, and what he probably does not realize.

Smith apparently does not know the living tradition of the official Catholic social teaching, for if he did, he would never propose one issue as the be-all and end-all of Catholic activism. A grounding in the social documents of the Church would give Smith a deeper understanding of the dignity of the human person and therefore a broader approach to respect for life.

Smith definitely does not display any concern for the plight of women in society. Claiming to want to defend innocent life, he does not seem to want to confront sexism, the feminization of poverty, and the second-class status of women, all of which kill innocent people. One reason, I think, why Smith does not confront these matters is because he does not care about the intricacies of living in a pluralistic society. Smith shows himself in his letter to be a fine Catholic, but one who lives in a Catholic ghetto, unable and/or unwilling to admit that the other side has anything at all to offer in the struggle for the coming of God's reign. Those on the other side are to be browbeat into submission by us Catholics, who have all the answers.

What Smith does not realize is that his thinking is dangerous. He thinks that by proclaiming, as he does in his essay, that he is not in favor of killing abortionists, he is absolved of any connection with the David Trosches of this world. He does not realize that the well-intentioned world of A. Russell Smith gives birth to the muddle-headed thinking of David Trosches; that as long as we Catholics are self-righteous and confrontational about the abortion issue and as long as we refuse any consideration of the issues important to the other side, we will continue, to our shame, to produce people like David Trosch.

SOURCE: Reprinted with permission of the author.

Children have the right to be born. They also have the right, when born, to live in a world in which people live decently and work together to solve their problems. Any attempt to preserve the first right without displaying equal concern for the second one remains unconvincing to me. I simply do not see it in the Gospel.

DISCUSSION QUESTIONS

1. Discuss these assumptions:
   a. Catholics should not believe in abortion.
   b. Pro-life is inimical to the plight of women and a pluralistic society.
   c. Pro-life thinking produces muddled and dangerous people like David Trosch.
   d. Catholics should "delink" abortion from other issues.
   Which of these does Darring attack most successfully? What evidence does he use to challenge them?
2. Darring has major assumptions of his own:
   a. Children have the right to be born.
   b. They "have the right . . . to live in a world in which people live decently and work together to solve their problems."
   What evidence does he offer?
3. What does Darring mean by "I simply do not see it in the Gospel"? What evidence is he trying to use?
4. Look at this syllogism in the author's argument:

   Catholics should not mindlessly oppose abortion.
   Smith is Catholic.
   Therefore, Smith should not mindlessly oppose abortion.

   What evidence supports the major premise?
5. The author believes his view is broad. Does the argument persuade you to adopt his "broader approach to respect for life"? Could any argument persuade you to change your mind in this area?

Stem Cell Research Needs to Proceed

It's time to overturn President Bush's limits on federal funding for embryonic stem cell research. The moral and medical issues connected to research on human embryos are indeed profound, but this nation has the capacity to fashion reasonable guidelines for research that offers so much promise for victims of deadly and debilitating diseases.

This month, scientists in South Korea announced success in what is known as "therapeutic cloning," one of the great hopes of the stem cell field and a process that many thought was still years away. That announcement not only invigorated the scientific community but also served as a reminder of the need to put the United States back in the forefront of this research.

In Congress, a bipartisan measure approved Tuesday by the U.S. House of Representatives would reauthorize the use of federal funds for research on stem cells available from the hundreds of thousands of frozen embryos stored in fertility clinics around the country. With the permission of the couples who no longer wish to use the embryos to get pregnant, scientists would be allowed to use them instead to harvest stem cells for research purposes. (In the vast majority of cases, those embryos would otherwise be destroyed. Only a tiny percentage are donated for other couples to use, and the success rate for pregnancy in such cases is dismally low.)

Unfortunately—despite widespread support within the public—the president has already promised to veto the House measure, as well as a similar bill that has gained widespread support in the Senate. In this country, unlike South Korea, Great Britain and other parts of the world, the federal government has virtually stymied stem cell research.

The Bush administration put up $25 million in funding for stem cell research lines derived from embryos before his 2001 ban. But that amount is paltry in the context of the federal science budget—the equivalent of what the country spends studying herbal remedies to cure diseases.

The National Institutes of Health, the agency at the forefront of most advances in American medicine, can and should be a major source of research in this field. Privately funded stem cell work will not be enough. The nation desperately needs the NIH's oversight of experiments now and in the future with embryonic stem cells.

SOURCE: Editorial, *Atlanta Journal-Constitution*, May 27, 2005. Reproduced with permission of *Atlanta Journal-Constitution* in the format Textbook via Copyright Clearance Center.

Stem cell research has been around for years, ranging from experiments using adult stem cells, to those harvested from umbilical cords discarded after childbirth, to those taken from embryos created in laboratory dishes. Adult stem cells exist to help the body repair and regenerate damaged cells, the way bone marrow regenerates blood cells and the way skin tissue grows back after a cut. But the best cells, the ones thought to have the most potential to develop the ability to heal or regenerate defective parts, come from embryos.

These cells exist only in human embryos, when a male's sperm is injected into the female egg in a laboratory process known as in vitro fertilization. Embryonic stem cells, in contrast to adult cells, have the ability to turn into all kinds of cells, including some—like brain and spinal cord cells—that an adult human body has no ability to make on its own.

In therapeutic cloning, the stem cells come from embryos that are clones of individuals and provide an exact genetic match for patients with certain disorders. The goal of researchers using this type of cloning is not to create a baby. They hope one day to use stem cells as replacement parts for diseased and injured organs. While that's probably decades away, research at this stage will help scientists understand diseases by watching the cells reproduce and change.

To harvest embryonic stem cells, scientists must first isolate them and then remove them from the embryo. In doing so, the embryo is destroyed. And that's where science and ethics collide.

As is often the case when science outpaces society, people search for moral absolutes to guide ethical decisionmaking before embarking on controversial research. The president, the Catholic Church and many others who oppose embryonic stem cell research believe there is no moral middle ground on the issue. The embryo represents human life, they say, and human life must be protected.

But when and where should that bright line of protection be drawn? It wasn't for the embryos destroyed in the rapidly dwindling stem cell lines harvested before August 2001, which the president's order still allows to be used in research. And it certainly hasn't been drawn in fertility labs around the country, where unused human embryos are thawed and destroyed because families no longer need them.

Have we, as a society, really decided there is a moral absolute in this? If human life is conceived in a Petri dish—and could never progress beyond a cluster of cells without a woman's womb to nurture it—do those cells destined, in most cases, to be discarded have the moral equivalency of a child who will suffer from diabetes the rest of her life or an adult who is permanently paralyzed by a spinal cord injury? Is that embryo frozen in liquid nitrogen a human being that must find a womb to be born, or might it also be human cells on their way to becoming a lifesaving treatment?

Last month, the National Academy of Sciences, acting in the absence of the NIH, issued a thoughtful set of guidelines for ethical research with embryonic stem cells for scientists in the private sector and those in states, such as California, where voters have approved state-funded experiments.

Among other things, the NAS guidelines prohibit payment for unfertilized eggs or embryos, require scientists to have their experiments overseen by ethics committees with citizen participation and create a national committee to tighten or relax regulatory constraints as new evidence warrants.

With these reasonable NAS guidelines and the ability to create new stem cell lines from thousands of embryos that might otherwise be wasted, the nation faces an important choice: Are we frozen now in this place, or can we find a moral and ethical framework within the miracle of human reproduction that has the potential to advance the health and happiness of humankind?

Research Not Equal to Sacrifice

Phil Gingrey

Not all stem cells are created equal.

Human stem cells come from a range of sources. Stem cells from adult blood, bone marrow and umbilical cords are harvested in an ethical way that does not harm the donor. Conversely, under current practices, the harvesting of embryonic stem cells results in the destruction of a human life.

Fortunately, for the millions of Americans suffering from debilitating diseases, the most ethical research is also the most promising. Adult stem cell and umbilical cord stem cell research has achieved preliminary success treating 67 diseases, including heart disease, leukemia, spinal cord injury, juvenile diabetes and stroke. On the other hand, scientists have not been able to develop any successful treatments using embryonic stem cells.

As an OB/GYN physician, I've witnessed the miracle of life from its most fragile, embryonic stage. We must have a culture that values life, including the lives of those who can't speak for themselves. After all, every one of us started life as an embryo.

Proponents of embryonic stem cell research say that frozen embryos will simply be thrown away if we don't use them for research. But I refuse to believe there are any "throwaway" lives. Certainly, the hundreds of parents who have successfully adopted frozen embryos and carried these "snowflake" babies to term don't think their children are disposable.

The notion of "throwaway embryos" is part of a larger problem that plagues the embryonic stem cell debate: misleading information and false promise. Let me set the record straight. Today, adult stem cells are providing usable treatments. Embryonic stem cells are being hyped by advocacy groups and the for-profit biotechnology sector trying to sell the "promise" of a cure to unsuspecting and vulnerable families.

America is unique among nations, in part because of the value we place on individual life. Our way—the American way—is to find treatments and cures that also uphold our highest ethical standards. America is home to some of the best scientists in the world, and I am confident they can achieve this goal.

For instance, scientists are researching methods of extracting embryonic stem cells without destroying human life. Currently, in-vitro fertilization

SOURCE: *Atlanta Journal-Constitution,* May 27, 2005. Reprinted with permission of the author.

clinics sometimes perform biopsies to test embryos for genetic abnormalities before implantation. A similar procedure could probably be used to extract stem cells without harming the embryo. I've signed on to legislation in the U.S. House that provides federal funding for scientists to further explore this possibility.

In the meantime, adult stem cells are getting results today.

We are presented with a choice between proven, successful adult stem cell research, and the current field of embryonic stem cell research, wrought with ethical concerns and medical uncertainties. If we cross a moral divide of this magnitude unnecessarily, the ends will not justify the means.

The choice, therefore, is clear: We don't have to sacrifice life in the hope of saving lives.

DISCUSSION QUESTIONS

Pro and Con: Stem Cell Research

1. Scientists want to use stem cells "as replacement cells for diseased and injured organs." What's wrong with this?
2. The President, the Catholic Church, and other conservative authorities take the opposite views. They hold that "the embryo represents human life . . . and human life must be protected." Do you feel that an embryo in a dish is, in fact, a human being?
3. Do these guidelines seem reasonable?
4. The author (Gingrey) makes the case that adult stem cells have been very successful working against disease. Why do you think medical establishments have come out in favor of federally funded research on embryonic stem cells?
5. "Proponents of embryonic stem cell research say that frozen embryos will simply be thrown away if we don't use them for research." How does the author respond to this?
6. The author refers to proponents of embryonic stem cell research— "advocacy groups and the for-profit biotechnology sector"—as hucksters trying to make money. What evidence does he offer to substantiate this?
7. Do you hear the author writing as a physician or as a member of the House of Representatives with a political agenda?
8. The author concludes "we don't have to sacrifice life to save life." Does he make a distinction between unborn potential life and adult active life? Should he make that distinction?

Fallacies

"How to Tune Up Your Marriage—Just Like a Car"

—ESSAY BY PRISCILLA KROGER

Some forms of misleading argument are so common they have been specifically labeled. Although most could be analyzed as faulty induction, deduction, and so on, they are treated separately here because the terms describing them should be familiar to you. You will meet them often; they are part of the language of argument.

■ FALSE ANALOGY

To argue by analogy is to compare two things known to be alike in one or more features and suggest that they will be alike in other features as well. This is a reasonable argument if the compared elements are genuinely similar. (Josh Woodward is an outstanding player and coach; he'll make a fine manager.) It is fallacious if the features are essentially different. (You have *fruit* for breakfast; why not try *Jell-O* for breakfast?)

You test an analogy by asking whether the comparison statement (if there is one) is true and whether the elements compared are sufficiently alike. A comparison statement is particularly questionable if it is simply an adage. Reelection campaigns regularly submit, for example, that "you wouldn't change horses in the middle of the stream." But even the smallest considerations will remind you of situations where you would be eager to change horses. Equally vulnerable are arguments insisting that "you can lead a horse to water but you can't make it drink" (meaning some people are unteachable) and that "where there's smoke, there's fire" (meaning some gossip is true). Hearing these analogies, you might want to point out that scientists (with brain probes) can make a horse drink itself sick and that where there's smoke, there could be dry ice.

More often, you reject an analogy by showing a fundamental difference between the things compared. A common argument insists, "We have pure food and drug laws. Why can't we have laws to keep moviemakers from

71

giving us filth?" Here you must examine the definitions relating to "pure" and "filth." Food is called "impure" when the person eating it gets physically sick. Because the individual who devours X-rated movies doesn't get sick, there is no comparable definition of pornographic "filth." Thus the analogy fails. The poster saying "I Don't Spit in Your Face—Please Don't Blow Smoke in Mine" seems excessive. The two actions aren't equally offensive.

Analogies can be dangerous. In the 1980s, the Ayatollah Khomeini executed prostitutes, adulterers, and homosexuals. His argument: Iran is like a human body, and these people are an infectious gangrene. They must be destroyed to preserve the health of the state.

Some analogies are complex. Here is an argument that has appeared in many temperance campaigns. "There are 10,000 deaths from alcohol poisoning to 1 from mad-dog bites in this country. In spite of this, we license liquor but shoot the dogs." Because it is desirable to get rid of any dogs or any liquor that proves deadly, this analogy seems reasonable. The argument, however, recommends that *all* liquor be outlawed. This is persuasive only if you are willing to pursue the comparison and shoot all dogs. Similarly, you should scrutinize popular arguments that compare independent nations with dominoes and federal deficit spending with a family budget.

In argument, analogies can be an effective way to make a point. Justice Byron White, rejecting a sweeping law restricting dial-a-porn, said "It is another case of burning the house down to roast the pig."

In writing persuasive essays, you will find such analogies useful. But be careful. The comparison may make your subject seem trivial. (Evangelist David Noebel wrote that "Sex education without morals is like breakfast without orange juice.") Or it may add strange dimensions of meaning. (Author Jessamyn West praised the book *Four Cats Make One Pride* by saying, "It is about cats in the same way that *Huckleberry Finn* is about boys and *Madame Bovary* is about women.")

Keep your analogies simple and direct. Elaborate comparisons are rarely effective as argument.

■ PRESUMED CAUSE-EFFECT

Relating an event to a cause can lead to three different fallacies.

Argument in a Circle

Circular argument occurs when speakers offer a restatement of their assertion as a reason for accepting it. They make a claim, add "because," then repeat the claim in different words. They say, "Smoking is injurious because it harms the human body," or "One phone is not enough in the modern home because modern homes have plenty of phones."

Sometimes the expression is more oblique, with the "because" implied rather than stated. William Jennings Bryan once declared, "There is only one argument that can be made to one who rejects the authority of the Bible, namely, that the Bible is true." It is hardly persuasive to argue that a thing is true because it is true. Repetition is not evidence.

Today, circular argument appears regularly in discussions of pornography. Definitions of obscenity never get beyond the one given by Supreme Court Justice William Brennan in *Roth* v. *United States:* "Obscene material is material which deals with sex in a manner appealing to prurient interest." This says that obscene material is obscene material. The issue was not clarified in 1989 when the Supreme Court rejected the congressional effort to shut down the dial-a-porn industry. The Court specified that "indecent" messages could not be outlawed, only those that were "obscene."

Post Hoc Ergo Propter Hoc

The post hoc fallacy ("After this, therefore because of this") occurs when a person mentions two past events and insists that because one happened first, it necessarily caused the second. Using such evidence, people have argued that Martin Luther left the Catholic priesthood to get married, that President Herbert Hoover caused the Great Depression, and that young people rioted during the 1960s because they were brought up under the permissive theories of Dr. Benjamin Spock. Such logic can make much of coincidence. *Christian Crusade* compared crime statistics for two six-week periods and headlined "Murder Rate Jumps 93 Percent in Oklahoma Following Death Penalty Ban." The cause-effect relationship was, it said, "self-evident."

Nothing illustrates the weakness of the post hoc fallacy better than Stephen J. Gould's example. He noted solemnly that as Halley's Comet approached the earth, the price of ice cream cones in Boston rose regularly.

Post hoc reasoning is fallacious because it ignores more complex factors that contribute to an event. Once, a Smith-Corona advertisement proclaimed that "Students Who Type Usually Receive Better Grades" and suggested that buying a child a typewriter will improve his or her schoolwork. (The same argument can apply to buying a computer.) Today, the fallacy is the implication that simply owning a typewriter or a computer makes the difference. Other factors seem more likely to account for the higher grades. Parents who buy their child a typewriter or a computer are concerned about the youngster's education, take pains to see that the child studies, and can afford to provide other cultural advantages as well. The writing instrument alone gives no one higher grades.

Recognizing the post hoc fallacy will keep you from jumping to unwarranted conclusions. No one can deny, for example, that some people who wear copper bracelets suffer no arthritis pain; that some heroin addicts have significantly fewer accidents than other drivers; that some patients who took the antidepressant Prozac have become homicidal, and that some individuals who witnessed John Kennedy's assassination have died in dramatic ways. Nevertheless, these cases do not justify sensational cause-effect conclusions. A post hoc judgment would ignore the range of other factors involved.

Another example: A 1985 study by Emory University psychologists reported that women who read romantic historical novels have sex 74 percent more often than those who don't. Here it is hard to establish what is cause and what is effect.

The post hoc fallacy is used particularly by people who write about curses. Many books describe the tragic events that occurred in the Romanov, Hapsburg, and Kennedy families after they were put under a curse. Stories tell the sad fate of people who owned the Hope diamond. Magazine articles appear regularly reporting that every person who was involved in breaking open King Tut's tomb is now either dead or sadly crippled. When reading such stories, you should remember Darrell Huff's wonderful line: "Post hoc rides again!"

Non Sequitur

Non sequitur means "it does not follow." This fallacy occurs when a person submits that a given fact has led or must inevitably lead to a particular consequence.

One can take a fact ("Arnold Schwarzenegger's father was a Nazi") and project a conclusion ("He should not be elected to public office"). Or one can take an anticipated fact ("If the Equal Rights Amendment becomes a law") and spell out the consequences ("American family life is doomed"). The reasonable objection, of course, is that the conclusion does not necessarily follow.

The term non sequitur is widely used. It lends itself to describing arguments with multiple causes ("The more you know—the more you do—the more you tax your nerves—the more important it is to relax tired nerves. Try safe, nonhabit-forming Sedquilin") or arguments so extreme that they fall outside the usual categories ("Of course Jehovah's Witnesses are communists; otherwise there wouldn't be so many of them"). But the term is of little value in defining general argument; almost any kind of fallacious reasoning is a non sequitur.

Still, it's useful to know the term when you read the ad for Emeraude perfume: "I love only one man. I wear only one fragrance."

▓ BEGGING THE QUESTION

People beg the question by assuming something it is their responsibility to prove. They build their argument on an undemonstrated claim. Generally it takes the form of a question. ("Have you stopped beating your wife?" or "Is it true blondes have more fun?") But it can appear as a declaration. ("Busing is no more the law of the land than any other communist doctrine.")

Another form of begging the question is to make a charge and then insist that someone else disprove it. ("How do you know that flying saucers haven't been visiting the earth for centuries?" or "If Jeane Dixon doesn't have psychic powers, how could she predict the assassination of President Kennedy?") In all argument, the burden of proof is on the person making the assertion. Never let yourself be put in a position where you have to disprove a claim that was never proven in the first place. One of the most common instances of begging the question today is the anti-abortionist's charge: "How can you favor slaughtering babies?"

▓ IGNORING THE QUESTION

People can ignore a question in different ways: They can leave the subject to attack their opponent, or they can leave the subject to discuss a different topic.

Ad Hominem Argument

An ad hominem argument attacks the opposing arguer rather than the question at issue. ("Senator Thurmond favored resumption of the draft because he was too old to have to serve," or "District Attorney Phillips wants to become famous prosecuting my client so he can run for governor"). Here, nothing is said of the main issue; the speaker ignores the question by attacking an adversary.

It should be noted, to avoid confusion, that an argument about a particular individual—a candidate, a defendant—is probably not ad hominem argument. In such a case, the person *is* the issue.

The fallacy often takes this form: "Of course you believe that—you're a woman" (or a Jew, Catholic, Southerner, business executive, etc.). It also can involve snarl words: "I expected this from a bleeding-heart liberal" (or a wild-eyed environmentalist, Bible-thumping fanatic, labor-union radical, simple-minded bastard, etc.).

A good rule: *Never make an ad hominem argument*. Attacking your opponent is always an admission that your case is weak. If you have a substantial argument and want people to know it, a good policy is to flatter your adversary.

Extension

The fallacy of extension has the same effect as an ad hominem argument. Here persuaders "extend" the question until they are arguing a different issue altogether. When a convict's execution is stayed, people ask, "What about the rights of the victim?" When women are admitted to medical schools under a quota system, the cry goes up, "What about the rights of men?" In both cases, the question is reasonable, but it moves the argument to a new topic.

A memorable example of extension happened during O. J. Simpson's criminal trial. As their defense, lawyers moved to exclude evidence found at the murder scene. They spoke for weeks about shortcomings of the Los Angeles Police Department.

Some famous examples of extension appear on bumper stickers. You see "Register Aliens, Not Guns." And "America: Love It or Leave It."

Sometimes you can see extension coming. When reporters ask an implicating question, a candidate might answer: "That's a good point. I'm glad you brought that up. Let me begin by putting the whole issue into perspective." The candidate, of course, will never return to the question. In politics, evasion is an art form.

Either-Or

The either-or fallacy is a form of extension. Here partisans distort an issue by insisting that only two alternatives exist: their recommendation and something worse. They describe a temperance election as a choice between Christianity and debauchery. They depict abortion as a choice between American family life and murder. Should you question any feature of American foreign policy, they challenge, "Which side are you on, anyway?"

To all such examples of ignoring the question, the reasonable response is "Let's get back to the issue."

■ FALLACIES IN OTHER FORMS

Most of the fallacies mentioned in this chapter could be analyzed as examples of induction, deduction, semantic argument, and so on. A false analogy, for example, is a deduction with invalid form; a post hoc claim is induction with an insufficient sample; and any bad argument can be called a non sequitur. But special terms do exist for these fallacies, and it may be valuable to have two ways of looking at them.

Unless you are championing a particularly weak cause, keep these fallacies out of your writing.

EXERCISES

Identify the fallacies in the following arguments.

1. If you pass out free condoms to high school kids, you might as well give free needles to drug addicts.
2. Of course you oppose no-fault auto insurance. You're a lawyer.
3. "I'm tired of being called a racist. I'm not a racist. The racists today are Jesse Jackson and the NAACP."—Rush Limbaugh
4. Of course, the Bible is true. St. Paul says, "All scripture is given by inspiration of God."
5. "I don't like the idea of abortion either, but I think it's better than having one poor woman kill herself trying to raise 11 or 12 children."
6. "Just two days after Liz Taylor announced plans to wed Larry Fortensky, her ex-husband Eddie Fisher took an overdose of painkillers and was rushed to a hospital in a life-and-death crisis."—*National Enquirer*
7. Arguing from the principle that a person is sick "when he fails to function in his appropriate gender identification," Dr. Charles Socarides, a New York psychoanalyst, concludes that homosexuality is a form of mental illness.
8. I oppose public smoking laws. If the government can make smokers stay in restricted places, can't they do the same for other groups: garlic eaters, children, gum chewers, crippled people, whistlers, senior citizens, and so on?
9. If evolution is true, why has it stopped?
10. Guilt is a terrible thing. Studies show that women who are promiscuous suffer feelings of low self-esteem.
11. I pay for my college education just the way I pay for my groceries in a supermarket. Why does the university think it can tell me what courses I have to take?

12. Gay people are essentially criminal. Look at the homosexuality that goes on in prison.

13. My father smoked a pack of Camels every day for 40 years. Then he died of lung cancer. I'm going to sue R. J. Reynolds for $5 million.

14. After receiving the Lourdes medal, this cash-starved woman received a $75,000 miracle.

15. Creationism in the public schools? Pretty soon we'll have to give equal time to the stork theory.

16. For over a century, every American president elected in a year ending in "0" died in office. But Ronald Reagan didn't. Astrologer Joan Quigley says her forecasts saved him.

17. "You'll love the Meat Lovers Pizza if you like meat and you like pizza."— Pizza Hut ad

18. It's not right to end the life of a terminally ill loved one. St. Paul wrote, "If we are to live like Christ, we must die like Christ."

19. Sure, veterans should have a G.I. bill to give them breaks getting a job or an education. But mothers who stayed home to raise their young children deserve a G.I. bill, too.

20. "Who are you to tell me that I shouldn't use literature to teach writing?"

21. "Millions of people are misnamed at birth, causing them problems and unhappiness throughout their lives."—Krishna Ram-Davi

22. After two LSU football players were arrested for stealing cash and credit cards worth more than $5000, basketball coach Dale Brown defended them. He said they were victims of a sick society that gave them homosexuals and drunks for role models.

ESSAY ASSIGNMENTS

Write an essay either affirming or opposing one of these statements. The arguments you encounter in your background reading may well include logical fallacies. Your essay should have none, or at least none you didn't intend.

1. We should never have deserted our allies in Vietnam.
2. A massive conspiracy led to the assassination of President Kennedy.
3. Prostitution should not be considered a crime; there is no victim.
4. Daylight saving time is unnatural.
5. If I had a different name, I'd be more successful.
6. America's space program is a waste of money.
7. The Hope diamond put a genuine curse on everyone who owned it.
8. X causes crime. (Fill in the X.)

Left-Handers (Those Sickos) Got No Reason To Live!

Roger L. Guffey

If you ask me, the U.S. Supreme Court ruling concerning certain sexual acts between consenting adults in the privacy of their own homes heralds a much welcome return to the right rather than an invasion of privacy and individual rights. To further this admirable goal of moving to the right, I want to encourage the Court now to go after one of the most despicable and un-American groups that threaten our great country today: left-handed people.

Ha, ha, you say. Most people do not realize how truly malevolent these subversive little perverts are. Look up the word "sinister" in the dictionary, and you find two meanings: evil or left-handed. Still not convinced, eh? Historically, the U.S. government has fought leftists worldwide, so let's do it in this country before we take on those in Nicaragua. In this century, every other English-speaking nation makes its citizens drive on the left (i.e., wrong) side of the road. If that doesn't prove how un-American left-handers are, I don't know what does.

Besides, left-handers are not normal. They are so unnatural that I can pick them out of a crowd a mile away. Our society has no use for their sick, twisted kind. Just think of all the things we have designed exclusively for the right-handers: scissors, shirt pockets, phone dials, wrist watches, toilet flush handles, books, etc. Have you ever seen a car with the ignition switch on the left side of the steering column? No, and you won't, because that's not the way God told Henry Ford to make them. You can even turn right against a red light, but if you try to make a left-hand turn against the light, you will find yourself going against society because it is not natural.

Oh, sure, the bleeding hearts will say that we need compassion for these sickos because they were born that way. Hogwash! It's a choice they make. If every mother would give her children a swift rap in the chops at the first sign of this filthy, disgusting left-handed behavior, this degenerate psychosis would vanish. Now, I am all for respecting everybody's rights to be different as long as I agree with what they are doing, but you have to draw the line somewhere. There won't be any left-handers in heaven, you can count on that.

SOURCE: Reprinted from the *Lexington Herald-Leader,* July 10, 1987.

The solution is not just social ostracism. We should all band together and pray fervently that God will strike these little perverts dead. Once this society returns to the moral character and justice that made this country great and prosecutes these deviant miscreants and genetic mistakes to the fullest extent of the law, everything will be all right. Act now before all go out and buy left-handed bicycles. Take heart. God is on our side.

DISCUSSION QUESTIONS

1. How far did you read before you realized the author is not writing about left-handers? What gave you the first clue?
2. What is a danger in writing irony, that is, saying one thing and meaning another?
3. If he isn't writing about left-handedness, what is he writing about?
4. If the analogy between left-handedness and homosexuality is valid, what does that say about homosexuality?
5. Do you think the analogy is valid?
6. Why does the author take such an extreme and angry position? Why all the emotional language? Whom is he mad at?
7. Why his references to God and heaven? Is the author religious? Is he irreligious?
8. Is the author a good writer? What makes this article easy to read?

Is This Intelligent Design or What?

Timothy Johnson

They're arguing about evolution again. I thought we gave that up years ago.

A New England high school is spearheading a national effort to downplay discussions of evolution. Biology teachers were ordered to read a statement in class. It said that evolution is only a theory and that the universe "shows evidence of intelligent design." By contrast, as you probably know, Darwin's Natural Selection suggests that life just started somehow and has muddled along mindlessly ever since.

Did the universe occur just by accident? I remember the Woody Allen story where an existentialist philosopher insisted that everything on earth had occurred by chance, except his breakfast, which he knew had been prepared by his landlady.

These are provocative areas. Last month, I finished "The Fifth Miracle" by Paul Davies, a book about biogenesis, the origin of life. After ranging analyses, the author's best guess was that, following the Big Bang explosion, gravity pulled dust and fragments together to form suns and stars and planets. Inside some of these were micro-organisms. They didn't need light or oxygen; they could live far underground or in ocean depths. Over the eons, these evolved and became plants, animals and human beings. Davies doesn't think life was ever created; he says it always was.

This may be true, but it doesn't answer many questions. We still wonder when and how life began. Where did these micro-organisms come from? And where in that Big Bang cataclysm is evidence of intelligent design?

For the people who use the phrase, "intelligent design" is a codeword for "God," for a divine presence watching over events. They quote Genesis: The Lord created everything, "and He saw that it was good."

Yes, but how good was it? Wasn't there a lot of waste? Why have a universe that was 14 billion years old before major life-forms appeared? Why is it so vast (millions of light-years across) and so empty? Current thought suggests that space is infinite. It has no outer limit and just goes on and on.

These origin questions may have an answer, but I don't know it. Me, I believe in God (because I need to) and in evolution (because the evidence is

SOURCE: Reprinted with permission of the author.

compelling)—but I'm uncomfortable speculating about divine purpose or intelligent design.

It isn't easy to accept the Garden of Eden story—or that Big Bang scenario. So I sit here with fundamental questions. Like Woody Allen's philosopher, I know my meals don't occur by chance. Theresa prepares them and she is a wonderful cook. (We had baked catfish last night.) But did Theresa occur by chance? Is she—like you and me and Thomas Aquinas and Shakespeare and Isaac Newton—is she the product of a cosmic accident, like a chemical spill out on the highway? Maybe—but I keep thinking, "There must be more to it than that."

I'm surest of intelligent design in the universe when I eat a tangerine. There it is. It fits in my hand. It peels easily. Inside, the fruit is separated into bite-size pieces. These divide without difficulty, and they taste delicious. (I always think, "Whoever made this knew what he was doing.")

Except for tangerines, I'm not sure about intelligent design, though Beethoven sonatas, Starbucks Coffee and golden retrievers would seem pretty good evidence.

I mention this issue because that's what Clint McCarty and I discussed at Hooters last week. Looking across our table, I couldn't imagine that Clint occurred just by chance. He is brilliant, sane, and morally concerned—a former CBS newsman. I didn't think the Budweiser we were drinking occurred by chance, that somebody just mixed it up in a back room. Carrie, our waitress, was a shapely beauty, an easy argument for intelligent design.

On the other hand, newspapers that day spoke of an AIDS epidemic and tsunami devastation. The man sitting at an adjacent table was obese. Food offered on the menu was unhealthy, mainly salt, fat and sugar. The music playing behind the bar was loud and cacophonous. I couldn't find intelligent design there.

I thought about these things for several minutes, then gave it up. This was no time for rational speculation. I called Carrie to our table and ordered another Budweiser. She smiled and said, "Sure thing, guys. I'll bring it right over."

DISCUSSION QUESTIONS

1. Do you feel the universe shows evidence of it? How could you argue for it, or how could you argue against it? Does it lend itself to evidence?
2. Do the author's wife and golden retriever and tangerines seem sufficient evidence to prove God?

3. Do the author's references to his personal life, to his wife, to his reading, to what he had for supper, make the essay more readable? More persuasive?

4. The author writes, "Me, I believe in God (because I need to) and in evolution (because the evidence is compelling)—but I'm uncomfortable speculating about divine purpose or intelligent design." Does this have to be an either-or choice?

5. What is the effect of using Hooters as the setting for the argument?

6. Does the last paragraph leave the argument or continue it?

How would you like the police to investigate your miscarriage?

So-called "pro-lifers" think nothing of invading women's privacy and jeopardizing their health. Their national campaign of violence and intimidation attracts plenty of media attention.

But the outrages they commit now are nothing compared to what would happen if they win.

Their Human Life Amendment to the Constitution treats the fetus as an independent human being from the very instant of fertilization. Abortion would be called murder under all circumstances. So would many effective birth control methods. And every miscarriage could be suspect.

While some anti-choice activists declare that only health professionals who assist with an abortion should be charged with murder, countless women could be caught up in police investigations and prosecutions even if they are never arraigned.

If the right to choose abortion is limited or eliminated, women who can afford to travel could probably evade the law.

Poor women and teenagers with no resources would be forced to induce their own abortions, or subject themselves to an illicit, dangerous back-alley procedure.

And thousands of them would be brutalized, maimed and killed.

How do we know what will happen if the extremists win? Because that's the way it was before abortion was made legal and safe in 1973. The choice they present isn't whether abortion should be stopped.

Prohibition never worked.

The choice is privacy...or punishment. Safety for women...or terrible danger. It's really not a choice we need to make again.

Make time to save your right to choose. Before the so-called "pro-lifers" start making your choices for you.

- - - - - - - - - - - - - - - - - -

Take action! Here's my urgent contribution to support Planned Parenthood's Campaign to Keep Abortion Safe and Legal:

NAME

ADDRESS

CITY   STATE   ZIP

Don't wait until women are dying again. Planned Parenthood®

DISCUSSION QUESTIONS

1. The author speaks of women being "brutalized, maimed and killed." Identify other examples of emotional language in this ad. Is the language appropriate for the message?

2. Does the ad speak of those opposing abortion as "pro-life"? What are they called?

3. "The choice is privacy . . . or punishment. Safety for women . . . or terrible danger." Is this an example of the either-or fallacy?

4. Do pro-life advocates really intend that police investigate miscarriages? Is this a likely prospect under any legal situation? What fallacy is illustrated here?

Sizism—One of the Last "Safe" Prejudices

Sally E. Smith

As obscene as it sounds, a generation or two ago, Black people were considered to be inherently ugly, stupid, unsanitary, lazy, and enslaved by creature comforts. Today, fat people are assumed to be inherently ugly, stupid, unsanitary, lazy, and enslaved by creature comforts. Such stereotypes are reinforced by both the media and the public. Even in "politically correct" circles, where one would never hear derogatory remarks about people of color, gays and lesbians, or people with disabilities, one continues to hear disparaging remarks about fat people.

Stereotypes, and the resulting prejudice, develop from a belief that a group of people share common characteristics. This belief is almost always grounded in myth. The central myth surrounding the prejudice against fat people is that, if fat people really wanted to, they could lose weight. It doesn't seem to matter that research indicates that fat people are fat because of heredity and metabolic factors; that 95–98% of all diets fail within three to five years; that much of the $33 billion that the diet industry earns annually comes at the expense of the health and well being of fat people; that more people will die from weight loss surgery than died in the Vietnam War; that yo-yo dieting makes a person fatter; that most fat people have no more choice in their size than a person does in the color of their skin. Our society, which accepts that in the bell curve of the human species, some people will be shorter or taller than average, and some people will be thinner than average, cannot accept that some people will be fatter than average.

This climate of non-acceptance creates a "blame the victim" mentality, wherein myths and stereotypes are used to justify treating fat people as second-class citizens. This has a devastating effect on the quality of life for fat people. Fat people are discriminated against in employment, in that they are denied employment, denied promotions and raises, denied benefits, and sometimes fired, all because of their weight. Fat people are discriminated against in education, in that they are not accepted into graduate programs, and are harassed and expelled because of their weight. Fat people cannot adopt children, solely because of their weight. Fat people are denied access to adequate medical care, in that they are denied treatment, misdiagnosed,

SOURCE: Reprinted from *California NOW*, July 1990. Reprinted by permission of the author.

harassed, and treated as though every medical condition, from a sore throat to a broken bone, is a weight-related condition. Fat people are denied access to public accommodations, such as public transportation, airline travel, theatres, and restaurants because seating is not available for them.

Because fat people are fair game for ridicule and public humiliation, they face substantial social discrimination. Epithets are screamed at fat people; ice cream cones are snatched out of the hands of fat people "for their own good"; fat people are run off of public beaches and out of health spas, because they do not look "acceptable."

This discrimination takes an enormous toll on a fat person's self-esteem, particularly when the person is a child. Unlike children in many other oppressed groups, fat children get little support from parents, teachers, or peers; instead of receiving support from her parents or teachers when other children make sizist remarks, a fat child will often be told, "If only you lost weight, you wouldn't have this problem."

Research has documented that women are most often the victims of size discrimination. Perhaps this is because men have traditionally garnered credibility through the power and wealth they accumulate, and women have garnered credibility through how closely they conform to society's ideals of beauty. Size discrimination is therefore linked to sexism. Because women of certain ethnic groups tend to be fatter than white women, size discrimination is linked to racism. Because women get fatter as they get older (a physiological phenomenon), size discrimination is linked to ageism. Because lower income women tend to be fatter than higher income women, size discrimination is linked to classism. There should be no doubt that size discrimination is a feminist issue.

In most places, discrimination against fat people is perfectly legal. Currently, there is only one state, Michigan, which has a statute prohibiting size discrimination. And there are only a few cities which have ordinances prohibiting discrimination based on personal appearance. When a fat person decides to fight size discrimination, she most often has to litigate using disability rights laws. But the truth is, while some fat people are disabled, most fat people aren't disabled, leading some courts to create a Catch-22 for fat people. There was a case in Pennsylvania, for example, where the court said that even though the employer didn't want to hire the person because of his/her physical problems, those problems were not a handicap, and therefore the fat person was not protected by the handicap law. Can you have it both ways? "We're not hiring you because you're physically inadequate, but you're not protected because you are physically adequate."

Fat people desperately need statutory protection, both to raise their quality of life, and to ensure an avenue of redress should they be discriminated against. The words "height and weight" should be added as a protected category, so that an employer cannot arbitrarily dismiss a candidate or an employee because of her size. Schools and universities should not receive state or federal funding if they discriminate against fat people. High school curriculum dealing with civil rights movements should include the size acceptance movement. Training for teachers should include material to raise sensitivity about size issues, and school health care professionals should have accurate information about fat and health, and the self-esteem issues of fat children. There should be a mandate that every public building, from jury boxes in courtrooms to desks in schools, be accessible to fat people.

Neither the California Legislature nor Congress has taken an interest in size discrimination issues. A Congressional subcommittee is holding a series of informational hearings on regulating the diet industry. Legislation coming out of these hearings may give fat people some consumer protection, but will do nothing for problems of size discrimination.

Because this is a feminist issue, NOW should take a public stance against size discrimination. An anti-size discrimination resolution, first passed by California NOW at our 1988 Conference, will be considered at the 1990 National NOW Conference in San Francisco.

DISCUSSION QUESTIONS

1. Why does the author describe her subjects as "fat people"? Why doesn't she call them "big" or "heavy"? Why doesn't she use the politically correct term "people of size"?
2. Do you discriminate against fat people? (Think of people who are 100 pounds overweight.) Will you accept them as your friends? Would you date one of them? Would you want your child to marry one of them? Would you blackball them from a private club? Would you hire them? Would you promote them to an important job? Discuss the issues involved here.
3. The author rejects the claim that fat people could be thinner if they wanted to. Does this mean that if they stopped eating, they wouldn't lose weight? What does it mean?
4. This is mainly an argument by analogy. It submits that people should not be penalized for conditions they didn't choose, that no one should be rejected because of size, gender, skin color, physical handicap, age, or national origin. Are these conditions analogous?
5. Should airlines, theaters, restaurants, and classrooms be legally required to have seats that will hold fat people? Is this different from the requirement that they have special facilities for handicapped people?

6. Is a fat person physically handicapped?
7. The author says that "lower income women tend to be fatter than higher income women" and thus sizism is a class distinction (one that shouldn't exist in a democracy). Why are higher income women thinner?
8. How prejudiced is the doctor who treats most of a fat person's ailments as if they were weight-related?

Pave the Stupid Rain Forests!

Ed Anger

I'm madder than a monkey with a rotten banana over all this hullabaloo about saving the stupid rain forests in South America.

Wimpy environmentalists are crying big fat tears because a bunch of headhunters in Brazil are chopping down some trees to make a little extra spending money.

These fruitcake Chicken Littles believe if we chop up jungles there won't be any more air and we'll all die.

Hogwash! They can PAVE the darn rain forests for all I care.

Let's face it. The first thing our Founding Fathers did when they landed on America's shores was start cutting down trees.

George Washington and Thomas Jefferson were farsighted enough to know that you can't build shopping malls in the woods, for crying out loud.

Our great nation doesn't have one single rain forest and I'm breathing just fine, thank you. If the rain forests are so healthy, then why in hell are all the people who live there trying to come here?

And another thing. The nuclear plant protesters who scream doom and gloom about the rain forests are the same nut cases who believe in this ozone stuff. You know, there's supposed to be a hole in the ozone layer over the North Pole or something and we're all supposed to get cancer and die because it lets too much sunshine in. Phooey!

It's supposed to be caused by all those cans of spray paint we've used to make America more beautiful. So let's just put ozone in spray cans and sell it to these scaredy-cat environmentalists.

These yellowbellies could just spray it into the air and patch the hole over the North Pole in no time flat. I mean, how difficult can it be to put ozone in a can?

And while I'm on the subject, I'll tell you another thing. These bleeding-heart nature freaks say they want to save the rain forests and all that stuff for our children. That's a crock.

Ask any red-blooded American teenager where he'd rather be—in a nice air-conditioned shopping mall playing video games or slapping mosquitoes in some godforsaken jungle?

SOURCE: *Weekly World News*, February 1, 2000. Reprinted with permission of the *Weekly World News*.

DISCUSSION QUESTIONS

1. What can you infer when an author named Ed Anger begins his essay "I'm madder than a monkey . . ."?
2. Do you think the author is genuinely angry about this issue? Why is he so hostile?
3. What evidence is there that Anger is more than an ignorant loudmouth?
4. Whom is this article addressed to?
5. Why does he invoke patriotic language: "Washington," "Jefferson," "our founding fathers," "our great nation"?
6. Does his argument against environmentalists seem genuine? How reasonable is his plan to patch the ozone layer?
7. Is this author a good writer?

Women Priests? Never!

S. L. Varnado

On May 30, Pope John Paul II issued an apostolic letter entitled "On Reserving Priestly Ordination to Men." The letter was intended to settle, once and for all, the controversy over "women priests," but thus far it has had the opposite effect. Like that annoying rabbit on the T. V. commercial, the controversy "just keeps going."

An editorial in *Commonweal*, for instance, described the letter as "an impetuous and Draconian response to a complex and still relatively unexplored development." The *New York Times* said the letter reinforces the impression of "a papacy wary of feminist intrusion." These and similar voices of dissent suggest that the Pope made a bad mistake in issuing his letter. I don't think he did, as the following arguments attempt to show.

1. John Paul II is a benevolent and flexible leader who has consistently demonstrated his concern for women's causes. His letter declares that the role of women in the church is "absolutely necessary and irreplaceable"; and to prove it, the Pope might point to the increasing involvement of women in church affairs. Thanks in large part to his influence, we now have women lectors, preachers, education directors, writers, theologians—even altar girls! If it would help matters, I feel sure the Pope would immediately fax a letter to the bishops recommending that women serve as bouncers at church bazaars! The idea that he is "Draconian" or "wary of feminist intrusion" is ludicrous.

2. The letter spends considerable time explaining why the tradition of a male priesthood—unlike altar boys, fish on Friday, on kneeling for communion—cannot be changed at will. The twelve men who were called to be apostles, it argues, "did not in fact receive only a function which could thereafter be exercised by any member of the church; rather they were specifically and intimately associated in the mission of the Incarnate Word." This teaching, it adds, is not a reflection on the "lesser dignity" of women. Even Mary, the Mother of the Church, was not appointed as an apostle. To change this ancient tradition would be far more than cosmetic surgery—it would amount to a major operation.

SOURCE: A letter to *Catholic Week* (Mobile, Alabama) July 8, 1994. Reprinted by permission of the author.

3. But such an operation, even if permitted, would trivialize Catholic theology beyond recognition. Our theology has historically affirmed that the priest stands as "representative" of The Son. The image of "maleness" is symbolic, to be sure, but it has the full force of scripture. If words mean anything at all, it is difficult to see how, after two thousand years of history, the word "Son" can suddenly be re-interpreted to mean "son or Daughter." This would amount to a kind of metaphysical sex change.

4. Moreover, such a change would imply that Catholic doctrine is something that can be altered whenever the mood suits us. We could abolish such difficult teachings as miracles, original sin, the Virgin Birth—and that troublesome business about Hell! If all this were possible, however, I see no reason why we shouldn't simply close down the institutional church and reorganize it as a civic club or a debating society. Then there would be no problems. Any doctrine that proved inconvenient or unfashionable could be changed by motion, second, and majority vote.

All talk about tradition and theology, however, will probably make little impression on the more extreme feminists in our midsts. As I see the matter, they suffer from a condition that might best be described as "cosmic dissatisfaction." The letter makes it perfectly clear that they are "equal" in every respect to men; but that apparently isn't enough for them. They don't want mere equality—they want to abolish sexual distinction itself.

Their attitude is a mystery to an old troglodyte like me and, I suspect, to a charitable gentleman like the Pope. He has tried to satisfy them, but it's like trying to satisfy an assembly line. They just keep coming at him with new demands. Sigmund Freud—scarcely a male chauvinist—said he could never quite figure out what women wanted. If he was talking about more ardent "feminists," I agree.

DISCUSSION QUESTIONS

1. The author describes the Pope "as a benevolent and flexible leader who has consistently demonstrated his concern for women's causes." Describe the author's attitude toward the idea of women priests. To what extent does he appear "benevolent" and "flexible" about "women's causes"?

2. Why does the Catholic church allow "increasing involvement of women in church affairs" but not allow women to become priests?

3. Find passages where the author editorializes about women's rights and the women's movement. Does editorializing enhance his argument? Why or why not?

4. The author gives four reasons in defense of the Pope's letter, "On Reserving Priestly Ordination to Men." What are they? Rank the reasons in order from most to least persuasive.

5. Do you see any fallacies among these four reasons? If so, what are they? How would you revise the reasons to eliminate the fallacies? What would you say?

6. The author refers to himself as an "old troglodyte." Who is his audience in this essay? To whom is an "old troglodyte" most likely to be persuasive?

Argument by Authority

"Thanks to the Buddha, I won $10,000.00."
—L. W., FLA

Much of what you believe—or are asked to believe—must be accepted simply on the word of an expert. Your doctor says you have glaucoma. Your mechanic says the car needs a valve job. Your newspaper reviews the film *Whale Rider* and calls it awful. Scientific authorities say the universe is expanding. In such instances, you are asked to accept a view on the basis of someone's authority.

It is reasonable to credit such testimony if it fulfills two conditions: (1) the speaker must be a genuine expert on the subject at hand, and (2) there must be no reasonable probability of bias. When Steve Young, for example, leaves his professional football career to praise the effects of Advil, you can justly question his expertise in the area. When Charles Barkley appears on television praising the excellence of Right Guard, you know he is being paid for the advertisement and infer a degree of bias.

Remember, however, that these unreliable arguments are not necessarily false. Steve Young may be expressing an important truth about Advil, and Charles Barkley may be giving his honest opinion of Right Guard. Nevertheless, it would be unreasonable to accept an argument—or to build a persuasive essay—solely on the authority of such speakers. You should compare their views to other evidence and to the word of other authorities.

■ EXPERT TESTIMONY

Many arguments raise the question of genuine expertness. Authorities may be unnamed. (Advertisements for health products often print testimony from "Brazilian researchers" or "five New York doctors.") They may be unfamiliar. ("*Promise of Saccharin* is a provocative book—readable and profoundly informed."—Colonel Winston X. Montgomery, III.) They may be known largely by their degrees. (A Kansas medico, in recommending goat gland surgery to restore vitality, signed himself "John R. Brinkley, M.D., C.M., Dr.P.H., Sc.D. . . . ") And they may appear with strange credentials. (A self-help book by Scott Reed describes him as "one of the nation's leading mind-power experts.") Persuaders always magnify the reputations of authorities who agree with them. A temperance circular quoting William Gladstone's condemnation of alcohol calls him "the greatest prime minister in English history."

Sometimes speakers of unquestioned authority express themselves in areas outside their competence. Actor Tony Randall praises Easy-Off Oven Pads. Actress Brooke Shields warns of the medical effects of cigarette smoking. Rural evangelists pinpoint weaknesses in evolutionary theory. And a U.S. Senate subcommittee (by a 3–1 vote) declares that human life begins at conception. You should judge such people on the quality of their evidence, not on their word as experts.

Religious Authority

Equally questionable as authorities are "God" and "everyone." Because the claim is not subject to verification with hard evidence, one can champion almost any opinion by saying it conforms to divine will. A correspondent to the *Mobile Press* once assured readers that Hurricane Danny was God's warning to Alabamians not to legalize gambling. Another correspondent declared it would violate "Christ's plan for the world" if the United States gave up its holdings in Panama. And during the 1980 and 1984 elections, the Moral Majority (and pro-life organizations) insisted that Ronald Reagan was God's choice for president of the United States.

Christian writers routinely quote passages from the Bible to declare the will of God and thus open up a rich area of argument. As mentioned earlier, religious questions seldom lend themselves to meaningful discussion because people cannot agree on necessary definitions. Clearly, an argument involving biblical authority can be persuasive only when addressed to someone who already accepts the truth of scripture and who interprets it in the same way as the speaker. There are large differences between those who claim the Bible *is* the word of God, those who say it *contains* the word of God, those who enjoy it as an anthology of Jewish literature, and those who reject it altogether.

Even when people agree on preliminary matters, problems remain. Because biblical texts were written by many authors over the course of 1300 years and include a wide variety of opinions, literary styles, and translations, persuaders can find a passage or two to support any argument they choose to make. Bishop James Pike illustrated this by asking ironically, "How many persons have been reborn from meditating on the last line of Psalm 137: 'Blessed shall he be that taketh and dasheth the little ones against the stone'?" Consequently, when facing a scriptural argument, you should take time to trace the references. You will find that authors often quote passages out of context (they might be championing the superficial counsel of Job's friends) and quote passages inaccurately from memory. They may cite lines scarcely related to the issue at hand. ("Only God can save America now. See Chronicles 7:14.")

An interesting modern claim says, "Of course, God favors capital punishment; otherwise He wouldn't have used it as a means to save the world." The problem with this argument is that it also puts God on the side of betrayal of friends, unjust trials, torture, and other atrocities.

Mass Authority

The authority of "everyone" is claimed in statements beginning, "They say," "Everyone knows," or "All fair-minded people agree."

Such arguments can be convincing in instances where "they" (some notable majority) have demonstrably committed themselves on a matter they are competent to judge. Arguments announcing "More women choose Simplicity than any other pattern" and "Budweiser—Largest Selling Beer in the World" are impressive because, in these areas, the opinion of a mass audience is superior to that of any particular expert. (In 1996, *Consumer Reports* announced that "Old Milwaukee and Stroh's are the best-tasting mass-market beers." You wonder if this persuaded anybody.)

It is important to remember that America's democratic procedures and its jury system both rely on the expertness of "everyone."

But mass authority can be distorted in a number of ways. It can be claimed arbitrarily. ("Everyone knows that Bill Clinton bought the 1996 election with foreign money.") It can be coupled with ambiguous language. ("More men get more pleasure out of Roi-Tan than any other cigar at its price.") And it can be invoked in areas that call for technical information. (A Gallup poll reported that 41 percent of Americans believe that cigarette smoking is a cause of birth defects.) In such instances, "everyone" is a dubious authority.

Still, mass opinion is worth listening to, especially when it becomes more or less unanimous. Remember the famous counsel, "If you can keep your head when all about you are losing theirs, probably you haven't grasped the situation."

Divided Authority

The word of a genuine expert will not, of course, settle every argument. Alexander Pope put the question best:

> Who shall decide when Doctors disagree.
> And soundest Casuists doubt, like you and me?

The plain fact is that many issues are complex, and experts hold opposing views. Legal authorities disagree over whether certain means of gathering evidence violate constitutional safeguards. (Was Marion Barry entrapped?) Eminent psychiatrists appear in court arguing the mental competence of particular defendants. (Was Theodore Kaczynski, the Unabomber, insane?) Medical experts do not agree on whether a month-old fetus is human. (Is abortion murder?)

Which authorities should you believe? In such cases, it's probably best to side with the majority of experts. However, when you hear a genuinely important authority voicing a minority view (for example, Rachel Carson on insecticides, or Linus Pauling on vitamin C), you would do well to withhold judgment altogether and await further evidence.

Critical Authority

You should recognize that some authorities have more established reputations than others. For example, many publications contain reviews of books, plays, and movies, but the reviews of the major New York newspapers, the television networks, and nationally circulated periodicals (*Time, Newsweek, Harpers,* and *Christian Science Monitor,* etc.) are generally considered more critically reliable.

If a book, movie, or play wins praise from critics writing in these publications, the reviews may be quoted in newspaper ads and on book jackets. If an advertisement quotes reviews from other sources, it strongly suggests that the work was not praised by the major critics. It may not be very good.

Of course, you can enjoy any book, play, or movie whatever the critics say, but you should recognize the varying standards of critical authorities. You should be warned, for example, when you see the cover of the paperback edition of Nancy Freeman's *Joshua Son of None* boasting rave reviews from the *El Paso Times,* the *San Gabriel Valley Tribune,* the *Macon Georgian,* and the *Oceanside Blade-Tribune.*

You should recognize these distinctions when writing a critical essay. If the book or movie you're championing is praised by the major critics, quote the reviews. If it found favor only with lesser authorities, you probably shouldn't mention the reviews at all.

■ BIASED TESTIMONY

Even when speakers are admitted experts in the field under discussion, an argument should be examined for the possibility of bias. An argument has a probable bias if the authority profits from expressing it or if it reflects the predictable loyalty or routine antagonism of a group. To dismiss the testimony of biased individuals does not mean calling them liars or even saying they are wrong; it means a condition exists that makes it unreasonable to accept a conclusion *solely* on their authority. You don't ask a barber whether you need a haircut.

Rewarded Opinions

Experts profit from making an argument when it brings them money or prestige. The financial incentive is easy to recognize when Bill Cosby recommends Jell-O pudding or Kodak film, when Uri Geller proclaims his psychic powers on lecture tours, and when owners of outdoor movies protest the unnaturalness of daylight saving time.

Today many people earn money by convincing you of preposterous "facts." Tabloid advertisers boast incredible products that will let you grow new hair, develop a larger bosom, win at the racetrack, lose 16 pounds in a week, and find true love by wearing Madame Zarina's talisman. Papers like the *Star* and the *National Enquirer* routinely carry stories of reincarnated housewives, arthritis cures, and space creatures that appeared in Canada. Recent best-selling books reveal that Errol Flynn was a Nazi spy, that Marilyn Monroe was murdered, that the Mafia killed President Kennedy, and that the Lindbergh baby is still alive. Such stories are fun to read, and there may be splinters of truth in some of them. But you can give no special belief to the authors of such tales. They are making money peddling their extravagant claims.

The effect of prestige is clear when individuals discuss their incomes, their reading habits, and their sex lives. In these areas, egos are threatened— and people lie.

The impact of money and prestige on an expert is sometimes difficult to establish. For example, few scientific authorities have affirmed the existence of Atlantis or of UFOs, but the few who do have won a level of recognition— along with television appearances, lecture tours, and book contracts—that they could never have won voicing more orthodox opinions. (You won't get on a talk show saying that fluoride prevents cavities.) These experts may be expressing their honest judgments, but you should remember all that acclaim when evaluating their testimony.

The 1987 revelations concerning TV evangelist Jim Bakker and church secretary Jessica Hahn illustrate problems relating to argument by authority. Both told of a sexual episode, though each remembered it differently. We know, however, that Bakker was trying to save his reputation as a religious leader. And we know Hahn changed her story twice when offered large sums of money. In such a case, you have to rely on outside evidence. You can't be comfortable believing either authority.

Things are settling down now, but for a long time, Americans heard dramatic misinformation about AIDS victims and the AIDS virus. Much of it came from tabloid reporters who wanted a sensational story and from zealous evangelists who wanted to announce God's vengeance. The place to get reliable facts about AIDS is the Centers for Disease Control and Prevention in Atlanta.

Predictable Judgments

An argument by authority is presumed to be biased if it is totally predictable—that is, when it reflects a traditional loyalty or antagonism. When you want to learn about the new Ford Explorers, you can't rely on the word of your Chevy dealer. You can't learn the truth about a woman's character by asking her ex-husband.

A classic example of a predictable and biased judgment occurred in 1977 when the University of Alabama's football team was ranked second in the final Associated Press and United Press International polls. Thereupon, the Alabama state legislature issued its own poll, and the Crimson Tide moved up to No. 1. Equally predictable are pamphlets on smoking and health distributed by the Tobacco Institute, articles on gun control and crime appearing in *American Rifleman,* and the publicized study of pain relievers produced by the makers of Bayer aspirin.

In 1986, when Attorney General Edwin Meese appointed a commission to investigate the effects of pornography on the social order, he remembered that a 1970 commission appointed by President Nixon had found that pornography did not cause dangerous behavior. So Meese selected a commission that would bring in a different ruling. Most of the members he chose were well known as militant opponents of pornography. And they brought in a report recommending controlling sexual images and texts. There may be merit in these recommendations, but they came from a biased source.

This presumption of bias appears most notably in political argument. When any Democrat is nominated for president, the candidate and the party's platform will be praised in liberal periodicals (*Washington Post, St. Louis Post Dispatch, Commonweal, The Progressive,* etc.) and condemned in conservative publications (*Chicago Tribune, U.S. News & World Report, American Spectator, National Review,* etc.). When any president finishes a State of the Union message, opposition speakers will call his program inadequate, wrongheaded, and potentially dangerous. You must judge these claims on specific evidence; such predictable views carry little authority.

■ DISTORTING QUOTATIONS

Besides a doubtful expert and a biased opinion, other misleading features attend argument by authority. Statements are sometimes abridged. (The advertisement for Kyle Onstott's *Mandingo* quotes a review from the *Dallas News:* ". . . like no other book ever written about the South. . . . ") Claims may be irrelevant to the issue at hand. (The paperback edition of *Nightmare in Pink* prints Richard Condon's opinion that "John D. MacDonald is the great American story-teller.") Quotations can appear without a source. (See *Hand in Hand*—"The Most Widely Praised Picture of Them All!") And undated quotations can be impressive. (During his presidential campaigns, opponents printed statements Ronald Reagan had made years before when he was a Democrat.)

Exact quotations can be presented in a distorting context. Under the heading "How L.B.J. Would Remake America," *Common Sense* printed a sentence from President Johnson's State of the Union message: "We are going to try to take all the money that we think is unnecessarily being spent and take it from the 'haves' and give it to the 'have nots' that need it so much." As the context of the speech made clear, the president did not advocate taking from the rich to give to the poor; he proposed taking money from the more heavily funded federal programs and putting it into those with smaller appropriations.

For decades, conservative speakers quoted Nikita Khrushchev's line "We will bury you," interpreting it as a Soviet threat to destroy the United States. The sentence is lifted totally out of context. Actually, Khrushchev was saying that the communist economic system would outproduce the capitalist system, and thus survive it. The statement wasn't addressed to the United States.

In the same way, temperance advocates like to strengthen their argument by quoting lines from Chaucer ("Character and shame depart when wine comes in") and Shakespeare ("O thou invisible spirit of wine, if thou hast no name to be known by, let us call thee devil!"). The lines, of course, are not direct expressions of these authors; they come from literary characters who are speaking in a dramatic context.

The hallmark of distorted quotations is the *Congressional Record,* which purports to be a record of what went on during House and Senate sessions. The periodical does record what the legislators said. But it also deletes what they said and reports what they wish they had said. It is a magnificently self-serving document and should be always be questioned when quoted as an argumentative source.

Audiotaped and Videotaped Evidence

With the advent of audio and video recorders, a persuader can produce new kinds of distorted testimony. In the 1972 senatorial campaign in Alabama, opponents broadcast Senator John Sparkman's voice saying, "Will the cause of desegregation be served? If so, then busing is all right." The two sentences were spliced together from separate parts of a taped interview. President Nixon recorded his phone calls and office conversations and produced the tapes that eventually implicated him in the Watergate scandal. Noting that the president made totally contradictory statements on the tape, Congressman Tip O'Neill speculated about Nixon's intention:

> Now that tells you what he was going to do with those tapes. He was going to take them with him when he left and spend years editing them, and then he could string together a record of his own which would show he was the greatest man ever to live. He'd be able to prove it with the tapes. You never would have known about any of the other tapes. That would have been thrown away. They would have only given you all these tapes with him making a hero of himself.

In the Abscam trials in the early 1980s, the FBI convicted government officials with the help of videotapes that showed them taking money and making incriminating promises to an agent posing as an Arab sheikh asking for favors. Here it is important to remember that the FBI agents had complete control of the situation. They could introduce topics, guide the conversation, stop it when convenient, tape some episodes, not tape others, and then choose which tapes they wanted to show in court. The Abscam defendants may not have been faultless, but it is hard to imagine Mother Teresa surviving such a test.

In 1984, a California jury saw films showing John DeLorean with quantities of illegal cocaine. They also saw a number of FBI agents who were taking part in an elaborate charade. The jury believed that DeLorean was a victim of entrapment. They found him not guilty.

In 1986, advocates produced a radio ad about cigarette companies and broadcast New York City Mayor Ed Koch's voice repeating, "They are selling death." In fact, Koch was talking about New York City bathhouses, which he thought were spreading AIDS.

You must take great care in analyzing audio and video evidence. There is a lot to consider besides the words and pictures you see.

Lies

Expert testimony can lend itself to bald misstatement of fact on the part of authorities or of those who quote them. A national columnist accused author Quentin Reynolds of being a Communist and a war profiteer. In the aftermath of Hurricane Katrina, both public officials and reporters for national television networks announced the number of dead in New Orleans to be in excess of 10,000. A U.S. senator called newsman Drew Pearson a child molester. Many have circulated the story that three Pennsylvania students on LSD became blind from staring at the sun for several hours and that a Michigan schoolteacher took off her clothes to demonstrate female anatomy to her coed sex education class. All these sensational claims were untrue.

Fictional quotations often appear as evidence. For many years the statement "We shall force the United States to spend itself to destruction" was attributed to V. I. Lenin and used to ground conservative political argument. Lenin never said that or anything like it. More recently, liberal sources circulated a paragraph protesting the communist threat and concluding, "We need law and order"; they ascribed this to Adolph Hitler. The quotation is pure fiction. Several years ago a tabloid headlined the news that marijuana may cure cancer. The story quoted Dr. James H. Kostinger, director of research for the Pittsburgh Academy of Forensic Medicine, who had been conducting studies in this area for four years. Investigation later revealed that the academy did not exist and that no medical school in Pittsburgh had ever heard of Dr. Kostinger.

Currently a number of famous women have announced they were abused by their fathers. They came to this conclusion through long periods of analysis which convinced them they had repressed traumatic memories. Some men "remembered" being abused by priests. Traditional psychiatrists call these memories suspect.

Although expert testimony can be misused by dishonest writers and speakers, it remains a forceful element of legitimate argument. When genuine authorities agree with you, quote them in your writing. Your case will be more persuasive.

How reliable are the following arguments from authority?

1. "I know UFOs are real because I've seen one."—Dennis Weaver
2. Baron Philippe de Rothschild's Mouton-Cadet—"Enjoyed more by discerning people than any other bordeaux wine in the world."
3. "The most disadvantaged peace is better than the most just war."—Erasmus
4. *Shakespeare of London* by Marchette Chute: "The best biography of Shakespeare"—Bernadine Kielty, *Book-of-the-Month Club News*
5. "72% of men have had sex by age 19."—Tom Biacree, *How Do You Rate?*
6. The Mont Blanc Diplomat—"Many pen experts here and abroad consider the Diplomat to be the finest pen ever designed. It's Europe's most prized pen, unmatched in writing ease."
7. "Causes of Cancer Remain Unknown"—headline in the *Tobacco Observer*
8. "O. J. Simpson's net worth is 33 million"—Prosecuting attorneys in the O. J. Simpson civil suit.
9. "O. J. Simpson's net worth is 5 million"—Defense attorneys in the O. J. Simpson civil suit.
10. "Adolf Hitler Is Alive!!!"—headline in the *National Examiner*
11. *Hitler's Daughter* by Gary Goss: "A brilliant academic satire"—Dennis Renault, *Sacramento Bee;* "A hilarious time"—Harry Cargas, *Buffalo Press;* "Raunchy and unfair"—Otto Tumiel, *Reading Intelligencer*
12. Pond's Cold Cream—"They say you can tell by a girl's complexion when she's in love."
13. "A bad peace is even worse than war."—Tacitus
14. "I might possibly be the Lindbergh child."—Harold Olson
15. "If I have a sore throat, or a rasp, or something that feels like laryngitis, I will visualize the color blue. Certain colors represent specific areas of the body, and blue is the color for the throat."—Shirley MacLaine.
16. *Vampire's Kiss:* "Just about the most interesting film of the year so far"—Andy Klein, *L. A. Herald Examiner*
17. "There's never an uncomfortable moment with the Plus 90i from Bryant. That's what I call having the right stuff."—Chuck Yeager, USAF, Ret.
18. "WordFinder has changed my life. I never used to use a thesaurus."—William J. Buckley, Jr.
19. "President James Garfield was able to write Latin with one hand and Greek with the other—and at the same time."—Dave Dutton, *Weird and Wacky Facts about Famous Oddballs*
20. "Cast thy bread upon the waters: For thou shalt find it after many days."—Ecclesiastes

21. "All reputable biologists have agreed that evolution of life on Earth is an established fact."—Vance and Miller, *Biology for You*
22. "The Veterans Administration has complained that the government is not doing enough to help victims of the Gulf War Syndrome." William J. Garrington, III.

ESSAY ASSIGNMENTS

Write an essay either affirming or opposing one of these statements. The arguments you encounter in your background reading will include expert testimony, and so should your essay.

1. Marijuana should be legalized.
2. Vitamin C pills are necessary for good health.
3. Speaking in tongues is a genuine spiritual gift.
4. Flying saucers are here.
5. Fluoridation of drinking water is dangerous.
6. A faith healer can help you.
7. Nuclear power is the answer.
8. Tobacco companies should pay smokers' medical expenses.
9. To remain healthy, one should avoid X. (Fill in the X.)

America's Founding Fathers on the Right to Keep and Bear Arms

National Rifle Association

Thomas Jefferson, of Virginia

"No free man shall ever be debarred the use of arms."
—PROPOSED VIRGINIA CONSTITUTION, 1776

"Laws that forbid the carrying of arms . . . disarm only those who are neither inclined nor determined to commit crimes . . . Such laws make things worse for the assaulted and better for the assailants; they serve rather to encourage than to prevent homicides, for an unarmed man may be attacked with greater confidence than an armed man."
—JEFFERSON'S "COMMONPLACE BOOK," 1774–1776, QUOTING FROM ON CRIMES AND PUNISHMENT, BY CRIMINOLOGIST CESARE BECCARIA, 1764

George Mason, of Virginia

"[W]hen the resolution of enslaving America was formed in Great Britain, the British Parliament was advised by an artful man, who was governor of Pennsylvania, to disarm the people; that it was the best and most effectual way to enslave them; but that they should not do it openly, but weaken them, and let them sink gradually." . . . I ask, who are the militia? They consist now of the whole people, except a few public officers."
—VIRGINIA'S U.S. CONSTITUTION RATIFICATION CONVENTION, 1788

"That the People have a right to keep and bear Arms; that a well regulated Militia, composed of the Body of the People, trained to arms, is the proper, natural and safe Defence of a free state."—Within Mason's declaration of "the essential and unalienable Rights of the People."
—LATER ADOPTED BY THE VIRGINIA RATIFICATION CONVENTION, 1788

Samuel Adams, of Massachusetts

"The said Constitution [shall] be never construed to authorize Congress to infringe the just liberty of the press, or the rights of conscience; or to prevent the people of the United States, who are peaceable citizens, from keeping their own arms."
—MASSACHUSETTS' U.S. CONSTITUTION RATIFICATION CONVENTION, 1788

William Grayson, of Virginia

"[A] string of amendments were presented to the lower House; these altogether respected personal liberty."
—LETTER TO PATRICK HENRY, JUNE 12, 1789, REFERRING TO THE INTRODUCTION OF WHAT BECAME THE BILL OF RIGHTS

Richard Henry Lee, of Virginia

"A militia when properly formed are in fact the people themselves . . . and include all men capable of bearing arms . . . To preserve liberty it is essential that the whole body of people always possess arms . . . The mind that aims at a select militia, must be influenced by a truly anti-republican principle."
—ADDITIONAL LETTERS FROM THE FEDERAL FARMER, 1788

James Madison, of Virginia

The Constitution preserves *"The advantage of being armed which Americans possess over the people of almost every other nation . . . (where) the governments are afraid to trust the people with arms."*
—THE FEDERALIST, NO. 46

Tench Coxe, of Pennsylvania

"The militia, who are in fact the effective part of the people at large, will render many troops quite unnecessary. They will form a powerful check upon the regular troops, and will generally be sufficient to over-awe them."
—AN AMERICAN CITIZEN, OCT. 21, 1787

"Who are the militia? Are they not ourselves? Congress have no power to disarm the militia. Their swords and every other terrible implement of the soldier, are the birthright of an American. . . . The unlimited power of the sword is not in the hands of either the federal or state governments, but, where I trust in God it will ever remain, in the hands of the people."
—THE PENNSYLVANIA GAZETTE, FEB. 20, 1788

"As the military forces which must occasionally be raised to defend our country, might pervert their power to the injury of their fellow citizens, the people are confirmed by the next article (of amendment) in their right to keep and bear their private arms."
—FEDERAL GAZETTE, JUNE 18, 1789

Noah Webster, of Pennsylvania

"Before a standing army can rule, the people must be disarmed; as they are in almost every kingdom in Europe. The supreme power in America cannot enforce unjust laws by the sword; because the whole body of the people are armed, and constitute a force superior to any band of regular troops that can be, on any pretence, raised in the United States. A military force, at the command of Congress, can execute no laws, but such as the people perceive to be just and constitutional; for they will possess the power."
—AN EXAMINATION OF THE LEADING PRINCIPLES OF THE FEDERAL CONSTITUTION, PHILADELPHIA, 1787

Alexander Hamilton, of New York

"[I]f circumstances should at any time oblige the government to form an army of any magnitude, that army can never be formidable to the liberties of the people while there is a large body of citizens, little if at all inferior to them in discipline and the use of arms, who stand ready to defend their rights and those of their fellow citizens."
—THE FEDERALIST, NO. 29

Thomas Paine, of Pennsylvania

"[A]rms discourage and keep the invader and plunderer in awe, and preserve order in the world as well as property . . . Horried mischief would ensue were the law-abiding deprived of the use of them."
—THOUGHTS ON DEFENSIVE WAR, 1775

Fisher Ames, of Massachusetts

"The rights of conscience, of bearing arms, of changing the government, are declared to be inherent in the people."
—LETTER TO F. R. MINOE, JUNE 12, 1789

Elbridge Gerry, of Massachusetts

"What, sir, is the use of militia? It is to prevent the establishment of a standing army, the bane of liberty . . . Whenever Government means to invade the rights

and liberties of the people, they always attempt to destroy the militia, in order to raise a standing army upon its ruins."
—DEBATE, U.S. HOUSE OF REPRESENTATIVES, AUGUST 17, 1789

Patrick Henry, of Virginia

"Guard with jealous attention the public liberty. Suspect everyone who approaches that jewel."
—VIRGINIA'S U.S. CONSTITUTION RATIFICATION CONVENTION

DISCUSSION QUESTIONS

1. Words of the Founding Fathers have a measure of authority in argument. But how relevant are these claims to experience in modern America?

   The English parliament was advised to disarm citizens during the British occupation of the colonies. (George Mason)

   "A string of amendments" which respected personal liberty were presented to the lower house. (William Grayson)

   "The mind that aims at a select militia must be influenced by a truly antirepublican principle." (Richard Henry Lee)

   An armed militia will render many troops unnecessary. "They will be a check upon the regular troops, and will generally be sufficient to over-awe them." (Tench Coxe)

   Military forces raised to defend our country might sometimes pervert their power. In this case, armed citizens can stand up against them. (Tench Coxe)

   The purpose of a militia is to prevent the establishment of a standing army. (Elbridge Gerry)

2. Argument by authority is considered reliable if the speaker is a genuine expert on the area being discussed. What do the Founding Fathers have to say about street crime, drug addiction, spouse abuse, road rage, and public-school shootings?

Tracking the Werewolf

Fred A. Dobson

As a longtime student of the tabloids, I'm used to seeing reports of vampires in Venezuela, space aliens in Borneo, and Elvis in Kalamazoo. So it was a rich surprise one day earlier this year when I picked up the *Weekly World News* (dated February 2, 1993) and discovered there was a werewolf downtown, right here in Mobile, Alabama, prowling the State Docks.

The report was written by Tim Skelly, identified as a "Special correspondent in Mobile, Ala." A small photo of Skelly appeared with the article.

The story was titled "Werewolf Battles Cops in Alabama," and the main facts were given in the opening paragraphs:

> MOBILE, Ala.—A howling, snarling werewolf escaped from a foreign freighter, savagely bit seven cops and turned a police cruiser over before he was captured in a darkened alley near the docks.
>
> Heavily armed police are now guarding the wolfman around the clock at an undisclosed location in Mobile County until he can be placed back aboard the ship he escaped from.

Much of this information came from "a police spokesman," who was quoted at length.

The most impressive evidence was photographic. There were four pictures:

- A profile of the creature's head, which took up most of one page of the two-page story. (He looks like Lon Chaney, Jr., in the Wolfman movies.) At the top of the picture is an identification number: "Mobile P.D. #702419–92."
- A photo of Laura Schindler, a 58-year-old housewife, who stood five feet from the werewolf when he jumped off the ship. She is quoted as saying, "I never saw anything so frightening." Schindler had come to the State Docks to pick up her husband, a merchant seaman.
- A picture of an overturned car, with four wheels pointing in the air and with a spare tire stored under the trunk.

SOURCE: Reprinted from *Skeptical Inquirer,* Summer 1993. Reprinted by permission of CSICOP (Committee for Scientific Examination of Claims of the Paranormal).

- A photo of a man with his entire head bandaged. Only his mouth is showing, and there are little slit spaces for his eyes. By the picture is a caption, "Ripped to Shreds."

The article fascinated me, and I was in a good position to check it out. Tom Jennings, who serves as Public Information Officer for the Mobile Police Department, is a former student of mine. So I phoned him to get the official version. Tom said, "We've had a lot of calls about that crazy story."

Then he gave me the facts.

- The police department couldn't find any "police spokesman" who told the story to the *Weekly World News*.
- They couldn't identify a foreign freighter that had lost a deckhand.
- The "undisclosed location in Mobile County" where the wolfman was being held remained undisclosed. Nobody in the department knew anything about it.
- The police had had no success in locating Laura Schindler. They could find no reference to her merchant-seaman husband.
- The identification number on the werewolf photo is not a sequence used by the Mobile Police Department.
- The police department has had no reports of an overturned vehicle, nor does it have a police cruiser that carries a spare tire under the car.
- There had been no injury reports relating to such an incident, certainly no report of a police officer "ripped to shreds."

Jennings was emphatic on the last two points. He said: "Around here, if an officer gets cut on the hand, there's a lot of paperwork that has to be filled out. If police property is destroyed, it's just the same. There are liability areas." He repeated that there were no reports relating to a werewolf incident. The article, he said, was a "total fabrication."

Jennings suggested I call Nancy Wilstach, a reporter for the *Birmingham News*. He said she had more information about the story.

Indeed she did. Wilstach had interviewed Eddie Clontz, editor of the *Weekly World News*. She found him pleasant and cooperative. He told her they got the werewolf report from Tim Skelly and that he considers Skelly a reliable source. He said, "Usually his stuff is right on the money."

According to Clontz, tabloids call these articles "harmless." They know that a werewolf story (or a vampire or space-alien story) won't offend anybody and won't bring a lawsuit. So the *Weekly World News* didn't try to verify the Mobile incident. They just got the report and published it. Clontz said, "We put it out there and let our readers decide."

He added, "Maybe it didn't happen."

Wilstach asked Clontz how she could get in touch with Tim Skelly. He told her it might be difficult, that Skelly is now doing research in Caracas, Venezuela. Clontz said. "He's covering our vampire beat."

DISCUSSION QUESTIONS

1. This story comes from reporters, editors, and eyewitnesses. How reliable are each of these authorities?
   a. *Weekly World News*
   b. Tim Skelly, special correspondent in Mobile
   c. "a police spokesman"
   d. Laura Schindler, 58-year-old housewife
   e. Tom Jennings, Public Relations Officer for the Mobile Police Department
   f. Nancy Wilstach, *Birmingham News* reporter
   g. Eddie Clontz, editor of the *Weekly World News*
   h. Fred A. Dobson
   i. *Skeptical Inquirer*
   j. Committee for Scientific Examination of Claims of the Paranormal
2. The author writes "The most impressive evidence was photographic." He is referring to the pictures showing the werewolf's head, Laura Schindler, the overturned police car, and the officer with his bandaged face. How impressive are these?

How Prozac Saved My Marriage

A True Story

Tanya Kowalsy

I used to be a real horror to live with. I nagged, and pestered Walter constantly trying to get him to pick up after himself, to get a job, or even just to acknowledge me when I spoke to him. But nothing seemed to work. Instead he just spent more time in front of the TV, drinking beer and polishing his guns.

I was getting more and more unhappy. My mother tried to console me by saying that at least he didn't cheat on me, but it only brought tears to my eyes. I yelled at myself for not being Christian enough to forget about those flings with the Hooter girls.

I turned to our priest, who said I should be more womanly and generous, so, I volunteered at the local old age home. Sure it was nice getting out of the house, and I managed to earn a bit of money beating the residents at poker, but I still didn't feel better.

It got so bad that I thought of leaving him, but thankfully my mother reminded me that no man is going to want a used woman. Heavens, I can only imagine what trouble I could have gotten myself into. Plus, I had the children to think about, too.

Then one day while I was re-shingling the roof, I spotted our 3-year-old Alex chasing a ball onto the street with a car coming straight towards him. I dropped my hammer, leaped to the nearest maple tree bough, swung over the fence and landed on the neighbor's trash cans which softened my fall. When I finally rushed out into the street, the car had seen Alex and managed to stop. Alex was OK—this time. But I knew something had to be done—my mothering capabilities had been affected. With every ounce of passion left in me I decided to try everything in my power to make the relationship work. I asked Walter to come to couple counseling, but he said the problem was me, that all he wanted was a woman to cook for him and to clean his underwear, and that I was making things so complicated.

So, I decided to go alone. I picked up the phone and made an appointment.

SOURCE: *Happy Woman Magazine.* Reprinted with permission of Irene Duma.

Sure, I was scared—nobody had ever been crazy in my family before. But you have to understand; it was my last hope.

Dr. Thicke wasn't kind or nice, but his gruffness and lack of interest in me as a human only assured me of his competence as a scientist.

I told him how I felt—that after a brief romance and courtship—a dance at the local hall and a dinner at Taco Bell—Walter and I fell in love. But things changed quickly after that. He paid less and less attention to me, demanded dinners be served in front of the TV, and started referring to me only as "woman."

I thought this would change after we married—if I kept the house tidy, got silicon implants and produced 2 perfect children, he'd come to appreciate me. But it only got worse—his friends were over almost every night to watch the game. I couldn't bring out the beer and perogies fast enough for them all.

Then when the children were born, the distance grew even wider. Walter believed children were women's work, and instead he spent his time in the garage polishing his vintage Camaro that he had bought with the trust fund I had saved for the children's education. (Which I'm not bitter about— I couldn't say anything—I was in the hospital recovering from a Caesarian and I missed his birthday.)

I didn't have to say any more—Dr. Thicke looked up from the TV guide he was reading and said that I shouldn't worry—he had seen this before and that it was common, I was suffering from depression.

He told me that depression is a disease suffered mostly by women, it makes us cranky and listless and a drag to be around. If I wanted to end my family's suffering, I should go on antidepressants.

I was so relieved—all these years I had thought that Walter was the problem, that his contempt for me was just a symptom of his misogynistic beliefs and our society's insistence on devaluing women.

But in fact, it turns out I was the problem. I was just too negative. I took the prescription without a moment's hesitation.

Within weeks things had changed dramatically, I skipped gaily through my chores, I sang while I scrubbed the toilet, attended to all my family's whims and fancies, and taught the old fogies at the home how to line dance.

Walter still didn't talk to me or seem to have any interest in me, the kids or the house—the difference was now I just didn't care. The antidepressants had effectively prevented me from feeling any of the effects of life. I didn't have to hurt after all. The marriage was saved.

Thank you Prozac, Dr. Thicke, and all the other doctors, scientists and pharmaceutical companies for changing my life. I couldn't be unhappy now if I tried.

DISCUSSION QUESTIONS

1. The argument is introduced as "a true story." Does it ring true to you?
2. What is the effect of the names "Tanya Kowalsy" and "Dr. Thicke"?
3. Many of the details sound fictional. Consider these:

> The husband who ignores her, eats his meals at the TV, drinks beer with his friends every night, doesn't have a job, has a gun collection, and just wants a wife to wash his underwear.
>
> The psychiatrist who ignores her and reads *TV Guide* during their session.
>
> The wife who was wooed at Taco Bell, got silicone implants to impress her husband, and was reshingling the roof when her child was almost hit by a car.
>
> The reformed wife who takes Prozac and is now singing while she scrubs the toilets.

   Doesn't this sound more like a fable than a true history?
4. What is the author's serious argument here?
5. Would it weaken the serious argument if we recognized the story is fabricated?
6. If the tale is not "a true story" in one sense, can't it be true in another? Can fiction be true?

WHAT JESUS SAID ABOUT HOMOSEXUALITY:

"   "

WHAT THE VATICAN HAS TO SAY:
"INTRINSIC MORAL EVIL... AN OBJECTIVE DISORDER...BEHAVIOR TO WHICH NO ONE HAS ANY CONCEIVABLE RIGHT"[1]

WHAT IN THE WORLD IS GOING ON HERE?

What Dignity/USA says about homosexuality: After serious study of our spiritual heritage, we believe that lesbian and gay Catholics are numbered among the People of God, and that they can express their sexuality in a manner that is responsible, loving and consonant with Christ's message.[2]

For nearly 20 years, Dignity has been the national organization fighting for equal rights for lesbians and gay men in the Catholic Church. In over 100 chapters across America, Dignity sponsors the Mass and Sacraments, along with educational and social programs, and a Biennial Convention.

But now, Dignity chapters are under attack. Ultraconservative forces in the Vatican and in America are seeking to turn the clock back to pre-Vatican II days. They are forbidding us to worship on Church property. Priests are prohibited from ministering to us. A whole group of the faithful is being ignored, discarded and despised—because of its sexual orientation.

But the Church is more than a building or a small group of men. The Church is black and white, women and men, gay and straight. The Church is the <u>whole</u> People of God.

When an institution as powerful as the Catholic Church discriminates, all people suffer. You know someone who is gay or lesbian. We are your brothers and sisters, your sons and daughters. We are lay people and clergy. We, too, are the People of God.

Dignity calls on the National Conference of Catholic Bishops to speak out against the expulsion of Dignity chapters, and to dialogue with us on the pastoral care of lesbian and gay Catholics.

Oppressive measures strengthen Dignity. We will continue our struggle. We invite you to join us.

Please use the coupon below or write: Dignity/USA, Suite 11-T, 1500 Massachusetts Avenue, N.W., Washington, D.C. 20005. Help support our work by making a tax-deductible contribution or request more information. Make checks payable to Dignity/USA. Our mailing list and all inquiries are held in strict confidence.

[1] Vatican Congregation for the Doctrine of the Faith, "Letter to the Bishops of the Catholic Church on the Pastoral Care of Homosexual Persons," October 1, 1986.
[2] See Dignity/USA, "Statement of Position and Purpose."

□ **YES!** I want to help Dignity. Here is my tax-deductible contribution:
    □ $15 □ $25 □ $50 □ $100 □ $500 □ Other: $_____
□ Please send me more information.
□ I want information about the Eighth Biennial Dignity Convention to be held in Miami, Florida, July 23–26, 1987.

Name _____

Address _____

City _____ State _____ Zip ____

Send to: Dignity/USA, Suite 11-T, 1500 Massachusetts Avenue, N.W., Washington, D.C. 20005. Make checks payable to Dignity/USA. Our mailing list and all inquiries are held in strict confidence.

Courtesy of Dignity/USA.

DISCUSSION QUESTIONS

1. The argument about homosexuality contrasts opinions of three authorities: (1) Jesus, (2) the Vatican, and (3) Dignity/USA. Evaluate these on the basis of their expertness and their freedom from bias.
2. How significant is it that Jesus made no statements rejecting gay people? Did he make any statements accepting gay people?
3. Why did the author limit quotations to those of Jesus in the gospels? Why didn't he quote Genesis and St. Paul? Are they equal authorities?
4. Are there many gay Catholics? Does the author emphasize the number of people involved in Dignity/USA? Why?
5. Under the current situation, the author claims, "Priests are prohibited from ministering to us." What is implicit in this statement?
6. The argument stresses that "The Church is the *whole* People of God." Who is it saying the Church is not?

Nudity Can't Separate Us From God, Sin Does
Robert Bahr

As both a Christian and a nudist, I'm indignant that letter-writer Kevin Randall equates clothes-optional bathing at Assateague with a decline in moral standards. The touchstone for Judeo-Christian morality is the Bible, a book which had a good deal to say about nudity, most of it positive.

For example, in Genesis we find God created Adam and Eve in his own image, naked: "And God saw every thing that he had made, and, behold, it was very good." (Genesis 1:31) Only after Adam and Eve ate the Tree of the Knowledge of Good and Evil were their eyes opened: "And they knew they were naked: and they sewed fig leaves together, and made themselves aprons." (Genesis 3:8)

But even covering himself with a fig leaf didn't relieve Adam of his newly discovered sense of shame. When God came to see him in the garden, Adam hid, and when God asked him why, he said, "I heard thy voice in the garden, and was afraid because I was naked. And I hid myself." (Genesis 3:10)

God immediately cut to the point: "Hast thou eaten of the tree, whereof I commanded thee that thou shouldst not eat?" (Genesis 3:11)

Nakedness was not the sin then, and it isn't the sin today. Disobedience to God is the sin. When David won a victory in battle, he danced naked in the street. God did not scold him. Isaiah spent years walking naked from town to town prophesying. St. Francis of Assisi wandered the land naked. Jesus was baptized naked. Not once are we told God disapproved.

It may come as a surprise to Christians of this era that the nude human body has been deeply respected by the Christian church. The Vatican has thousands of sculptures and paintings of the nude human form. Only in the past 200 years, more or less, have we bought the mind-boggling proposal that somehow a God who cannot commit sin created an indecent human body which is also, somehow, God's temple.

I have a proposal for Randall and those who think as he does: Spend an hour at a clothes-optional beach or nudist resort. You will discover that there is nothing at all lustful or sinful about the experience. In fact, many have testified that nudism is a spiritual experience. It is sin that separates us from God—and from our own bodies.

SOURCE: Reprinted with permission of the author.

DISCUSSION QUESTIONS

1. In the first paragraph, the author announces he is a nudist and a Christian. How does this affect the authority of his argument?
2. The author champions nudism by offering exact quotations from the Bible. Do you feel these make his case?
3. "Only in the past 200 years, more or less, have we bought the mind-boggling proposal that somehow a God who cannot commit sin created an indecent human body which is, also, somehow God's temple." Is this in fact a "mind-boggling proposal"? Does this seem persuasive to you?
4. Do you think this argument will change anybody's mind? Discuss.

There Is No Safe Sex

Robert C. Noble

The other night on the evening news, there was a piece about condoms. Someone wanted to provide free condoms to high-school students. A perky, fresh-faced teenage girl interviewed said everyone her age was having sex, so what was the big deal about giving out condoms? Her principal replied that giving out condoms set a bad example. Then two experts commented. One was a lady who sat very straight in her chair, white hair in a tight perm, and, in a prudish voice, declared that condoms didn't work very well; teenagers shouldn't be having sex anyway. The other expert, a young, attractive woman, said that since teenagers were sexually active, they shouldn't be denied the protection that condoms afforded. I found myself agreeing with the prude.

What do I know about all this? I'm an infectious-diseases physician and an AIDS doctor to the poor. Passing out condoms to teenagers is like issuing them squirt guns for a four-alarm blaze. Condoms just don't hack it. We should stop kidding ourselves.

I'm taking care of a 21-year-old boy with AIDS. He could have been the model for Donatello's David, androgynous, deep blue eyes, long blond hair, as sweet and gentle as he can be. His mom's in shock. He called her the other day and gave her two messages. I'm gay. I've got AIDS. His lover looks like a fellow you'd see in Sunday school; he works in a bank. He's had sex with only one person, my patient (*his* second partner), and they've been together for more than a year. These fellows aren't dummies. They read newspapers. You think condoms would have saved them?

Smart people don't wear condoms. I read a study about the sexual habits of college women. In 1975, 12 percent of college women used condoms when they had sexual intercourse. In 1989, the percentage had risen to only 41 percent. Why don't college women and their partners use condoms? They know about herpes. They know about genital warts and cervical cancer. All the public-health messages of the past 15 years have been sent, and only 41 percent of the college women use condoms. Maybe your brain has to be working to use one. In the heat of passion, the brain shuts down. You have to use a condom every time. *Every time.* That's hard to do.

SOURCE: Reprinted from *Newsweek*, April 1, 1991. Reprinted by permission of the author.

I can't say I'm comforted reading a government pamphlet called "Condoms and Sexually Transmitted Diseases, Especially AIDS." "Condoms are not 100 percent safe," it says, "but if used properly will reduce the risk of sexually transmitted diseases, including AIDS." *Reduce* the risk of a disease that is 100 percent fatal! That's all that's available between us and death? How much do condoms reduce the risk? They don't say. So much for Safe Sex. Safe Sex was a dumb idea anyway. I've noticed that the catchword now is "Safer Sex." So much for truth in advertising. Other nuggets of advice: "If you know your partner is infected, the best rule is to avoid intercourse (including oral sex). If you do decide to have sex with an infected partner, you should *always* be sure a condom is used from start to finish, every time." Seems reasonable, but is it really helpful? Most folks don't know when their partner is infected. It's not as if their nose is purple. Lots of men and women with herpes and wart-virus infections are having sex right now lying their heads off to their sexual partners—that is, to those who ask. At our place we are taking care of a guy with AIDS who is back visiting the bars and having sex. "Well, did your partner use a condom?" I ask. "Did you tell him that you're infected with the virus?" "Oh, no, Dr. Noble," he replies. "It would have broken the mood." You bet it would have broken the mood. It's not only the mood that gets broken. "Condoms may be more likely to break during anal intercourse than during other types of sex . . ." Condoms also break in heterosexual sex; one study shows a 4 percent breakage rate. "Government testing can *not* guarantee that condoms will always prevent the spread of sexually transmitted diseases." That's what the pamphlet says. Condoms are all we've got.

Nobody these days lobbies for abstinence, virginity or single lifetime sexual partners. That would be boring. Abstinence and sexual intercourse with one mutually faithful uninfected partner are the only totally effective prevention strategies. That's from another recently published government report.

Media Messages

What am I going to tell my daughters? I'm going to tell them that condoms give a false sense of security and that having sex is dangerous. *Reducing* the risk is not the same as *eliminating* the risk. My message will fly in the face of all other media messages they receive. In the movie "The Tall Guy," a nurse goes to bed with the "Guy" character on their first date, boasting that she likes to get the sex thing out of the way at the beginning of the relationship. His roommate is a nymphomaniac who is always in bed with one or more men. This was supposed to be cute. "Pretty Woman" says you can find happiness with a prostitute. Who are the people that write this stuff? Have the '80s passed and everyone forgotten sexually transmitted diseases?

Syphilis is on the rise. Gonorrhea is harder to treat and increasing among black teenagers and adults. Ectopic pregnancies and infertility from sexually transmitted diseases are mounting every year. Giving condoms to high-school kids isn't going to reverse all this.

That prim little old lady on TV had it right. Unmarried people shouldn't be having sex. Few people have the courage to say this publicly. In the context of our culture, they sound like cranks. Doctors can't fix most of the things you can catch out there. There's no cure for AIDS. There's no cure for herpes or genital warts. Gonorrhea and chlamydial infection can ruin your chances of ever getting pregnant and can harm your baby if you do. That afternoon in the motel may leave you with an infection that you'll have to explain to your spouse. Your doctor can't cover up for you. Your spouse's lawyer may sue him if he tries. There is no safe sex. Condoms aren't going to make a dent in the sexual epidemics that we are facing. If the condom breaks, you may die.

DISCUSSION QUESTIONS

1. What are Dr. Noble's credentials? Is he competent to talk on this issue? Is he speaking as a moral or religious authority?
2. How impressive are the other authorities mentioned in the essay? Consider each of these:
   a. "two experts" speaking on the evening news
   b. "a study" about the sexual habits of college women
   c. a government pamphlet "Condoms and Sexually Transmitted Diseases, Especially AIDS"
   d. Dr. Noble's patients: "a 21-year-old boy with AIDS" and "a guy with AIDS"
   e. "one study" on the breakage rate of condoms
   f. a "recently published government report"
   g. two movies: *The Tall Guy* and *Pretty Woman*
3. How threatening are the diseases Dr. Noble mentions? How does he emphasize the problems involved?
4. What is the difference between "safe sex" and "safer sex"?
5. The author mentions half a dozen reasons why "Condoms just don't hack it." What are these?
6. Dr. Noble says, "Condoms just don't hack it" and "Safe sex was a dumb idea anyway." Is this appropriate language for a physician writing on a serious medical subject?
7. Did you find the article easy to read? Is Dr. Noble an effective writer?

Semantic Argument

"Buick Electra. The name alone speaks volumes."

Semantic argument tries to make a persuasive point by using impressive language rather than by presenting or arranging evidence. It should convince no one.

Semantic argument always sounds good. Its effectiveness derives from the nature of words. A word can have two levels of meaning: a denotative meaning—that is, some specific thing or condition to which it refers *(paper, swim, beige)*; and a connotative meaning—that is, certain emotional responses that it arouses. Connotations can be affirmative *(national leader, negotiation, right of unlimited debate)* or negative *(politician, deal, filibuster)*. Semantic argument uses connotative words to characterize an issue or to enhance the tone of a discussion.

■ SNARL AND PURR WORDS

Connotative words (sometimes called purr words and snarl words) do not prove anything; they just call something good or bad. American politicians of both parties regularly run for office, for example, on a program favoring *obedience to God, family, and country; adherence to law and order; separation of powers; fiscal responsibility; personal integrity; economic progress without inflation;* and *faith in the American dream.* They oppose *absenteeism, wasteful spending, anarchy, economic floundering,* and *terrorism.* The essence of such argument is its vagueness—and its usefulness. When asked for an opinion on a controversial issue like school prayer, a candidate can hide behind language:

> First, let me put this issue in perspective. My record shows I have always fought for the cause of education and for our children, who are the hope of this great nation. I recognize the profound complexities in this area and the honest differences presently existing between good men. I assure you I will work for a positive, fair, and democratic solution. Trust me.

What is the speaker's view on school prayer? You can't even guess.

This kind of argument can praise any entity—a party platform, a current novel, a union demand—as *authentic, just, reasonable, natural,* and *realistic* or condemn it as *irresponsible, asinine, phony, dangerous,* and *superficial.* It can celebrate one citizen as a *Samaritan,* a *patriot,* and an *independent thinker* and reject another as a *do-gooder,* a *reactionary,* and a *pseudo-intellectual.* Such terms have little specific meaning. A rich variety highlights every election. In Alabama, Fob James, a little-known candidate, won the governorship with a campaign that affirmed "the politics of compassion and a renaissance of common sense." In the 1988 national campaign, George Bush assured us that America was sustained by "a thousand points of light." In the 1996 presidential campaign, Bill Clinton promised his democratic platform would "build a bridge to the 21st century accessible for all Americans."

Semantic language depends on its emotional associations. An automobile is more appealing when named a *Hummer;* a bill, when called a *right-to-work law;* and a military settlement, when termed *peace with honor.* In successful argument, much depends on finding the right words. It is easy to champion *baseball, hot dogs, apple pie, and Chevrolet,* and it is hard to attack a position bulwarked with powerful language. How can anyone oppose *fair-trade* laws, the *right-to-life* movement, or a *clean air* act? Who can question the importance of the *miracle nutrient coenzyme Q10?* And what about George W. Bush's campaign offering "compassionate conservatism"?

Currently a favorite advertising word is *nature.* A laxative is called *Nature's Remedy;* a shoe, *The Naturalizer;* and Rheingold, "the natural beer." L.A. Beer was particularly celebrated. It boasted that "a special natural brewing process along with the finest natural ingredients and slow natural aging produces a beer with less alcohol, that tastes as good as a regular beer." Beer hardly seems to qualify as natural, since it takes a chemist to make it. Still, if you look at things in a broad perspective, every process and ingredient can be called natural.

The word *light* is equally popular, and equally chancy. Sometimes it means a product has significantly fewer calories; sometimes it doesn't. The Wesson Oil that's called "light and natural" has the same calories as regular Wesson Oil—it's just paler in color. While most light beers have 50 to 80 fewer calories than regular beer, Michelob Light shed only 15.

Another word to watch for is *best.* Some products—like gasoline, aspirin, and toothpaste—are called parity products. This means all brands are essentially the same. None can claim to be *better* without offering a body of evidence. But because none is superior to the others, all can claim to be *best.* Every one of them. Remember this when you hear "Nestlé makes the very best," or "Gillette—the best a man can get," or "Minute Maid—the best there is." Such products are indeed the best, just like their competitors are.

There is a special group of words you should look out for—words like *helps, virtually, up to,* and *relatively.* These modify any claim they appear with. You've seen the promises. Product A *helps* control dandruff, Product B leaves dishes *virtually* spotless, Product C lets you lose *up to* 15 pounds in a week, and Product D is *relatively* inexpensive.

Advertisers have called up an impressive range of associations to offer Blue Cross, Lemon-fresh Joy, Cashmere Bouquet, Old Grand-Dad, and Lincoln Continental Mark VIII—plus Obsession, Canadian Mist, 350Z, English Leather, and Brut 33 by Fabergé. Such names often make the difference. Millions of dollars have been earned and lost as Carnation Slender won the market from Metrecal, as DieHard outsold the J. C. Penney battery, and as Taster's Choice defeated Maxim instant coffee. For some time, the best-selling perfume in the world was called Charlie.

Names make a difference. A weight-loss book titled *The New Dimensions II Bio-Imagery Programming Figure Enhancement System* has a lot going for it (perhaps too much). Products like Algemarin soap, Mr. Turkey luncheon meats, Jhirmack shampoo, Hyundai Scoupe, and Volkswagen Facade seem to labor under a handicap. But a creative persuader can do wonders. Who can forget the jam advertisement "With a name like Smucker's, it has to be good"?

Recent administrations have done wonders with semantic argument. Did President Reagan order the Army, Marines, and Air Force to invade Grenada? No, the "Caribbean Peace Keeping Forces" made a "pre-dawn vertical insertion" into Grenada. When American troops marched into Somalia, President Clinton called it a "relief effort" and a "mission of mercy." In 2003, U.S. troops moved into Iraq on a mission of "Operation Iraqi Freedom."

Names

Even people's names carry associations. In comic fiction, you know immediately that Mary Worth is good and that Snidely Whiplash is bad. Real-life examples demonstrate the American rejection of vague or foreign-sounding names. For years Hollywood hired performers like Charles Buchinsky and Doris von Kappelhoff and made them stars as Charles Bronson and Doris Day. For a long time, Household Finance Corporation presented loan officers to the public as "friendly Bob Adams." Currently, men with mild names like Scott Simpson, Robert Remus, and Jim Harris appear on the professional wrestling circuit as "Nikita Kiloff," "Sergeant Slaughter," and "Kamala, the Ugandan Giant." Sylvester Ritter wrestles as "the Junkyard Dog."

Names are important in politics. John Varick Tunney had always been called Varick until he chose to run for office. After Opinion Research of California polled citizen response to the name Varick, he reverted to his unused first name and became Senator John Tunney. It is noteworthy that the serious candidates for the presidency in 1976 (Senators Udall and Jackson, President Ford, Governors Reagan and Carter) were introduced as Mo, Scoop, Jerry, Ron, and Jimmy. In the 1980s race, the candidates were Jimmy, Ted, Ron, George, Bob, John, and Big John. Only Senator Baker (Howard) had a name that needed work.

In 1984, the candidates were Ron and Walter (called Fritz), though much attention was given to Jesse (a fine biblical name for a minister) and to Gary Hart (formerly Gary Hartpence). Jesse ran again in 1988, as did a number of candidates with safe names—George, Bob, Al, Jack, Pat, Paul, Joe, Bill, Pete, and Sam. However, the American public also faced more complicated ethnic names like Mario Cuomo and Mike Dukakis. (His close friends called him Michael.) In 1992, Bill Clinton's Democratic competitors were Bob and Paul. George H. Bush easily won the conservative vote over H. Ross Perot. In 1992 and 1996, Bill Clinton beat George and Bob, H. Ross Perot ran third. The candidates in the 2000 election had uncomplicated names—George and Al. (Nobody spoke of Albert Gore.) In 2004, George easily defeated John. Ralph ran a distant third.

Political Correctness

Politically correct language involves purr words.

For generations, minorities have been insulted with snarl words. They were called *niggers, spicks, broads, queers, fatties, old geezers, retards, gimps,* and so on. To avoid this (and, indeed, to compensate for it), academicians, ethnic voices, and social critics have produced a new vocabulary to discuss minority groups. We now speak of *African Americans, Hispanics, spokespersons, people of color, alternative lifestyles, senior citizens, people of size,* and individuals who are *physically challenged* or *intellectually challenged.*

As a writer, you can expect problems in this area. Of course, you want to use politically correct language where you can. First because it is the civilized thing to do, and second because there is a broad audience that expects it (as well as a hostile audience that demands it). It's always a mistake to offend someone you didn't want to offend.

But don't let political correctness cripple your prose. You still want to write with specific details. You want to sound like a speaking voice. Therefore, you shouldn't write, "At school yesterday, I talked to an African American, a senior citizen, and two people of size. One had a child who is physically challenged." This language calls too much attention to itself, and your reader won't know what you're talking about. You can do better than this.

Political correctness is a worthy goal, but it can be a minefield for writers and persuaders. Walk with care.

▪ INDIRECT STATEMENT

Semantic argument can also work indirectly; that is, in a particular context, a purr word expressed is also a snarl word implied. To advertise "Oil Heat Is Safe," for example, is to imply that gas and electric heat are dangerous. To describe a movie as "not recommended for immature audiences" is to boast that it is impressively sexual or violent. When Tampax was advertised as a "natural cotton" product, it was reminding readers that it was not one of the sponge tampons that had been associated with toxic shock syndrome and several deaths.

In the years before things became explicit, commercial advertisers used many indirect attacks. Diners Club said, "Why go abroad with a credit card you've outgrown?" Playtex asked, "Are you still using the same brand of tampons they invented for your grandmother?" And Scope mouthwash boasted it was "Minty-fresh, not mediciney."

Such argument produces rich paradoxes. The ad for *Valley of the Dolls* reported that "Any similarity between any person, living or dead, and the characters portrayed in this film is purely coincidental and not intended"; this told moviegoers that the film was about real-life Hollywood stars. Another ad declared that the "United States Supreme Court has ruled that *Carnal Knowledge* is NOT OBSCENE," which meant it was.

When George Wallace ran for governor of Alabama in 1980, his two opponents in the Democratic primary could not tastefully point out that he had recently married a country singer and that he was crippled. So one opponent produced television ads showing his own elegant wife and saying "When you elect a governor, you elect a first lady." The other opponent was less subtle. His TV ads showed him running up the steps to the statehouse.

Sometimes, semantic claims are not meant to be penetrated. This is especially true when impressive language is used to mask a negative admission. For example, when government economists announce that the inflation rate is "slowing down," they wish to communicate optimistic reassurance rather than what the words really say, that prices are still high and still climbing. When manufacturers label a garment "shrink-resistant," they want to suggest that it will not shrink, not what the term literally says, that the garment will resist shrinking, and thus that shrinkage will certainly occur. Advertisers for an inexpensive portable radio wish to imply that it is powerful and can pull in signals from distant stations. What they say is, "You can take it anywhere."

You have to admire the creative language that public relations experts use to mask problems. When the Reagan administration admitted giving the media false stories about Libyan unrest, it called the stories "disinformation." One corporation specified a large sum of money on its annual balance-sheet and declared it a "negative investment increment." You know what that means. When responding to accusations about his relationship to Monica Lewinsky, President Clinton confessed to "inappropriate activity."

■ PERSUASIVE STYLE

The attempt to communicate more than is literally said also occurs when persuaders use impressive language to add character to an argument. Couching their views in religious allusions, folksy talk, or esoteric jargon, they argue more with style than with facts. In a letter to the *Saturday Review,* for example, Gelett Burgess maintained that Shakespeare did not write the plays attributed to him. His language was intellectual:

> Sir:
>   My recent communication relative to Oxford-is-Shakespeare elicited responses which evince and hypostatize the bigoted renitency usual in orthodox addicts. For the Stratfordian mythology has engendered a strange nympholepsy like a fanatical religion which is not amenable to reason or logic and abrogates all scientific methods.

As a contrast, consider the tone of this fund-raising letter sent out some years ago by Senator Jesse Helms:

> Dear Friend:
>   Will you do me a personal favor and place the enclosed bumper sticker on your car today?
>   And, will you use the enclosed form to let me know if I can send you a Reagan for President button to wear?
>   I'll be deeply gratified if I could hear from you immediately. . . .
>   Won't you please, please dig down deep and give as you have never given before?
>   Whether Ronald Reagan wins or loses is up to folks like you and me. The decision rests in our hands.
>   I pray that you will answer this call for help. God bless you.

The senator tried to make his message more persuasive by speaking as a Christian Southern gentleman.

You should, of course, judge an argument solely on the evidence brought forward to support a conclusion, not on the effect of connotative language. Similarly, in writing argument, fight the temptation to overuse snarl and purr words. Avoid pedantic language and high-sounding phrases. Your reader will think, perhaps rightly, that you are compensating for weaknesses in your case.

Connotative language defies meaningful analysis. Is it true that "Education without God produces a nation without freedom," that Nike running shoes are "faster than the fastest feet," that Fleishmann's Gin is "Clean . . . Clean . . . Clean"? Who can say? Until the claims are clarified and documented, such vague language can produce only empty and repetitive argument. Fleishmann advertisements, it should be noted, once offered to explain "What do they mean CLEAN . . . CLEAN . . . CLEAN?" The answer: "They mean the crispest, brightest drinks under the sun are made with clean-tasting Fleishmann's Gin." This is about as meaningful as semantic argument gets.

EXERCISES

How effective are the following semantic arguments?

1. I want to distinguish my program from that of Senator Williams. My position has been firm where his has been pig-headed. My actions have been energetic and creative where his have been manic and bizarre. I am much concerned in these areas where he is obsessive.
2. "At Ford, Quality is Job 1"; "Nobody sweats the details like GM."
3. The human organism is a homeostatic mechanism; that is, all behavior is an attempt to preserve organismic integrity by homeostatic restoration of equilibrium, as that equilibrium is disturbed by biologically significant organizations of energies in the external or internal environments of the organism.
4. Macho cologne—"It's b-a-a-a-d."
5. I can't decide which car to buy. I'm choosing between a Dodge Intrepid, a Honda Accord EX, an Olds Cutlass Ciera, a Caprice Classic, a Chevrolet Lumina, a Geo Prizm, an Isuzu Trooper, and a Continental Mark VIII.
6. Night Repair was scientifically formulated in Estée Lauder's U.S. laboratories as part of the Swiss Age-Controlling Skincare Program. Although only nature controls the aging process, this program helps control the signs of aging and encourages skin to look and feel younger.
7. When a correspondent wrote to *Personality Parade* asking whether Elvis Presley had learned to act, columnist Walter Scott responded, "Mr. Presley has always been good to his mother."

8. Christian Dior's Eau Sauvage—"Virile. Discreet. Refreshing. Uncompromising. A fragrance of masculine refinement."
9. We guarantee our product will reduce your waist by up to three inches in the first two weeks, or double your money back.
10. The abortion issue comes down to this: Should a baby be mutilated for the convenience of its mother?
11. Try Naturade Conditioning Mascara with Natural Protein. (Contains stearic acid, PUP, butylene glycol, sorbitan sesquioleate, triethanolamine, imidazolidinyl urea, methylparaben, and prophylparaben.)
12. Miller beer. Made the American way.
13. As a resident of this city for some time, I have become accustomed to the pathetic whining your paper is prone to whenever city government fails to apishly follow your always myopic and generally self-defeating plans for civic "betterment." Tolerating such infantile and retrograde twaddle was the price, I told myself, of a free and unshackled press.
14. A problematic of canon-formation, in contradistinction to an ideology of tradition, must assimilate the concept of tradition within an objective history, as an effect of monumentalization by which a canon of works confronts an author over against the contemporary social conditions of literary production, as simply given.
15. Fahrvernügen—It's what makes a car a Volkswagen.
16. "Part of the great pleasure one gets from Dewar's 'White Label' Scotch is the reassuring knowledge that you have chosen something authentic."
17. The men confined at Guantanamo are not prisoners of war; they're detainees.

ESSAY ASSIGNMENTS

Write an essay either affirming or opposing one of these statements. The material you encounter in your background reading will include a good deal of semantic argument, and so may your essay.

1. Abortion is murder.
2. Feminist organizations want to destroy the American family.
3. Who needs poetry?
4. Capital punishment is necessary.
5. The publishers of *Hustler* and *Penthouse* should be sent to jail.
6. America needs some old-fashioned patriotism.
7. We should make "America the Beautiful" our national anthem.
8. X should be abolished. (Fill in the X.)

Offices Revolve Around Doughnuts

Nancy Hauge

In an eye-opening survey conducted several months ago by a leading business think tank called the Boston Consulting Group, three out of four top executives from 68 countries said they planned to increase research and development spending this year. Fewer than half of the 940 respondents, however, thought the increases would produce the necessary profit or competitive advantage to justify the expenditures.

Why such a disconnect? Perhaps it's because they're spending too much of their money on the wrong things: technology, rather than Twinkies.

My experience tells me that the rapidity with which an enterprise creates value is directly related to how well it stocks the company kitchen. The lower the nutritional value of the food choices, the greater the intellectual property produced.

I have spent time in a variety of industries: software, hardware, compression technology, storage technology, outsourced manufacturing and digital media. What they all have in common is this: They all run on junk food.

During my career, I have spent hundreds of all-night sessions alongside my entrepreneurial colleagues as we prepared for market launches, product launches, term sheets, due diligence reviews, tape outs, quarterly results, auditors and initial public offerings.

When engineers, scientists and technologists have to stay up all night, they don't reach for No-Doz; they reach for Cheetos.

It's always a sign of decline when a company slows down on junk-food purchases. Many CEOs and CFOs deny the value of the kitchen. It is an easy expense to control or cut when money gets tight. It seems like no big deal. People can bring food in or buy their drinks from a vending machine.

But the purpose of junk food is not just to give the team a little blood sugar bump at 3 p.m. When you stop supplying fun food, morale and productivity decline.

As soon as your supply of Twizzlers and Diet Coke runs out, so do your people. They leave the office to go home or go out to eat. And when people leave, even for a short lunch break, you can lose the rhythm . . . the hum of execution . . . to say nothing of that esprit d'corps that comes with foraging for Pop Tarts at 2 a.m.

SOURCE: *Atlanta Journal-Constitution*, January 9, 2006. Reprinted with permission of the author.

I once worked for a start-up computing company that grew to $7 billion in annual revenue during my stint. In the early years we brought in doughnuts every morning. As time went on, the doughnut bill got to be pretty outrageous. So we cut back to doughnuts only on Wednesday mornings. Funny thing, our product launches began to stretch out. We were not moving as fast as we once had.

When I asked the vice president of engineering what had happened, he said, "My guys used to get in here by 8 a.m. every day to get their favorite doughnut before it was gone. Now they come in around 9. I have 600 engineers in this organization and I lost about 600 man hours per day because you stopped the doughnuts!"

Why should junk food have this effect? Can a doughnut really motivate folks to come to work earlier? Sure. It's simple: People eat stuff at work they would never be caught dead buying and never allow themselves at home. It is compensation for long hours. And wholesome food really doesn't cut it.

No one goes to the community kitchen to fix themselves a salad and then go back to work. People do not bond over broccoli spears and cottage cheese.

Junk food in the kitchen is designed to keep your most important asset at work.

Do I really promote enticing employees to spend too many hours at work and eat junk food to boot? You bet. Junk food is the enabler of an unbalanced lifestyle and an unbalanced lifestyle is crucial to success, especially at start-up companies.

Maybe we can seek balance and nutrition after the company starts producing $500 million in annual revenues. Until then, pass the pork rinds and beef jerky (I'm on Atkins).

DISCUSSION QUESTIONS

1. Is this a serious argument? Is the author seriously claiming that junk food at work will increase productivity? Does this argument seem reasonable to you?
2. Would you come to work an hour early simply to get your favorite doughnut?
3. Cheetos, pork rinds, beef jerky, Twinkies, doughnuts: Do these examples enhance her argument? Are they purr words, snarl words, or neither?
4. Consider the length the author goes to identify herself as an authority. Do you feel she *is* an authority?
5. Is the author really trying to persuade anybody? Or is this merely an expression of an amusing paradox?

Psychometry: Getting the Vibrations
David St. Clair

That fancy ten-dollar word means holding something in your hand and getting the vibrations from it—no more than that.

After a while, all objects take on the personality of their owner, and just as fingerprints cling to a drinking glass, your psychic print remains on things you wear and touch. Don't ask me why, because I don't know. This phenomenon, like so many others in this field, has yet to be investigated scientifically.

Quite often a good medium will be able to give you a reading just by holding an object belonging to you. Again, like the radio set, she tunes out the world around her—especially her own thoughts—and tunes in to what the object is transmitting. Then she reports what is coming through to her. If she is right, you should tell her so and she'll know she has tuned in to your particular vibrations. Then the reading will continue with ease and (one hopes) with accuracy.

In Los Angeles there is one well-known medium, the Baroness Lotta von Strahl, who has helped the Los Angeles police solve innumerable cases by the exclusive use of psychometry.

One of her most famous cases was that of the Manson killings. The day after they found the bodies of Sharon Tate and her friends in all that blood and gore, the police came (secretly, of course!) knocking at Lotta's door. They had objects that belonged to the victims and also a knife or two that they were sure must have been dropped by the killers. What could she see?

Lotta took the objects and began to have horrible pains. She felt the stabbings in her back and stomach and, a few times, was tempted to ask the police to go away and not force her to go through this torment. But she kept on. She said that she picked up the name "Mason" or "Maxon," and that the man was small, with piercing dark eyes. She also said that the killers were not just men but that there were women with them, and young girls at that. She was puzzled when she kept getting "the same last name. You know," she told the officers, "it's almost as if they were all members of the same *family*." Then she saw something that puzzled her. It was an old town in the days of the

SOURCE: Reprinted by permission. From *David St. Clair's Lessons in Instant ESP.* New York: New American Library (Signet Books), 1978.

Wild West but "nobody lives there. It's strange, but the doors are open and the houses have no substance."

Of course, when Charles Manson was finally caught, he did have several girls with him who formed his "family." They had been living at a ranch that served as a location for shooting Western films. What Lotta had seen was the empty false fronts of the movie set.

Another case involved a violent murder at a Mexican-American wedding. The groom had been stabbed and the bride was wounded. The police had arrested several suspects, but none of them admitted committing the crime. The police gave Lotta the dead man's shirt, all torn and brown with dried blood, and she picked up something about a man with a birthmark on his upper-right shoulder. The police had photographs of the corpse. No, he didn't have such a mark. "Then," said the medium, "the murderer has such a mark. If you find the man with this birthmark, he will confess."

The police called in all the suspects and asked them to remove their shirts. One had a birthmark just where Lotta had said it would be. He denied killing the bridegroom, but when the police told him about Lotta and what she had seen, he began to scream about witchcraft, broke down, and confessed.

Psychometry is easy, especially if you practice and if you—what's the magic word?—*listen*.

Here it is terribly important to *listen* to the information you get from the object. Don't hesitate to say something because *you* don't feel it applies. *You must stay out of it.* It is vitally important for your success that you keep *yourself* out of it as much as possible. Once again, you are only the radio receiving the message—and radios don't think or decide what they will broadcast.

The first time I ever tried psychometry, I was interviewing two wonderful mediums in San Jose, California: Marcia Warzek and Norma Dart, for my book *The Psychic World of California*. Both women had been doing psychometry for a large audience that afternoon, going from row to row and telling people things about themselves no stranger could possibly have known. The audience was amazed and, I'll confess, I was impressed. Later that evening I said to Norma, "That must be very difficult to do, isn't it?"

"Not at all," she said, and promptly took off her bracelet and handed it to me. "Just relax, close your eyes, and tell me the first thing that comes to your mind. Don't force it and don't try to analyze it. Just let the images come and I'll tell you if you're right or not."

I took that bracelet (a little self-consciously, for after all, they were the psychics, not I!) and as I held it, I started to smile.

"What's so funny?" Norma asked.

"I've got a dumb picture here," I said with some embarrassment. "It couldn't possibly mean anything, because it doesn't have anything to do with you."

"Well, what is it? You let me decide if it's for me or not."

"I see a large sailing ship," I said, "with its sails unfurled, and its going across choppy water." I opened my eyes and handed her the bracelet. "See? That meant nothing at all."

"Oh no?" Norma got up and went out of the room. In a few minutes she was back with a book in her hand. "When my husband died recently, I decided to take all his books and incorporate them into my own library. I wanted to have the same bookplate in them that I had in my own books. I've been combing San Jose for the past month trying to find that bookplate. Look!" She opened her book and pointed to the bookplate. It was a picture of a ship, its sails unfurled, going against a rough sea.

After that, I did psychometry for my family and acquaintances, even saved a friend of mine a few dollars on the purchase of an antique Chinese vase. She was anxious to have it, but the dealer wanted $500 for it. She took me with her to help her make up her mind. I know quite a bit about American and English antiques but nothing about Oriental art. Yet as I picked up the vase I decided to do some psychometry on it. The first words I got were "not old."

"Should I buy it?" she asked me, with the dealer standing right there.

"No," I said with great authority. "It's not old. It's a fake."

The dealer looked thunderstruck. "What do you know about the Ming period?" he asked haughtily.

"A great deal," I lied, "and this vase is not more than thirty years old and not worth more than fifty dollars."

He was sure I was from the police and began to apologize for having tried to sell us something that wasn't genuine. We walked out in righteous indignation and had a good laugh about it in a nearby bar. My friend bought the drinks with some of the $500 I had saved her.

One of the first times I ever did psychometry in public was in Dallas, Texas. I was lecturing on various aspects of psychic phenomena and when I mentioned that it was possible to get information from inanimate objects, a lady in the front row got up and handed me a very expensive diamond wristwatch. "Let's see what you can get from that," she said.

I held the watch and looked at the lady. She was superbly dressed in the very latest fashion—Gucci shoes, diamond necklace, Louis Vuitton handbag, the works. There I stood before over four hundred people and what did I get? A tumbledown shack, an old Ford up on cinder blocks, and two or three small children running around with bare feet, dirty clothes, and ratted hair.

"Well?" she said.

I gulped, trying to get out of this public fiasco and wondering if Texans still used guns to run charlatans out of town. I decided to play it honest. "What I get can't have anything to do with you. There is a shack, an old Ford, and some dirty half-naked children playing around it."

"Oh yes," she beamed. "That does mean something to me. That was the way we lived until Daddy struck oil!"

I repeat: Keep *yourself* out of the reading!

The longer an object has been worn, the stronger the vibrations will be. When giving a reading, ask for something the person has carried with him for a while. A key ring bought just a few days ago won't tell you anything, but a pair of glasses worn for five years will be an encyclopedia of information.

Also make sure that the object has had only one owner. If someone gives you a ring that has also been worn by her mother or her sister, you may well get conflicting vibrations. Often I've been telling someone things and she'll say, "No, that doesn't mean a thing," and *then* she'll tell me that she bought that object in a secondhand store or antique shop. I have no way, then, of knowing *who* the vibrations belong to.

When you are giving a reading, insist that the person be entirely honest with you. If you say that he drives a green car, and he drives a brown car, tell him to say so. Many people will want to please you, and they will stretch the truth (or just plain lie) to "help" you along. They are only confusing things because until you start getting the truthful "Yes, that makes sense" answers, you have no idea whether you have tuned in to that person or not. Insist that people be honest with you; it'll help you give them a better reading.

Every now and then, you'll find yourself telling someone things, they'll go along and admit that you are absolutely right, and then you'll hit one item and they'll balk: "No. That isn't me. I don't know what you're talking about." If the image in question fades away and doesn't repeat itself in the reading, then most likely you were wrong. But if it *keeps* returning or won't go away, and the person keeps denying it, it is almost 100 percent certain that this person doesn't know or doesn't remember what he or she is talking about.

I've had people tell me, as much as a month later, that I had been correct and they just hadn't realized it then. I remember with one woman I kept getting the name Sarah. No, she didn't know any Sarah. The name came back and wouldn't go away. "I have the impression that this Sarah is in spirit and is guiding you, protecting you," I said. No, she had never had a Sarah in her life. I must be wrong.

Then, about three months later, I got a letter from the woman. She had gone back to visit her aged mother and had told her of the reading. When she mentioned the name Sarah, her mother almost fainted. The first child the mother had ever had was named Sarah, but she was born with a severe deformity and only lived a few days. The mother had never told any of the children that came after Sarah that they had had a sister who died.

The information may be given to you in many different ways. You may get names, dates, places, and so on—by "get" I mean you'll *hear* them inside your head or else you'll *see* them written out in your mind's eye.

You may get colors, or heat or cold. You may get symbols. You may see an eagle, for example, and know this person doesn't keep eagles as pets or shoot eagles on her days off, so the big bird must be symbolic of something. Don't try to interpret the eagle symbol *unless* the interpretation is given to you immediately after the image. If all you get is the bird, then give her the bird and let her interpret it to her own satisfaction.

One last thing that is *very important*. *Never* give someone a reading who doesn't want it! It will only end in disaster, with you looking like the main candidate for the Nobel Prize for Jerks. If someone says that he doesn't want to have anything psychometrized, then *don't* insist. You will get no cooperation from this negative soul but be blocked at every level by his negativity. Don't say I didn't warn you!

Any further questions, dear students? Good. Let's get to *work*. Find yourself someone (the less well you know them, the better) who has an object and wants a reading. Have that person take off the object and hold it in her hands. Tell her to close her eyes and imagine currents of electricity running down both her arms into her palms. Have her recharge the object to put even more of herself into it. Then, when you feel ready to begin, ask her to hand it to you.

Say whatever comes into your head. You may start to get words or names even before the object touches your own hands. Fine—say what you get. Keep asking for confirmation of your facts. Make the person say yes or no or maybe, but get her confirmation in some way or else you won't know if you're on the right track.

If you don't get anything at all, ask for another object and hold *both* those objects together. You can pass the objects from one hand to another if you choose, press them against your forehead, do anything with them (within reason!) to make you closer and more in touch with their vibrations.

If you still don't get anything, pass the objects back. Either ask for another item to hold or forget the whole thing with that particular person. And remember, just because you bomb out with one person doesn't mean you'll do it with another. Maybe you just couldn't find that first person's wavelength.

Keep at it until you get it right . . . and you will.

Okay, you may say, this is all very nice but what *good* is it? Why bother to learn this spooky stuff with the long name?

Good question! I've already cited two of the reasons: to help track down a murderer and to decide if something, like the fake antique vase, is really worth the price.

But there are other reasons. You are about to sign a contract, say. You hold it for a few minutes and "something" just doesn't feel right to you. You ask to take it home and study it overnight. Then, in the calmness of your own study, you read the small print at the bottom! No way do you agree with those terms!

You get a letter from a friend. He is saying one thing but by holding his letter and "listening," you get what he was *thinking* as he was writing—and that was something completely different. I'm not suggesting that you'll get his exact words, but you'll get his mood and his emotions, and you'll be able to judge for yourself whether or not to take his letter at face value.

On being introduced to someone, you reach out and take his hand. Blaaahhh! comes back the response in quick psychometric fashion. Uh-huh, you say to yourself, I'd better *watch* this fellow.

I've had students who were collectors of various and sundry things use their psychometry to cut through all the muddle at flea markets and head straight for the items they would be interested in. It saves a lot of time and shoe leather.

I myself like to collect occult and psychic books, especially those written before 1940. I've gotten so that I can go directly to such books in the most jumbled shop and my hand will reach for the interesting ones first. Furthermore, if the book has been signed by the author, I *know* the signature is in there before I open the cover.

There are many ways psychometry can be used in your daily life. After all, that's why you are taking this course, correct?

DISCUSSION QUESTIONS

1. What biographical facts does this essay tell you about David St. Clair? Does he seem to be someone you'd like to know? Do you feel you can trust him?
2. What does the writing style tell you about the author? Does he use many big words, many long sentences? Does he seem concerned about communicating with *you*?
3. If you wanted to verify the story of Baroness Lotta von Strahl's helping the police solve the two crimes, how could you do it?

4. What keeps you from being too impressed by the fact the Baroness guessed the name "Maxon" and knew of Charles Manson's eyes and his family? When are you learning about these facts?

5. What advantages does a psychic have because of these features of psychometry?
   a. The subject hands the psychic an object.
   b. The subject comments about right and wrong facts as the reading progresses.
   c. Some images can be interpreted either literally or symbolically.
   d. Some subjects try to help the psychic by lying or by exaggerating things about themselves.
   e. One should never do a reading for a "negative" person.

6. If you tried a psychometry exercise and a psychic saw a ship on a choppy sea and the name "Sarah," could you find a way to tie these into your life story?

7. If you tried to do a reading on some other member of your class, what advantages (besides psychic power) would you have to help you make correct statements?

Stauer EMC² Analog Atomic Watch

We apologize that it loses 1 second every 20 million years...

The classic watch built with German precision to 1 billionth of a second?

There is a new super-accurate government device that gives you a perfect use for atomic theory. The US government has engineered the most ingenious, most accurate clock in the world, the new F-1 U.S. Atomic Clock in Boulder, Colorado. Our extraordinary new Stauer EMC² watch uses this clock to report the exact time from this remarkable cesium fission clock. So you are on time…all the time. This amazing clock will gain or lose only one second over a twenty million-year period. It is that accurate!

This perfectly tuned technological invention is now available for UNDER $100. And you'll never have to set this watch…the hands set themselves. Just push one of the buttons and you are synchronized with the F-1 and the hands of the watch move to the exact time position. The Stauer EMC² exceeds the accuracy of any Swiss luxury automatic so you can be more accurate and keep most of your money in your wallet… not on your wrist.

There are some unattractive plastic digital atomic watches on the market, but when our German movement maker made it possible for us to break the $100 price barrier with a beautiful, classically styled stainless steel

analog watch, we were truly excited.

The EMC² features precise atomic time with an automatic Standard time and Daylight Saving Time adjustment. It will adjust for leap years and even leap seconds! A breakthrough in technology at a breakthrough price.

The large numeric markers are luminescent and extremely easy to read so the watch is perfect for low light situation. The EMC² is water-resistant to 5 atms as well. The small readout shows you the date and has a digital second counter. This watch is rugged enough to take to the gym but handsome enough to wear to the boardroom or out to dinner. The designers built this watch for those who prefer their watches to be practical and sharp-looking rather than overrated and overpriced.

How can it be so accurate? The new F-1 clock uses laser beams to measure the photons emitted from the cesium atom to measure the resonance frequency. This laser-cooling clock makes it about 20 times more accurate than any other clock on earth. This timepiece is a great gift for anyone who values precision and technology. Know precisely when the markets open and close. Know

the times for landings and take offs or when the train is leaving the station. If punctuality and accuracy matter, then this watch was built for you.

We're still perfecting atomic theory. We must apologize that our Stauer EMC² Atomic Watch loses 1 second every 20,000,000 years. Our scientists are working diligently to correct this problem; but in the interim if you are not thrilled with the design and the accuracy of the EMC², return it in the next 30 days for a full refund of the purchase price.

This watch is not available in stores and it comes with our 30 day money-back guarantee. If you're not completely satisfied with the accuracy, simply return the watch for the full purchase price.

Not Available in Stores

Call now to take advantage of this limited offer.

Stauer EMC² Analog Atomic Watch
Three EXACT Payments of $33 +S&H

800-482-7995

Promotional Code AAW100
Please mention this when you call.
To order by mail, please call for details.

14101 Southcross Drive W.,
Dept. AAW100
Burnsville, Minnesota 55337

The operation of atomic precision depends on an electrical oscillator regulated by the natural vibration frequencies of an atomic system (as a beam of cesium atoms) accuracy to about one second in 20 million years, making it the most accurate clock ever made

SOURCE: *Atlanta Journal-Constitution.* Reprinted with permission of NEXTEN, Inc.

DISCUSSION QUESTIONS

1. Count the purr words in the ad: EMC², German precision, ingenious, extraordinary, exact, remarkable, amazing, luxury, practical, etc. Do these make for impressive argument?
2. If the watch is, in fact, as good as it is purported to be, why do the makers feel they have to hype it with the language?
3. Granting that the watch may keep super accurate time, how long do you think the watch will last?
4. Do you feel this argument needs to be a half-page ad? Why did the advertisers go to the expense of giving it so much space?

WHICH WOULD YOU RATHER PUT ON YOUR KIDS' CEREAL?

The decision is in your hands. But before you make it, here are some things to think about.

SUGAR IS SAFE
Unlike any artificial sweetener, sugar is on the government's FDA GRAS list (Generally Recognized As Safe).

100% NATURAL
Sugar is pure and 100% natural. It contains no mysterious, unnatural ingredients. No man-made chemicals. And no warning labels.

ONLY 16 CALORIES
Surprisingly, real sugar has only 16 calories per teaspoon—16 naturally satisfying calories.

SUGAR TASTES BEST
In a recent taste test, sugar was preferred nearly 3 to 1 over the leading artificial sweetener.

So if you want your kids to have a low calorie sweetener that's 100% natural and perfectly safe, give them real sugar. After all, don't they deserve to have it as good as you did?

100% NATURAL SUGAR.

THERE'S REALLY NO SUBSTITUTE.

The Sugar Association, Inc. 1511 K St. NW, Washington, D.C. 20005. (202) 628-0189

SOURCE: Courtesy of the Sugar Association, Inc.

DISCUSSION QUESTIONS

1. The advertisement attacks chemicals with long names, calling them "artificial" and "man-made." Can it be argued that these *are* natural products?
2. Is sugar a natural product? Does one dig it out of a mine and bring it to the table?
3. Why does the author attack "tribasic calcium phosphate" rather than "NutraSweet"?
4. What is the effect of the modifiers "pure," "100%," and "natural"?
5. Whom is the author addressing? Is the ad making a rational or an emotional argument?
6. How effective are the picture and the lines in bold print? How many readers would read down into the small print?

SAT Has Outlived Its Usefulness—If It Ever Had Any, That Is

Joe Rodriguez

They're trying to reform the SAT again, which is like trying to turn a pit bull into a toy poodle. What they ought to do is euthanize this mutt.

This time they've added a writing section to the Scholastic Aptitude Test. That's because educators have been saying that writing is critical for success in college. Actually, university professors have been saying this for centuries. You have to wonder why the College Board, which administers the test, has only now caught on.

Oh well, an essay question can't hurt, can it? I wish the SAT had used one when I was a senior at Garfield High School in East Los Angeles. All I remember are algebra formulas I had never seen before, and multiple-choice, verbal questions that looked suspiciously like an IQ test.

The highest possible SAT score is 1600. I can't remember my exact score, because I don't want to, but it was under 900.

On second thought, I don't think a writing test would have jacked up my score all that much. And it won't make much difference today for students in schools like mine. They don't have as many advanced placement classes or experienced teachers. Nor do they have affluent parents who can pay for expensive SAT preparation courses, as they do at privileged schools.

Did I forget to mention that the poorest schools in Latino and black neighborhoods often don't have enough textbooks and other basics? That helps explain the growing gap between Latino and black SAT scores, and white and Asian scores.

Since 1990, according to the College Board's own study, the average verbal score among Mexican-American students has dropped four points and their math scores have stayed flat. Meanwhile, white students have increased their verbal scores by nine points and math by 15. Asian scores have risen by 16 on verbal and 19 in math.

Some college systems, including the University of California and Texas, try to compensate by accepting the top 10 percent or so of each high school's

SOURCE: *Atlanta Journal-Constitution*, August 24, 2004. Reprinted with permission.

graduating class, but with mixed results. The fact is, most colleges across the country rely too heavily on the SAT. So do many scholarship programs.

Instead of tinkering with the SAT, we should kill it.

Although the test has its roots in the racist eugenics movement of the early 20th century—they thought Jews and African-Americans were inherently dumb and college incapable—the supporters of scholastic testing doggedly pursued an exam that would measure how much a student had learned in 12 years.

It wasn't a bad idea if it weren't so simplistic, lazy and easily exploited.

A major flaw of today's SAT is that it's vulnerable to coaching and short-term improvements. How can you trust a test that, for the $800 price of a quickie prep course, can produce a gain of 100 points?

A test isn't much good if it can't predict something, and the SAT hasn't been proved to be a reliable predictor of college success.

A few years ago, plucky little Muhlenberg College in Pennsylvania measured the first-semester grades of freshmen with SAT scores of about 1000 against freshmen with 1200 scores or better. The results were virtually identical.

But the absolute, worst assumption of the SAT is that any young person's potential can be reduced to a number. It assumes that, after four years of college, a 900-point student from a poor school cannot catch up to or surpass the 1400-point student from a wealthy school.

I don't know about the rest of you, but I'm sure glad my boss didn't ask for my SAT score when I applied. Come to think of it, none of my employers has ever asked.

Some years ago, former University of California President Richard Atkinson called for replacing the SAT with tests that try to measure achievement in specific subjects. The testocrats shot him down, but it's still a good idea and much better than a one-size-fits-all test that doesn't live up to its promise.

DISCUSSION QUESTIONS

1. Count the examples of snarl words in this essay. Do they make the argument more persuasive?
2. Does the author's personal experience—information about his high school, college, jobs, test scores—strengthen his argument?
3. What is the author's tone? Does it enhance the argument?
4. Do you think universities should use any kind of testing before admitting students? What is the value of testing?
5. Granted that well-to-do students and students from affluent backgrounds will do well in college, will having the SAT or not having the SAT change this?

Women Can Dump Jerks Without Help of Lawyers

Judy Jarvis

The date escapes me. At what point did women in America become victims? Exactly when did females, who are, after all, the majority in this country, forget how to tell pathetic and sexually clumsy men "no"? At what point did we give up our drive for equality, let out a collective whine and ask the government for special help? Probably about the same time we stopped calling men who employed tactless sexual come-ons harmless jerks and began calling them criminals.

I know this isn't very fashionable these days, but I'm having a hard time understanding this country's hysteria over sexual harassment. I find it very hard to think of Bob Packwood, for example, as a criminal. He's a guy who apparently couldn't stop himself from slobbering over women who had no interest in him, who made a fool of himself. This is a criminal? All Packwood was—and still is, for all we know—was a tactless, sexually maladjusted old man. Is that a crime worth running the man out of the U.S. Senate?

And, of course, there's the lecher of the hour, our unfaithful president. He may well be a criminal for other reasons, for lying under oath, for asking others to lie for him, but was his alleged pitch to Paula Jones criminal? Was it worth putting our nation's business on hold for a year or more?

As a woman who's dealt for years with guys like Bill Clinton who can't wait to show you their private parts, or ask to see yours, he's more pathetic than criminal. I'm not a lawyer. And I'm not a member of Congress. Clinton may well deserve to be impeached if Congress thinks he's abused the power of the presidency. But as a woman, all I see is a case born of a woman's inability to tell an overly aggressive man where to go.

Ditto with Clarence Thomas. Maybe he talked dirty to Anita Hill. Maybe he didn't. Something obviously went on between the two of them that was sexually charged. But if he did leave pubic hairs on her Coke can or talk to her about X-rated films, isn't that a pretty sad way to get a date?

Look what the Hill-Thomas hearings brought: the most regulated workplaces in the world. You can't tell dirty jokes. You can't put up pictures

SOURCE: *Mobile Register,* October 16, 1998. Reprinted with permission.

of your loved ones in bikinis, especially if her breasts are bigger than your female co-workers'. You can't look at someone with a glint in your eye.

But, the most chilling aspect of this sexual harassment movement is the indoctrination of our young into the culture of victimhood. Our children are being told now that if they are bullied by the opposite sex, this is sexual harassment. The Supreme Court has accepted a case in which a 10-year-old was allegedly sexually harassed.

Apparently, the young girl was bothered repeatedly by a boy who said nasty things to her, who touched her and whose teacher was a moron and didn't help her at all. The girl's parents sued, and now the school may end up being responsible for this boy's crummy behavior. But as they say, bad cases make bad law. And if the Supremes decide that the school is responsible any time a kid is offended or bullied or taunted, or, yes, in extreme cases, actually touched, maybe even assaulted, then say goodbye to the normal, experimental, groping, hormonally charged lifestyle of the American kid. Imagine a world where bra-snapping, wedgies, graffiti in the bathrooms about Susie and Tom, playground taunts about who's gay and who is not will be prosecuted as criminal offenses.

For those of you who think that's progress, think again. Do we really want our girls to grow up believing that they can't tell a jerky boy to get lost without hiring a lawyer? Do we really want an aggressive girl who bothers the hell out of a teen-age crush, who sends sexy notes to him, who corners him in the hall, to be a criminal? Because that's the direction we're headed. In fact, we're already halfway there.

My husband likes to tease me that I think sex makes the world go round, that I see most of life's dramas and many of life's news stories as having a sexual plot. I do. And that's just life. Boy meets girl. Girl meets boy. Either they get together or they don't. Can't we keep the lawyers out of it?

DISCUSSION QUESTIONS

1. Consider the snarl words in this essay:

   dump
   jerks
   pathetic [used twice]
   sexually clumsy
   a collective whine
   hysteria
   slobbering
   sexually maladjusted
   old man
   lecher of the hour

sad way to get a date
a jerky boy
a moron

2. What more denotative words might the author have used in these instances? Would they have been effective?
3. "Look what the Hill-Thomas hearings brought: the most regulated workplaces in the world." Is this a real problem?
4. How hard is it to accuse a employer or a co-worker of sexual harassment? Why might a person do it?
5. Are women the only victims of harassment? Can men be sexually harassed? If a man can't put up a picture of his wife or girlfriend, isn't that harassment?
6. What about men who are falsely accused of harassment? Can they call a lawyer too?

Statistics

"I'll remember this as the night Michael Jordan and I combined to score 70 points."

—STACY KING, CHICAGO BULLS

There are many ways in which statistics can be used to distort argument. Persuaders can cite impressive averages, irrelevant totals, and homemade figures. They can offer a number in a context that makes it appear larger or smaller, according to their wish.

■ AVERAGES

A common fallacy involves the use of so-called average figures: average income, average price, average audience size, and so on. It is easy to argue from such statistics because the word *average* can mean different things.

What, for example, is the average if a group of 15 homemakers, responding to a poll question, say they watch television 48, 40, 30, 26, 22, 18, 12, 10, 9, 8, 5, 5, 5, 1, and 0 hours a week? From these numbers, one can claim the group watches television an average of 15.933 hours a week, or 10 hours a week, or 5 hours a week. The 15.933 figure is the *mean* (the total number of hours watched divided by the number of viewers); the 10 figure is the *median* (the middle number in the series); and the 5 figure is the *mode* (the number that appears most frequently).

Each kind of average has its value, depending on the type of material being measured. But all three are available to the persuader who wants to manipulate an argument.

■ QUESTIONABLE FIGURES

Vague statistics can produce impressive averages. Numbers derived from memory, guesswork, and exaggeration can be averaged with amazing precision. (In the preceding paragraph, the 15.933 average was computed after

149

15 homemakers made rough guesses of their television viewing time.) Dr. Kinsey interviewed American men and reported that those without a high school education averaged 3.21 sexual experiences a week. The annual FBI report *Crime in the United States*, which compiles material from police departments across the country, showed that Baltimore in one year had suffered a crime increase of 71 percent. But police departments report crimes differently and with different degrees of accuracy. The sensational Baltimore figure wasn't caused by a crime wave; it came from more accurate police reporting in the second year.

Crime statistics produce strange news stories. Though the FBI warns its numbers are not reliable, *Dateline NBC* believed them and, in January 1994, announced that Mobile, Alabama, was the third most violent city in America— right after Miami and Atlanta. (The Mobile Police Department had grouped simple assaults with aggravated assaults and recorded 5768 aggravated assaults—a figure six times too high.) The television story brought a lot of angry complaints, and three weeks later *Dateline NBC* apologized for its mistake. The problem is the media circulated the sensational claim, and ignored the apology. Among those who missed the retraction were the authors of *Crime at College*, who listed Mobile's University of South Alabama as the fifth most dangerous college in the United States. South Alabama—which has had one major crime in its 28-year history—ranked ahead of the University of Florida, which had five murders in 1990. And two months later, *Money* magazine recalled the inflated FBI statistics and, in its story on "The Best Places to Live," ranked Mobile as No. 190. Never underestimate the longevity of a false statistic.

Amazing claims can be drawn from a small or partial sample. Some years ago a survey reported that 33.3 percent of all coeds at Johns Hopkins University had married faculty members. Johns Hopkins had three women students at the time. Advocates of extrasensory perception thrive on partial samples. They like to report cases of a gifted individual (Hubert Pearce, Basil Shakleton, or another) who has produced laboratory results for which the odds are 10,000,000 to 1 against chance being the explanation. Commonly, those who bother to question such claims discover that the individual cases were part of a longer series of tests and that the results of the entire experiment were not given.

Comparisons can produce misleading statistics. Commentators note that, in a given year, two million Americans get married, and one million get divorced. Then they claim that half of U.S. marriages are failing. (Actually, the marriages are a one-year statistic; the divorces involve people who wed during the previous 40 years.) Similarly, because of a dated norm, every state in the nation now reports its public-school students score "above the national average." (This has been called "the Lake Wobegon effect.")

▪ IRRELEVANT NUMBERS

An argument can be bolstered with irrelevant statistics. Some years ago tobacco companies responded to evidence that smoking may cause cancer by counting filter traps. Viceroy boasted 20,000 filters ("twice as many as the other two largest-selling brands") until Parliament began claiming 30,000, and Hit Parade overwhelmed both with 400,000. (That was an average figure. The testing lab reported that one Hit Parade filter had 597,000 filter traps.) These were impressive numbers, but they were meaningless. There was no evidence that *any* filter protected a person from the effects of smoking. And no one had defined "filter trap."

Many arguments assign numbers to undefined objects. When you're told that Americans reported 550 UFOs last month, you wonder what these people saw. When you face the sensational headline "Asthma Deaths in U.S. Double in Seven Years," you read on and see the reason: Authorities changed the definition of "asthma."

Advertisers take the practice a step further and employ numbers without references. You see a travel ad for Martinique offering "Four times the pleasure" and one for Montreal boasting "It's four times better." Better than what? Don't ask.

For a long time, cigarette advertisements offered precise numbers and irrelevant statistics. One ad boasted "Carlton is lowest." Another said Now is "lowest in tar and nicotine." These contradictions were possible because Carlton was referring to its King Size Soft Pack, and Now to its Soft Pack 100's. Neither ad showed how the figures made any difference to the average smoker.

Even when counting clearly defined items, speakers can offer irrelevant numbers. Responding to a demonstrated statistical relationship between cigarette smoking and an increased incidence of lung cancer, they can observe that the vast majority of smokers do not get cancer. As violent crimes increase, they can oppose gun control laws by calculating that only 0.0034 percent of American handguns are involved in homicides.

Equally creative computation goes into the unemployment figures produced by the U.S. Bureau of Labor Statistics. Because any administration can be faulted if unemployment is too high, the Bureau uses polling techniques that systematically underestimate the economic hardship within the labor force. A person is not "unemployed" unless he or she has actively looked for work in the preceding month. This method of counting eliminates people who have been sick, who have been forced into early retirement, and who have looked for months and have given up in despair.

However, a person can be looking regularly for work and still not be "unemployed." If an out-of-work longshoreman mows lawns two afternoons a month, he counts as being fully employed. If he helps out his brother in a family business and works for nothing, he is fully employed. If his daughter works an hour a month as a babysitter, she is just as employed (in administration figures) as a chemist who works 60 hours a week at Monsanto.

In an inspired move, the Reagan administration chose to enlarge the work force to include people in military service. Because all those added had jobs, the percentage of Americans who were unemployed dropped significantly. In its report on unemployment in August 2003, the U.S. Department of Labor did not include 1.7 million persons because they had not looked for work in the four weeks prior to the survey. Of the 1.7 million, 503,000 were "discouraged workers" who did not seek employment because they believed there were no jobs available for them.

A rich example of irrelevant statistics occurred in 1985 when corporate officers at the Coca-Cola Company changed the taste of Coke. They had 200,000 tests demonstrating that the public preferred the taste of the new Coke to the old Coke and preferred it to Pepsi. Still, the change produced a nationwide protest that forced them to bring back the old Coke (now called Coca-Cola Classic). Nobody cared about 200,000 tests. As one critic said, "It's like they redesigned the flag."

There is a kind of irrelevance in statistics derived from a singular sample. Hollywood Bread, for example, advertised that it had fewer calories per slice than other breads; this was true because its slices were thinner. Carlton cigarettes boasted that it had been tested as the lowest in "tar" of all filter kings; one reason was that it had a longer filter than other cigarettes of the same length and therefore contained less tobacco. Television personality Hugh Downs announced that he got 28.3 miles per gallon while driving a Mustang II from Phoenix to Los Angeles. The trip is largely downhill.

◼ HOMEMADE STATISTICS

The preceding examples indicate that people don't have to make up statistics to create a misleading argument. But, of course, they can make up statistics if they want to. For example, the temperance advocate who built an analogy on the claim that there were 10,000 deaths from alcohol poisoning to 1 death from mad-dog bites was using figures that exist nowhere else.

Homemade statistics usually relate to things that have not been measured or are impossible to measure. Authorities can be suspiciously precise about events too trivial to have been counted. (Dr. Joyce Brothers reported that the "American girl kisses an average of 79 men before getting married." A Lane cedar chest advertisement warned that moths destroy $400,000,000 worth of goods each year.) They can be glibly confident about obscure facts. (A *Nation* article said that there were 9,000,000 rats in New York City; Massachusetts Congressman Paul White, introducing a bill to make swearing illegal, announced that Americans curse 700,000 times a second.)

Imaginary numbers like these usually relate to areas in which it is impossible to get real figures. To make an impressive argument, advocates may want to specify the number of HIV-positive people in America today—or the number of pot smokers or abused wives. They may want to report how much money was spent on pornography last year—or on welfare fraud. The writers can find some information in these areas, but because exact counts remain unavailable, they are strongly tempted to produce a number that supports the case they are trying to make. Many give in. Remember this the next time you see headlines announcing that a rail strike in Chicago is costing the city $2,000,000 a day.

Even in instances where a measure of scientific computation occurred, resulting statistics often seem singularly creative. Consider these examples, taken from recent news stories:

1. Seventeen percent of the babies born to near-affluent parents are unwanted.
2. Americans eat 38,000,000,000 hamburgers a year.
3. Up to 30 percent of American coeds are harassed by their professors.
4. Five percent of Americans dream in color.
5. Men aged 35 to 50 average one sexual thought every 25 minutes.
6. Every five seconds a woman is beaten in the United States.
7. Fifty percent of people don't ask for help from a librarian.

An instructive example of homemade statistics occurred in July 1994 when Disney announced that *The Lion King* had grossed $23 million over the weekend. Immediately Paramount reported *Forrest Gump* had brought in $24 million and thus was the nation's No. 1 movie. The next day, Paramount boasted the final *Gump* figure was $24.415 million. Within minutes, Disney announced a new calculation: *The Lion King* had grossed $24.425 million. Shortly thereafter, Paramount reported its "final" figures didn't include receipts from some theaters in San Francisco and New York, and that *Forrest Gump* had actually grossed $24.45 million. Later, when reporters asked about these numbers, Paramount's distribution chief admitted the totals "involve some guesswork."

Maybe you saw the Planned Parenthood ad that appeared in leading newspapers. It said, "They did it 9000 times on television last year. How come nobody got pregnant?" Or maybe you saw the ad as it appeared later in *USA Today*. It began, "They did it 20,000 times on television last year." With a little practice, you can identify homemade statistics with the naked eye.

■ ENHANCING A STATISTIC

With careful presentation, people can make any number seem bigger or smaller, as their argument requires. For example, many newspapers reported an Oberlin College poll that claimed that 40 percent of the unmarried coeds had engaged in sex, that 1 in 13 of these women became pregnant, and that 80 percent of the pregnancies were terminated by abortion. The "80 percent" figure seems startling until you ask, "80 percent of what?" Relatively modest statistics appear sensational when given as percentages of percentages of percentages.

More commonly, persuaders change the character of a statistic by simple comparison. They relate it to a smaller number to make it seem large or to a larger number to make it seem small. The contrasting number need have no relevance aside from offering a useful comparison.

In presidential primaries, candidates routinely predict weak results. They point out that the contest is not in their strongest state, that other duties have limited their public appearances, and that, all in all, they will do well to win 8 percent of the vote. Then when they win 11 percent, their followers announce, "He did well. His vote exceeded expectations." One reverses the process to dwarf a statistic. When Governor George Wallace—a law-and-order spokesman—had to face the fact that Alabama had the highest murder rate of any state in the nation (11.4 murders per 100,000 people), his office explained that this figure was not nearly so high as that for Detroit, Los Angeles, and other major cities.

In a summary statement on statistical manipulation, Darrell Huff (*How to Lie with Statistics*, New York, Norton, 1954) counseled the business community:

> There are often many ways of expressing any figure. You can, for instance, express exactly the same fact by calling it a one percent return on sales, a fifteen percent return on investment, a ten-million-dollar profit, an increase of profits of forty percent (compared with 1935–39 average), and a decrease of sixty percent from last year. The method is to choose which one sounds best for the purpose at hand and trust that few who read it will recognize how imperfectly it reflects the situation.

In a society subject to political controversy, social argument, and Madison Avenue rhetoric, such argument is common.

You should recognize examples of distorted statistics and avoid them as much as possible in your writing.

Of course you won't want to use specific numbers when they hurt the case you are making. Consider the diamond-industry ad urging the purchase of an expensive engagement ring: "Is two months' salary too much to spend for something that will last forever?" (One might answer, "Is $4000 too much to spend on a marriage that will last two months?")

Even when numbers favor your case, do not use them too extensively. A mass audience is rarely persuaded by a body of statistics. This explains why they are used so infrequently in the antismoking campaigns of the American Cancer Society and the American Heart Association.

You should remember, finally, that a number by itself means little or nothing. If in a particular year Philadelphia's baseball team leads the major leagues with 179 double plays, what does that mean? That it has a fine second baseman? That it has poor pitchers? That its home park has an Astroturf infield? Who knows? When 46 of 100 beer drinkers who "regularly drink Budweiser" preferred an unmarked mug of Schlitz (in a 1980 New Orleans test), what did that prove? Probably that most drinkers can't tell one beer from another. What can you conclude about a $58,000 annual salary, a 150-word poem, a $12.95 meal? Not much. An important quality of statistical argument was expressed in a scene in the film *Annie Hall:* The lovers, played by Diane Keaton and Woody Allen, are asked by their psychiatrists how often they have sex. She responds, "All the time. Three times a week." And he says, "Hardly at all. Three times a week."

EXERCISES

How reliable are the following statistical arguments?

1. "There are 53 vampires in America today."—Headline in *The Sun*
2. If you begin having your hair styled, are people going to think you've gone soft? Half the Los Angeles Rams' line has their hair styled. If you want to laugh at them, go ahead. We don't.
3. Listening mistakes in the United States cost $10 billion a year.
4. Listerine Antiseptic stops bad breath four times better than toothpaste.
5. According to Rodale Press, cigarette smoking costs Americans $50 billion a year.
6. "One out of six college women will be sexually assaulted this year."—Rape Treatment Center, Santa Monica Hospital

7. Using a simple cipher (A = 6, B = 12, C = 18, etc.), the words KISSINGER and COMPUTER both total 666, the number of the Antichrist. Certainly this proves something.

8. Leo Guild's book *What Are the Odds?* reports that a young man with a broken engagement behind him is "75 percent as happy" as one who has never been engaged.

9. It is estimated that each year some 10 million wise Americans spend $500 million on essential life-building food supplements and vitamin capsules. Can 10 million Americans be wrong?

10. "27 million Americans can't read a bedtime story to a child."

11. Mennen Speed Stick offers "110 percent protection."

12. "Banging your head against a wall burns 150 calories an hour."— *National Enquirer* (July 15, 1986).

13. "Over 10 million men suffer impotence problems in the U.S. today."— Ken Druck

14. In her heyday, Clara Bow received more mail per week than the average town of 5000.

15. Studies show that therapy which includes an aspirin a day reduces heart attacks as much as 50 percent for some people. Aspirin, combined with exercise and the right foods, could save as many as 50,000 lives a year.

16. "1 in 10 have psychic power."—Uri Geller

17. "With 200,000,000 of us, God had something good in mind."—Poster displayed at a Gay Rights demonstration, New York.

18. Some car dealers offer purchasers no-interest loans. Others offer loans at 0 interest and 0.0 interest and 0.00 interest.

ESSAY ASSIGNMENTS

Write an essay either affirming or opposing one of these statements. The material you encounter in your background reading will include statistical argument, and so should your essay.

1. American industry is fighting pollution.
2. We need gun control laws to curtail crime.
3. Sex education leads to promiscuity, pregnancy, and disease.
4. It's proved: Cigarette smoking causes genetic defects.
5. IQ tests do not prove anything.
6. American income tax laws should be revised.
7. Viagra is an effective treatment for AIDS.
8. Statistics prove that X is a mistake. (Fill in the X.)

Terrorism and You—The Real Odds
Michael L. Rothschild

The odds of dying in an automobile accident each year are about one in 7,000, yet we continue to drive. The odds of dying from heart disease in any given year are one in 400 and of dying from cancer one in 600, yet many of us fail to exercise or maintain a healthy diet. We have learned to live with these common threats to our health. Yet we have been afraid to return to the malls and the skies.

What are the odds of dying on our next flight or next trip to a shopping mall? There are more than 40,000 malls in this country, and each is open about 75 hours per week. If a person shopped for two hours each week and terrorists were able to destroy one mall per week, the odds of being at the wrong place at the wrong time would be approximately 1.5 million to 1. If terrorists destroyed one mall each month, the odds would climb to one in 6 million. This assumes the total destruction of the entire mall; if that unlikely event didn't occur, the odds would become even more favorable.

In another hypothetical but horrible scenario, let us assume that each week one commercial aircraft was hijacked and crashed. What are the odds that a person who goes on one trip per month would be in that plane? There are currently about 18,000 commercial flights a day, and if that person's trip has four flights associated with it, the odds against that person's being on a crashed plane are about 135,000 to 1. If there were only one hijacked plane per month, the odds would be about 540,000 to 1.

Stories in the news media have begun to consider the virtue of a public relations campaign in Muslim nations to bring our side of the war to the populations of these countries. While this can be an important strategy, I would like to suggest that we need an information campaign in this country as well, because a key element of life after Sept. 11 has not been well presented to the public: Our leaders and media have not done a good job of discussing the risks that citizens need to consider when making choices in their daily lives.

We are presented with a continuous stream of stories telling us about the most recent horrible incident and the possibilities of future terrors.

SOURCE: *Washington Post*, national weekly edition, December 3–9, 2001, p. 27. Reprinted by permission of the author.

Frequent repetition of these stories may lead people to overestimate the likelihood of future dire events. While we need to be made aware of potential dangers, we also need to understand the true probabilities of these risks. In the above examples, the scenarios were pretty extreme; the odds of any one of us being directly affected by a lesser event would be even more remote.

People tend to underestimate the probability of a common event's occurring but overestimate the probability of a rare event. These findings may be due in part to the frequency with which we are exposed to news stories about the remote versus the common event. Anthrax, which has so far claimed five lives out of a population of 275 million, is a continuous story, while smoking-related illnesses, which claim about 400,000 lives per year, are not a news story at all.

Anthrax is a big story and is worthy of media attention, but people may be overreacting in changing their personal behavior because of this remote event. Perhaps they overestimate the potential probabilities that an anthrax related incident could happen to them because of the frequency with which they see anthrax-related news stories. In Madison, Wis., it was reported that in some neighborhoods parents didn't allow their children to go trick-or-treating at Halloween because of the heightened risks of terrorism. What are the odds that any single child would be affected by terrorists on that one night?

We need to separate the probability that an event may occur in our country and the probability that it will occur to us as individuals. In making an informed decision about my own behavior, I need to know the probability that I will be personally affected by a terrorist act, not what the probability is that such an act may occur at some place and some time.

We each have many opportunities to take various actions each day. Each opportunity has multiple choices and multiple outcomes. Each of us must independently make our own decisions, but we are being given incomplete information on which to base these decisions. As a result we may have been unnecessarily cautious.

The economic cost to our nation in lost expenditures, resulting in lost jobs and lost businesses, has been enormous. While the impact of any potential event on any one of us is slight, the impact of the sum of our individual behaviors is great. There is a key question that we need to consider: What are the odds that I, myself, will be at the exact wrong place at the exact wrong time?

While any terrorist event is horrible, if I act with respect to my own real risk and the probability that I, personally, will be affected, then I can return to a more normal life. If I act as if each terrorist act will be directed specifically at me, then I will hide, and collectively we will all hide.

DISCUSSION QUESTIONS

1. "Our leaders and media have not done a good job of discussing the risks that citizens need to consider when making choices in their daily lives." Is the argument claiming this persuasive?
2. Do the author's statistics seem reliable? Why so?
3. Frequent repetition of terrorists' stories can lead people to overestimate the dangers involved. Why so many news stories? Why so many political warnings?
4. If terrorists destroy one mall per month, the odds of one individual being killed are one in six million. How many American shopping malls have been destroyed in the past year?

100,000 Beer Commercials?

Anheuser-Busch

Have you heard the one about the average 18-year-old and the 100,000 beer commercials?

We'd almost be surprised if you hadn't. Since they first made the accusation in 1987, critics of the beer industry have repeated again and again that by the time the average American turns 18, he or she has seen 100,000 beer commercials on television. By now, no doubt, many people believe it. After all, spokesmen for such groups as the Center for Science in the Public Interest, which are widely perceived as interested only in the truth, have said it. Congress has heard witnesses testify to it. And reputable newspapers and magazines have reported it as gospel. So why shouldn't people believe it?

For just one reason. It isn't true.

We'd like to set the record straight. We'd like to explain how ridiculous the "100,000 beer commercials" accusation happens to be. And while we're at it, we'd like to raise some questions about the whole climate in which serious public issues are debated in this country. Specifically, we'd like to show how readily misinformation can achieve wide distribution—and ultimately, win acceptance by the public—if it suits some group's political agenda.

The origin of the "100,000 beer commercials" accusation is "Myths, Men & Beer," a lengthy and highly critical report on 40 beer commercials that appeared on network television in 1987. Although written by four university faculty members, "Myths, Men & Beer" was published and paid for by the American Automobile Association Foundation for Traffic Study in Falls Church, Va. It did not receive academic peer review, nor was it ever published in a professional journal.

"Myths, Men & Beer" alleges that beer advertising presents a "powerful, distorted, and dangerous message . . . to young people." It urges that "the policy permitting the televising of commercials for beer be revised to prohibit such commercials."

The authors, of course, have a right to their opinion. They should, however, stick to the facts in arriving at their opinions. And that's where we take issue.

SOURCE: Courtesy of Anheuser-Busch.

Let's think for a moment about the authors' assertion: "Between the ages of 2 and 18, American children see something like 100,000 television commercials for beer." Let's analyze this claim—for which, we hasten to point out, not one shred of evidence is provided in the report.

Sixteen years lie between a child's 2nd and 18th birthdays. Sixteen years represents about 5844 days, give or take a few for the vagaries of leap year. To see 100,000 beer commercials in that time, a young person would have to see an average of more than 17 beer commercials a day.

We say that's ridiculous on the face of it. But let's walk it through to prove how absurd it is.

On average, beer commercials represent about 3.4 percent of the total number of commercials aired in any given market, according to figures supplied by the Arbitron Co., the authoritative source on the subject. So if 17 beer commercials a day represents 3.4 percent of the total, it takes only a little arithmetic to show that the average viewer is seeing a total of 503 commercials a day. Actually, that's a conservative figure, because children tend to watch less TV at the times when beer commercials are scheduled. But we'll use the most conservative figures to make our point all the stronger.

How much daily viewing would 503 commercials require? Well, the average network commercial runs about 23 to 25 seconds. Given that local commercials are often a bit shorter, we use 20 seconds as a conservative, low estimate of the length of the average TV commercial. We'll multiply 503 by 20 and then divide by 60 to get the number of minutes of commercials our kids are allegedly seeing each day: 168 minutes.

We suspect we've already made our point, but indulge us, please, to the end. How much TV would someone have to see in a day, on average, to witness 168 minutes of commercials? The answer can be calculated from this information:

A conservative—in this case, high—estimate on the number of minutes of commercials shown each hour on TV is 12. Dividing 168 by 12 gives the answer: 14 hours per day—on average for 16 years.

Now we know our children watch a lot of TV. And we know that a lot of them don't get their proper rest. But most of them, we are convinced, still sleep several hours a night. Many, we're quite certain, also attend school. Our own powers of observation also disclose the following: Many children still go outside and play, and whole flocks of them visit shopping malls.

Emboldened by this skepticism, we checked with A. C. Neilsen Co., which we consider a credible authority on these matters. And what do you know—they reported that average **weekly** TV viewing by 2- and 17-year-olds in 1988 was a little more than 23.5 hours, or less than 3.5 hours per day.

Pardon our sarcasm: the fact is, there are even more problems with the authors' claim. Nowhere, for example, is there any indication that the authors have taken into account **when children are watching TV, or what they're seeing.** (As we mentioned, we haven't either—but only to be conservative and give the authors a better chance to prove their claim.) The reality is, beer is advertised primarily during evenings and sporting events— and never on "Pee-Wee's Playhouse" or the "Wonderful World of Disney." The authors of "Myths, Men & Beer" don't seem to be aware, or care.

One more note along these lines. As we've noted, sporting events are a focus for beer advertising. But, in a typical major league baseball game, 11 is a high estimate of the number of beer commercials that might be shown. So according to the authors of "Myths, Men & Beer," the average child is see-ing—on a daily basis for 16 years—the equivalent of about one and one-half baseball games worth of beer commercials. And that's on top of the viewing this child is doing of shows without beer advertisements.

In short, the "100,000 beer commercials" charge is not just wrong; it's absurd and shoddy. It is, you'll excuse the expression, false advertising.

Now let's go on to the deeper issues. Why is it that an accusation as patently false as the one relating to 100,000 beer commercials gets leveled? And why does it then get repeated again and again and again—by people who obviously don't bother to check it—until it takes on the mantle of con-ventional wisdom?

The answer relates to the fact that the alcohol-related issues are emo-tional ones that are heavily freighted with value judgments. In the minds of its critics, beer industry advertising is bad. Therefore, any information that would reflect negatively on this advertising—information, for instance, that would suggest that young people are being inundated and corrupted by it— gains an eager reception.

In saying this, we don't question the sincerity of the critics. We do, how-ever, object to the way in which their deeply held views seem to interfere with their research and analysis—the way, in other words, in which their views seem to affect their intellectual standards. And we do question the willingness of some of our critics to leap enthusiastically upon such obvi-ously flawed research if it advances their political agenda.

It's well known that if falsehood is repeated often enough, many people will believe it. But in this country, a strong media often puts the lie to would-be propagandists' claims. It's therefore also important to ask—why hasn't the media exposed the "100,000 commercials" canard for what it is?

In our view, it's because groups like Remove Intoxicated Drivers and the Center for Science in the Public Interest enjoy so much credibility with the public. Groups like RID are widely perceived as noble champions of good causes: Who wouldn't fight against drunk driving? (The beer industry certainly opposes it, but that fact can be easily overlooked.) Groups like the Center for Science in the Public Interest, meanwhile, are seen as above-the-battle guardians of society's broader concerns. (How many people understand that the CSPI has a minimal scientific staff and is essentially a political organization?) The upshot is that most people believe whatever these groups say.

In the end, it all boils down to a simple chain of events: Sloppy research, compromised by an underlying political agenda, produces a simple, quotable "fact" that meets the political needs of organizations which enjoy a wide public and journalistic following. The "fact" is repeated and repeated until, in short order, everybody "knows" it—even though it happens not to be true.

We could give many more examples, but we'll confine ourselves to a few that are central to the overall issue: specifically, to the critics' contention that advertising results in higher levels of beer consumption, underage drinking, and abuse.

In 1985, the Federal Trade Commission investigated these allegations in response to a petition by the CSPI and other parties. The FTC subsequently reported: "Our staffs' review of the literature regarding the quantitative effect of alcohol advertising on consumption and abuse found no reliable basis to conclude that alcohol advertising significantly affects consumption, let alone abuse." At a Senate hearing just last year, the FTC reiterated its position.

The FTC's findings shouldn't have come as too much of a surprise to at least one of the groups seeking advertising restrictions. In its petition to the FTC, the CSPI conceded that "the available literature does not demonstrate a causal connection between advertising and harm."

In effect, the FTC inquiry—and a similar one conducted in 1985 by the U.S. Senate's Subcommittee on Alcoholism and Drug Abuse—gave support to our view: Beer advertising doesn't significantly affect consumption, underage drinking, or abuse. It affects market share.

Ironically, this is a fact that even the authors of "Myths, Men & Beer" acknowledge. In their report, they write: "It would be a grave error to believe, for example, that advertising causes the people of a culture to behave as they do, in any but trivial ways (selecting Brand X, perhaps, over Brand Y)."

Hurrah—sort of. Allow us to add that the "trivial ways" to which the authors refer are the difference between success and failure to us. In the beer industry, each point of market share is worth about $440 million at the retail level. That's the whole reason members of the industry spend as much as they do on advertising—to try to win market share.

Let us add, too, that while beer advertising rose in the 1980s, per capita consumption of beer actually declined 2.5 percent between 1980 and 1988, the last year for which figures are available; that the number of people killed in drunk driving accidents fell 9 percent between 1982 and 1988; and that the beer industry has played a substantial part in the public awareness and education campaigns that are apparently helping to reduce the abuse of alcohol.

In short, let us observe that reality is more complicated—and in many cases quite different—from what our critics would have us all believe.

Alcohol abuse is a serious problem in this country, inflicting substantial damage on individuals and society. How we deal with alcohol abuse also raises serious issues—involving such matters as commercial free speech, individual freedoms versus society's interest in self-protection, and appropriate assignments of responsibility for individual conduct.

To resolve these questions rationally will require all the intelligence and solid information we can muster. Flawed information, fueled by emotion and exploited for political ends, will make news. It may even shape policy.

But it won't help.

DISCUSSION QUESTIONS

1. At one point in challenging the "100,000 commercials" claim, the author writes, "We suspect we've already made our point, but indulge us, please, to the end." Why such an exhaustive analysis of the claim?
2. Does the argument make effective use of authorities? What does it say about each of these:
   a. Center for Science in the Public Interest
   b. American Automobile Association Foundation for Traffic Study
   c. Arbitron Company
   d. A. C. Neilsen Company
   e. Remove Intoxicated Drivers
   f. Federal Trade Commission
   g. U.S. Senate's Subcommittee on Alcoholism and Drug Abuse
3. Is the author angry at beer-industry critics? What is the tone of the essay? Does this tone help the argument?
4. How does the argument challenge the view that beer ads lead young people to drink dangerously? Is the argument persuasive?
5. How formal is this essay? What is the effect of lines like "Hurrah—sort of" and "But it won't help"?
6. Is the author an effective writer? Why do you think so?

Barry Bonds, Your Records Will Stand

Mike Luckovich

SOURCE: *Atlanta Journal-Constitution*, March 9, 2005. Reprinted with permission of Creators Syndicate.

DISCUSSION QUESTIONS

1. Is it reasonable to compare real-life achievement with comic strip adventure?
2. Why shouldn't athletes use steroids if it improves their game? Where is the problem?
3. Is it fair to compare a drug-enhanced record with records of regular athletes, such as Babe Ruth and Henry Aaron? Does fairness make a difference here?

Is It Sports, the Weather or Love of God That Keeps Us Married?

William R. Mattox, Jr.

As every ball player preparing for Opening Day knows, the game of baseball revolves around home. Pitchers try to throw the ball over home plate. Batters try to hit home runs. Runners try to make it home safely. And fans root, root, root for the home team.

Apparently, baseball's preoccupation with home is no accident. A research study by Denver University psychologist Howard Markman shows that the average divorce rate in cities that have a major league baseball team is 28 percent lower than in cities that lack a Major League franchise.

While Markman insists this finding is just a coincidence, his research does raise a rather intriguing question: What geographic differences do exist in divorce rates?

Perhaps the easiest way to answer this question is to think not of baseball, but of another warm weather accompaniment—bathing suits. Strangely enough, the divorce rate of any place in the continental United States can be reliably predicted by knowing the number of days out of the year that women there can wear swimsuits. Generally, the more warm weather days suitable for bathing attire, the higher the divorce rate; the more cold weather days unsuitable for swimwear, the lower the divorce rate.

To illustrate, draw a line across the midsection of the continental United States (along the northern border of North Carolina, Tennessee, Arkansas. Oklahoma, New Mexico and Arizona, and continuing through southern Nevada and central California). More than 60 percent of the total U.S. population lives above what might be called "the tan line." Yet less than half of all divorces occur here, and all of the 10 states with the lowest divorce rates are above the tan line.

In fact, believe it or not, Teddy Kennedy's home state of Massachusetts is number one in marital stability. Donald Trump's New York follows close behind. Conversely, almost all of the states with the highest divorce rates are found below the tan line. And four of these states—Alabama, Arkansas. Oklahoma and Tennessee—are located right in the heart of the Bible Belt.

SOURCE: *Mobile Register*, April 2, 1999. Reprinted with permission.

The irony here, of course, is that the Bible is hardly neutral on the subject of divorce. The Old Testament prophet Malachi reports that God "hates divorce." And in the New Testament, Jesus condemns divorce "for any reason except sexual immorality" (Matthew 5:32).

In truth, the National Institute for Healthcare Research says weekly churchgoers throughout the U.S. are less apt to divorce than people who claim "no religion" and those who attend religious services less than once a week. Devout Catholics have especially low divorce rates—apparently because Catholic parishes often take the responsibility of marriage preparation and enrichment more seriously than Protestant churches do.

Thus, one of the reasons for the relatively low divorce rates in the Northeast and Midwest is because these regions tend to have a higher concentration of Catholics than do other geographic areas.

University of Texas sociologist Norval Glenn says another factor affecting regional differences in divorce is "social rootedness." His research shows that people who live in stable communities are less apt to divorce because they are more likely to be enmeshed in an inter-generational social network that helps them evaluate potential mates, offers them marital advice and support, and expects them to work through any domestic problems that may arise.

Thus, the Sun Belt's higher divorce rates are due, in part, to the fact that this region has more social instability than less-transient areas in the Northeast and Midwest.

In many ways, it is too bad that America's divorce problem isn't attributable to the absence of professional baseball. Because it would be far easier to expand the number of professional baseball teams than to make the kind of changes needed to dramatically reduce the number of divorces in America.

But if we are serious about strengthening marriages in this country—and we should be—then we should be encouraging churches to make marriage preparation, enrichment and restoration a high priority.

We should be imploring businesses to reduce the volume of forced geographic transfers and job-related travel.

And we should be helping couples to see that divorce rarely solves problems; it usually just exchanges one set of problems for another.

Obviously, changing cultural attitudes about divorce will not be easy. But a nation that still fondly remembers "old school" ballplayers like Joltin' Joe DiMaggio—and still cherishes historic ballparks like Chicago's Wrigley Field—ought to be able to regain its commitment to the time-honored ideal of lifelong marriage.

We ought to be able to renew our appreciation for the idea that "diamonds are forever." We ought to be able to find our way home.

DISCUSSION QUESTIONS

1. The author presents statistical relationships:

   "The average divorce rate in cities that have a major league baseball team is 28 percent lower than in cities that lack a Major League franchise."
   "The divorce rate of any place in the continental United States can be reliably predicted by knowing the number of days out of the year that women there can wear swimsuits."
   What do these examples tell you about statistical evidence?

2. The author gives paradoxical facts:

   Four of the states with the highest divorce rates are located in the heart of the Bible Belt.
   Ted Kennedy's home state and Donald Trump's home state are ranked numbers one and two in marital stability.

   Why does he state the facts this way?
3. Devout Catholics have "an especially low divorce rate." How does the author explain this? Does the explanation make sense to you?
4. Why are there more divorces south of the "tan line"? Does geography have much to do with it?
5. "Divorce rarely solves problems; it usually just exchanges one set of problems for another." What kind of evidence might support this claim?

Consider the Bulk Rate for Wide-Bodied Airline Passengers

Marc Fisher

Two pounds of apples cost more than one. Mailing a big, fat envelope is more expensive than mailing a letter. Smokers pay more for life insurance than do non-smokers.

So why shouldn't you pay an airline according to how much you weigh and how much space you take up?

A report the other day from the National Center for Environmental Health tells us that our collective national belt-loosening is costing the airlines big money—an extra $275 million in fuel costs in one year to account for the 10-pound average increase in Americans' weight over the past decade.

The airlines are desperately trying to cut fuel costs by cutting the weight they carry—replacing metal utensils with plastic ones, scrapping heavy magazines. But the solution lies directly beneath the floor of the passenger cabin: Charge passengers by the pound, just as freight in the cargo hold is priced.

That would not only help the airlines but, more important, would create a social and financial disincentive for becoming or staying obese.

As things stand, the one-third of Americans who are not overweight subsidize the two-thirds who are. It's in everyone's interest to shift the balance back toward healthier, slimmer lives.

Advocates for the obese—yes, they have a Washington lobby, too—reject solutions that put the responsibility for obesity squarely on the bellies of the big. The American Obesity Association argues that our commercial and entertainment culture bears a good part of the blame for our becoming a nation of wide loads.

With almost any other malady, we distinguish between people's behavior and their affliction. You might behave in ways that make it more likely that you'll get cancer, but when you do get cancer, it's generally perceived as a really bad break that deserves oceans of sympathy. But if you're large, the public reaction is that it's your own darn fault and maybe you should lay off the Mars bars.

"We suspend the compassion that we normally feel," as Morgan Downey, director of the obesity group, put it. Instead, we laugh in the general

SOURCE: *Atlanta Journal-Constitution*, November 22, 2004. Reprinted with permission from the *Atlanta Journal-Constitution,* copyright © 2004.

direction of fat people, making a "moral judgment of laziness, lack of self-control, weakness," Downey said.

Fair enough. But accepting the idea that obesity is a community problem actually strengthens the case for creating such disincentives as paying by the pound for air travel.

Yet when Southwest Airlines tried to draw the line against corpulent passengers flowing over onto someone else's seat, the obesity lobby rolled into action. Southwest's policy is simple and fair: If you take up more than one seat, you need to buy the extra seat. The airline refunds the extra charge if there are empty seats on a given flight.

The Obesity Association reacted by asking Southwest to install wider seats for the extra large. No way, said Southwest, which went ahead with its policy, noting that only six seats per airplane account for their profit margin. Replacing only three rows of seats per plane with extra-wide seats would suck up all their profits, Southwest's president argued.

All that extra weight we're carrying is a burden not only on the airlines' bottom line, but also on our very survival. After a commuter plane crashed last year in Charlotte, federal investigators said it might have been overloaded. So the FAA ordered airlines to revise the formula they use to estimate the weights of passengers. The feds tacked an extra 10 pounds onto the assumed average weight of an American adult.

The answer: Public weigh-ins before every flight. Heck, it'll add some entertainment while we wait at the security checkpoints. Shame, a nearly-lost tool of social persuasion in this society, is good: Line 'em up, weigh 'em in and watch the pounds come off.

DISCUSSION QUESTIONS

1. To whom is this argument addressed? Is it aimed at fat people?
2. The claim is that additional weight has cost the airlines $275 million in fuel costs. How could anyone measure this? Does this number seem suspicious to you?
3. The American Obesity Association is disturbed that the public is blaming being overweight on laziness, lack of self control, weakness. Isn't this the cause of the problem?
4. Why do obese citizens have a lobby at all?
5. Is it reasonable to blame obesity on the culture rather than on the individual?
6. Would a public weigh-in be successful? Who would complain about that?

Courtesy of Brady Campaign to Prevent Gun Violence.

DISCUSSION QUESTIONS

1. What is the unstated conclusion of this ad? What is the author advocating?
2. Is the argument persuasive?
3. Would the argument be less persuasive if you were told the number of stabbings in Britain, the number of bombings in Ireland, the number of fatal beatings in West Germany, and so on?
4. If the sale of handguns was made illegal tomorrow, do you think the figures on the ad would be significantly different a year from now? Why or why not?

No, Virginia, There *Isn't* a Santa Claus!
Bruce Handy

Do you believe in Santa Claus? This is a complex theological question that each child must decide for him- or herself. Until now, that is. With the aid of computers, *spy jr.* has conducted a rigorous **statistical** investigation into the question of Santa's existence. Be forewarned: you may not like our conclusions.

We begin our investigation by assuming that Santa Claus really does exist. Now, if you've learned anything about human nature, you know it's highly unlikely that a normal man would choose, for no particular reason, to devote his life to making toys and delivering them to boys and girls the world over. But this is an **objective** inquiry, and questions of motivation aren't relevant. We want only to know whether such a man could accomplish his mission.

Santa's first obstacle is that *no known species of reindeer can fly*. However, scientists estimate that out of the earth's roughly 2 million species of living organisms, 30,000 or so have yet to be classified. So, even though most of these undiscovered species are insects and germs, we can't rule out the slight possibility that a species of flying reindeer does, in fact, exist. And that no one besides Santa has ever seen one.

A bigger obstacle for Santa is that there are 2 billion children under the age of 18 in the world. The good news is that he needs to deliver presents only to *Christian* children, of whom there are approximately 378 million (according to figures provided by the Population Reference Bureau). Let's assume that 15 percent of these Christian children have been bad and are thus—like Muslim, Hindu, Jewish and Buddhist children—ineligible for gift getting. Still, at an average rate of 3.5 children per household, Santa has a backbreaking 91.8 million homes to visit on any given Christmas Eve.

Fortunately, Santa has 31 hours of Christmas Eve darkness to visit all these homes if he travels from east to west, thanks to the rotation of the earth. Unfortunately, this still works out to 822.6 visits per second. So, for each Christian household with good children, Santa has just over a thousandth of a second to land, hop out of his sleigh, jump down the chimney, fill the stockings, distribute the rest of the presents under the tree, eat whatever

SOURCE: Reprinted by permission from *Spy*, January 1991.

snacks have been left out, get back up the chimney, climb back into his sleigh, take off and fly to the next house.

How fast is Santa moving? Assuming all 91.8 million stops are spread evenly over the earth's landmass, Santa must travel 0.79 miles per household—a total trip of 72,522,000 miles. (This is a conservative estimate. It doesn't include trips across oceans, feeding stops for the reindeer, etc.) Given the 31-hour time period, Santa's sleigh must maintain an average speed of 650 miles per second, or more than 3,000 times the speed of sound. To give you an idea how fast that is, the fastest man-made vehicle ever built, the *Ulysses* space probe, travels at a relatively poky pace of 27.4 miles per second, and conventional land-bound reindeer travel at a top speed of 15 miles per hour. But let's just assume that Santa's flying reindeer are somehow able to reach hypersonic speeds—thanks, say, to the magical spirit of Christmas giving.

Let's take a closer look at Santa's vehicle. First of all, assuming a cheapo 2 pounds of presents per child (that's like one crummy Lego set), the sleigh must still be able to carry a load of 321,300 tons—plus Santa, an overweight man. On land, a reindeer can't pull more than 300 pounds of freight, and even assuming that flying reindeer could pull ten times that amount, Santa's massive sleigh has to be drawn by 214,200 beasts. They increase the weight of the overall Santa payload to 353,430 tons (not including the weight of the sleigh itself). This is more than four times the weight of the *Queen Elizabeth* ocean liner. Imagine: Santa skimming over rooftops in a gargantuan hypersonic aircraft with even less maneuverability than a Big Wheel.

Here's where things get fun.

Three hundred fifty-three thousand tons of reindeer and presents are going to create an enormous amount of air-resistance—especially at 650 miles per second. This air resistance will heat the reindeer in the same way that spaceships are heated up when they reenter the earth's atmosphere. According to our calculations, the lead pair of reindeer will absorb 14.3-quintillion joules of energy per second each. This means they will burst into spectacular, multicolored flames almost instantaneously, exposing the reindeer behind them. As Santa continues on his mission—leaving deafening sonic booms in his wake—charred reindeer will constantly be sloughed off. All 214,200 reindeer will be dead within 4.26 thousandths of a second.

As for Santa, he will be subjected to centrifugal forces 17,500.06 times greater than gravity. A 250-pound Santa will be pinned to the back of his sleigh by 4,375,015 pounds of force (after we deduct his weight). This force will kill Santa instantly, crushing his bones, pulverizing his flesh, turning him into pink goo. In other words, if Santa tries to deliver presents on Christmas Eve to every qualified boy and girl on the face of the earth, he will be liquefied.

If he even exists, he's already dead.

So where *do* the presents come from? Weirdly kindhearted intruders? Stupid robbers? Magic? Your parents, maybe?

We won't insult your intelligence with the answer.

DISCUSSION QUESTIONS

1. What is the purpose of this essay? Is it to discourage the reader from believing in Santa Claus?
2. Look at the use of lines like "rigorous statistical investigation," "an objective inquiry," "a conservative estimate," etc. What do these contribute to the tone of the essay? What is their purpose?
3. Do the scientific numbers and the mathematical analyses seem reliable to you?
4. Do they seem relevant?
5. Does Santa Claus exist? What is the problem when one offers a statistical analysis of love, beauty, or religious or traditional beliefs?
6. Is this essay well-written? Why do you think so?

PART TWO

Argument for Analysis

Do not despise prophesying, but test everything; hold fast what is good.
—St. Paul, *I Thessalonians*

The Ugliness Problem

Dan Seligman

Is it Irrational to Discriminate against the Appearance-Challenged? Not Entirely.

A sizeable and growing body of literature attests to the fact that homely people confront disadvantages not only in the competition for spouses but in many other areas of life. They have lower incomes than handsome types. When accused of crime, they tend to be dealt with more harshly by judges and juries. One recent report, sorrowfully dwelt upon by *New York Times* columnist Maureen Dowd, concludes that less attractive children are discriminated against by their own parents. (Parents are alleged to be less mindful of the safety of unattractive tots.)

In most academic venues and popular media the reaction has been to emphasize the irrational thinking that underlies discrimination against the ugly.

The alternative perspective, about to be advanced on this page, questions whether the discrimination really is so irrational.

The classic article about the economic effects of physical appearance, published in the December 1994 *American Economic Review*, was written by Daniel S. Hamermesh (University of Texas, Austin) and Jeff E. Biddle (Michigan State). It relies on three studies (two American, one Canadian) in which interviewers visited people's homes, asked the occupants a lot of questions about their education, training and job histories, and discreetly (one hopes) rated each man or woman on physical attractiveness. The ratings were on a scale of one (best) to five (worst). In the larger of the two American samples 15% of interviewees were rated "quite plain" or "homely"—categories four and five.

Hamermesh and Biddle found that men in the top two categories enjoyed incomes 5% above those of men rated merely average in appearance. The unfortunate fellows in the two bottom categories were paid 9% below the average. The results for women workers were somewhat similar, except that the workplace effects were smaller. The study controlled for differences in education, experience and several other factors affecting pay but did not measure (and thus did not adjust for) intelligence.

Hamermesh and Biddle agree that it's rational to pay more for good looks in some occupations, e.g., salesperson, but deny that this explains much of the pay gap. They leave you thinking that the basic dynamic is pure employer discrimination—a simple preference for good-looking people. Their paper says nothing about the policy implications of this perspective, but in a recent conversation with Hamermesh I discovered that he is sympathetic to ugly people who want laws to bar the discrimination.

But is it entirely irrational to view ugly people as generally less competent than beautiful people? It is hard to accept that employers in a competitive economy would irrationally persist in paying a premium for beauty—while somehow never noticing that all those lookers were in fact no more intelligent and reliable than the ugly characters being turned down. In the standard economic model of discrimination put forward years ago by Gary Becker of the University of Chicago, employers who discriminate irrationally get punished by the market, i.e., by competitors able to hire competence at lower rates.

The mating practices of human beings offer a reason for thinking beauty and intelligence might come in the same package. The logic of this covariance was explained to me years ago by a Harvard psychologist who had been reading a history of the Rothschild family. His mischievous but astute observation: The family founders, in 18th-century Frankfurt, were supremely ugly, but several generations later, after successive marriages to supremely beautiful women, the men in the family were indistinguishable from movie stars. The Rothschild effect, as you could call it, is well established in sociology research: Men everywhere want to marry beautiful women, and women everywhere want socially dominant (i.e., intelligent) husbands. When competent men marry pretty women, the couple tends to have children above average in both competence and looks. Covariance is everywhere. At the other end of the scale, too, there is a connection between looks and smarts. According to Erdal Tekin, a research fellow at the National Bureau of Economic Research, low attractiveness ratings predict lower test scores and a greater likelihood of criminal activity.

Antidiscrimination laws being what they are, it is sometimes difficult for an employer to give intelligence tests or even to ascertain criminal histories. So maybe the managers who subconsciously award a few extra points to the handsome applicants are rational. Or at least not quite as stupid as they look.

Would You Take a House Call from Dr. Kevorkian?

Faye Girsh, Ed. D.

What Is This All About?

Some people suffer a lot at the end of their lives. Most of us have had experience with loved ones whose death took a long time and was agonizing. There are some times when a hastened death is the only way out of that kind of agony. Many patients beg their doctor, "Can you please help me die, doc? I can't stand this suffering any more. Why is this taking so long?" Many doctors will help. But, if they do they risk going to jail and/or losing their license. Even if someone you love helps you die, he or she is taking a chance. It is against the law in this country to help someone else to die.

Do you agree with such a law which prevents a compassionate doctor from granting the request of his or her dying patient. Seventy-five percent of Americans say Yes when asked: Should doctors be allowed by law to end a patient's life if the patient has a terminal illness and requests it?

Are You Trying to Change the Law?

Yes! The Hemlock Society and other groups have been tying to make it legal for doctors to help a dying patient. They are suggesting strict safeguards to make sure that, the patient is really dying, that he or she is mentally competent to make the decision, and that it is an "enduring request" not an impulsive act. The doctor would have to be willing to do it and the request from the patient would have to be voluntary. In most of these proposals the doctor would prescribe a large amount of medicine that would cause death and the patient would take it when they felt their suffering had gotten unbearable.

Four states have voted on this kind of law: Washington, California, Oregon, and Michigan. It was passed by the people of Oregon in 1994, and again in 1997 and has been in effect since November 1997 but various groups have tried to stop it from going into effect.

SOURCE: Reprinted by permission of the author.

More than 20 states have had bills like Oregon's introduced but, so far, they have not passed. The Supreme Court ruled that it is not constitutional for a state to make it a crime for a doctor to help a dying patient who makes the request. Two courts said people had a constitutional right to decide the time and manner of their death; but the Supreme Court said it is not an issue that has anything to do with the federal constitution. It will be up to each state to decide.

If Most People Want It, Why Isn't It OK?

Some people, notably the hierarchy of the Catholic Church, the Right to Life organizations, and the American Medical Association (AMA) oppose physician aid in dying. They believe in the sanctity of life, worry about abuse of such a law and where it will lead.

These organizations do not necessarily speak for their members. Two recent national surveys show that more than half of the Catholics surveyed favor legal physician aid in dying. People who care about the right to life for an unborn child have different ideas about hastening death. This is not a situation where a decision is made by someone else to discontinue a life that could be lived fully. This is a request from the patient him/herself to hasten a death which is inevitable. And, the three recent surveys of doctors in Oregon, Michigan, and Washington show a majority would like to see the practice legalized. Many doctors already do it: for example, 53% of doctors in San Francisco who work with AIDS patients admit to having helped their patients die, many more than once.

Actually, we don't know how many Kevorkians there are out there. He was the only doctor who publicly says who he helped, why, and how. What we have now is chaos with doctors helping people die in a completely unregulated way with no accountability. Until Dr. Kevorkian's conviction in 1999, no doctor has ever been convicted for helping, but still most fear doing it because of what might happen. And, we have loved ones who either help and risk their freedom or who don't respond to the desperate pleas and feel guilty the rest of their lives.

Why Do We Need a Doctor to Help Anyway?

The Hemlock Society believes a person has the right to a gentle, dignified death surrounded by people s/he loves and a death which is quick and certain—if that is his or her choice. The only way to achieve that is with the medications a doctor can prescribe.

Assistance in dying should be part of the care provided by a doctor anyway. We discuss all the treatment possibilities with our doctors; then, when there is no more treatment, we should be able to talk about all the ways our death can be as comfortable as possible. If a person does not want a lingering death, then there should be a choice of asking for help.

Most doctors do not take the Hippocratic Oath nowadays. They take an oath which emphasizes the relief of suffering and respecting their patient's wishes. Even in the days of Hippocrates people died from accidents and infections; now we have conquered most of the causes of a premature death and people die from chronic diseases where death can be long and difficult. Cancer, stroke, AIDS, and neurological diseases are what people fear most.

What About Living Wills? Isn't That Enough to Protect Me Against Treatment I Don't Want?

The Living Will and another document, the Durable Power of Attorney for Health Care, will let you refuse or stop treatment. The problem is that some people who are dying do not have treatment they can refuse and then die. The only way they can die is linger on and die "naturally" or to get help. Even when they stop treatment, like dialysis or chemotherapy, dying can take a long time and be hard for a small percentage of people.

A law allowing a doctor to help would be the additional piece in the dying process that would reassure people that they would not have to endure a horrible death. Many people would live longer once they knew they had that assurance.

I Hear a Lot About Hospice. Isn't That a Good Thing for Dying People?

Yes, it's a wonderful thing. Hospice provides humane and compassionate care; it furnishes good pain relief and it helps family members adjust to the dying process. Hospice neither prolongs nor hastens the dying process.

The problem is that for some people the disease has caused so much devastation, their condition is so weakened, or they do not want to be diapered, sedated, and completely dependent that they would like the process to be over. They want to call their loved ones in, say good-bye and make a graceful exit while they still can. They do not want their family to have to care for them while they starve to death or are in a state of "terminal sedation." These are the only things hospice can do to make dying quicker. Hospice care is not available to everyone but even when it is people should have a choice about this last right, how they die.

What Should People Do Who Agree With the Idea That Doctors Should Be Allowed to Help?

They should write, call, or talk to their representatives in Congress and in their own state legislatures. The opponents are a vocal, well-organized minority and legislators are afraid to sponsor bills that might cause these organizations to campaign against them. They need to hear from regular people about what their wishes are at the end of life.

They can join and support organizations that are trying to get the law changed. The Hemlock Society is a 19-year-old organization with members in 60 chapters all over the country. We teach people how to plan their death and we push for laws which will make it possible to get a doctor's help. We are on the Web at www.hemlock.org/ or you can get information or you can join by calling us at 800-247-7421. It is with your support that the law will reflect what you want for yourself and your loved ones—choice and dignity in the dying process.

*I could have spent all day
on the treadmill.*

I could have worn one-size-fits-all.

Actual Plastic Surgery Patient

I had liposuction instead.

Proper diet and exercise are essential to keep your body in the best shape possible.
But sometimes they're not enough. Liposuction can provide the perfect complement.

If you're considering liposuction, the
American Society of Plastic and Reconstructive Surgeons
wants to help you make the right decision. One that can boost your confidence.
One that can improve the way you feel about yourself.

Call 1-800-635-0635 for a list of our surgeons in your area.

AMERICAN SOCIETY OF
PLASTIC AND RECONSTRUCTIVE
SURGEONS

1-800-635-0635   Visit our website: http://www.plasticsurgery.org

Courtesy of the American Society of Plastic and Reconstructive Surgeons.

JOHN DE ROSIER/Mobile Register

SOURCE: *Mobile Register.* Reprinted with permission.

Give Hotel Guests a Bible-Free Room

Annie Laurie Gaylor

February 14, 1989

Kenneth F. Hine, Executive Vice President
American HOTEL & Motel Association
888 7th Ave.
New York, NY 10106

Dear Mr. Hine:

We urge your Association to inaugurate a simple and much-needed reform. Just as the better establishments now offer smoke-free rooms, our association of freethinkers is requesting "bible-free" rooms.

Currently, a missionary organization with a poor track record of respecting state/church separation uses your member establishments to proselytize a captive audience. We believe it is time that the lodging industry "just say NO" to the Gideons. The Gideons glorify a bible character who is a villain and mass murderer (see enclosed "Gideon Exposed!" bible sticker).

Twenty million Americans are free from religion, and millions more follow other faiths. Many atheists and agnostics are deeply offended that they are paying high fees in order to be proselytized in the privacy of their own bedrooms! Fanatics who must read the bible every day will surely take precautions to travel with their own bibles. The rest of us deserve a break from mindless evangelizing when we are on vacation.

If hoteliers wish to serve customers in possible crisis, it would be far more useful to compile a list of local secular resource numbers: the police, battered woman's shelter, Red Cross, mental health hotline, nearby hospitals, etc. In fact, the bible itself offers not just gruesome bedtime reading (blood is splashed on nearly every page), but potentially violence-inciting and lethal advice. Murderers, child molesters, rapists, sexists, racists and even slaveholders have turned to bible verses to justify crimes. Jesus promotes self-mutilation, the terrifying myth of hell, and the dangerous,

SOURCE: Reprinted by permission of the author.

primitive belief that sickness results from "demons." The bible also offends by its often pornographic and bloodthirsty language. Why align your association with this image, and insult customers of other faiths, or no faith?

Sincerely,

Annie Laurie Gaylor
Freedom From Religion, Inc.
P.O. Box 750

Let's Not Blame Wrestling for All the Violence

R. W. Peterson

All right already. Enough is enough. Letter writer John Hoekje and others who want to blame professional wrestling for all of the violence that is going on can just stop right there ("Shootings reveal a 'cruel world going mad,'" Letters, Friday).

I have been around pro wrestling for more than 40 years. Granted, people say it's fake, and we do have a script. But the broken bones, heart attacks, pulled muscles and the mental state required of the wrestler make the sport far from fake.

I agree that some of the bigger shows are using bad writing with sexual content, but, as we all know, sex sells.

All of the independent shows that I have dealt with throughout my lifetime and all of the pro wrestlers I know do this for the kids and families as entertainment.

Most of us are professionals in other aspects of life, but pro wrestling is an anger-management outlet for some. For others, it's just a way to fame. If you want to blame something for the violence that children see from day to day, look at the video games, cartoons, movies and common everyday life that surrounds them—from violence in a dysfunctional family to the violence they see at the corner grocery store or even at their schools.

Don't blame wrestling. If people don't like it, they don't have to watch it.

What's going to be next? Are we going to blame lingerie ads in newspapers for sexual crimes, too?

SOURCE: *USA Today,* March 9, 2000. Reprinted with permission of the author.

The Supreme Court Also Legalized Slavery

SOURCE: *Mobile Press Register*. Reprinted from Asbury Park Press © 2000. www.injersey.com/ Breen. Copley News Service.

Entrance to High School Should Not Be Automatic

Carol Jago

Santa Monica, Calif.—Watching friends' children applying to private high school wait nervously for their acceptance letters, it dawned on me that this is what public school students should be doing as well. Why is entrance to high school automatic? If every eighth-grader had to demonstrate minimum competency in math, reading and writing before being allowed to enroll in high school, more students might pay attention in middle school. Some might get the message that taking up space at a desk doesn't equal learning. A few might even begin to realize that free public education is a privilege.

Seventy percent of any public high school administrator's time is spent tending to discipline problems caused by 10 percent of the students. One of the most obvious reasons teen-agers disrupt class is that they simply can't keep up with the course work. The troublemakers figure that it's better to play the fool and cover up what they don't know. These ninth-graders then bring home a bouquet of D's and F's on the first report card, setting a pattern for the next four years. It seems to me that screening and remediation does these students a greater justice than punishing them for acting out.

I am not suggesting that youngsters who cannot meet standards remain in middle school. If three years in an institution had little impact on their learning, a fourth is unlikely to either. Students who do not qualify for high school entrance should be offered two alternatives. The first would be the option to enroll in an accelerated program focusing on basic skills. Small, intensive classes would help students catch up, pass the entrance test and get on with their education.

The second option would be for students who have no interest, at least at the moment, in education. These 14-year-olds would be able to enroll in apprenticeship programs where they could learn job skills in a field of their choice. Attendance would be mandatory until they are 16, but once they demonstrate their worth to an employer, there would be no reason

SOURCE: Reprinted with permission of the author.

why they couldn't be paid as they learn. The option to go back for the accelerated program would always be open and from there the door to high school or community college.

High school is no place for students who don't know their multiplication tables. Can you picture a college prep high school accepting a student who didn't know fractions? I believe it is a reasonable expectation that entering freshmen should be able to read and write. It also is reasonable to expect that students will carry books and pencils and paper. Depending on when you last visited a public high school, you may or may not be surprised to see how many teen-agers don't. The problem with this stance is that, unencumbered by the accouterments of a scholar, let alone his habits of mind, there is little incentive to behave like one.

English teachers turn themselves inside out trying to figure out innovative ways of teaching a novel to students who won't read 10 pages for homework. Can you imagine reading all of "Lord of the Flies" aloud in class? No wonder both teachers and students are yawning.

Rather than redesign curricula, let's first make sure everyone in class has the skills necessary to complete the work assigned. Once this has been ascertained, expect performance of each and every one. No coach would do less.

When eighth-graders apply for entrance to high school, they and their parents should be asked to sign a contract. The agreement would spell out both what the student can expect from the school and what the teachers can expect from the student. Repeated failure to meet these terms on the part of the child would end not with rancor and an ugly expulsion but with admission to the internship program. If the evidence is that the teen-ager isn't in the mood for school, he shouldn't be there.

A public education, while free, is expensive. We should start treating it as such.

Women Don't Belong in the Cockpit!
Ed Anger

I'm madder than Charles Lindbergh with a busted propeller over the biggest cover-up in American aviation today—the danger of women pilots!

Let's face it. A gal has about as much business flying an airplane as Zippy the chimp.

But those yappy women's libbers screamed so loud for females to get men's jobs that every broad who isn't afraid of heights and doesn't wear Coke-bottle glasses has a chance to captain a Boeing 747 these days!

Hey, that's great as long as nobody else has to ride along with them. But letting a woman pilot a plane with paying customers on board is criminal.

What if a mouse runs into the cockpit? Who's going to fly the plane when the lady pilot screams and jumps into the copilot's lap, for crying out loud?

And what about premenstrual syndrome (PMS)?

Who's gonna pry her hands off the stick when she gets in a bitchy mood and puts the plane into an intentional nosedive?

And if she's been spayed or going through menopause, how would you like to fly from New York to L.A. with a pilot who's having hot flashes every 10 seconds?

But what really scares the bejesus out of me is the way women pilots almost always distract male members of the crew.

Let's face it. A male copilot just ain't gonna keep an eye on the instrument panel with a nice set of 38 double-Ds bouncing around two feet to his left. And, of course, it's going to be worse during air turbulence, when he should be paying the most attention to his job.

But, hey, I'm more liberal than I used to be. I think women should be allowed to make their living in the air—but as stewardesses, for Pete's sake.

That way they get to satisfy their natural instinct to serve meals, fluff pillows and show people how to put on life jackets.

I'll tell you, yours truly is never going to get on another plane with a captain named Bambi, Chastity, or Sissy. I want an ex-Marine fighter pilot with big, hairy arms at the controls, folks.

And I'm not alone. The latest Carnegie-Atex poll found that nearly 94 percent of Americans are "concerned" about flying with a female pilot.

SOURCE: *Weekly World News*, February 17, 1999. Reprinted with permission.

You haven't heard much said about it, of course, because it's not politically correct to talk about things like that.

But hey, even Amelia Earhart, the greatest lady pilot of them all, couldn't island-hop the Pacific without crashing somewhere out there. The truth is, how do you expect a woman to fly a plane when they can't even drive a dadblamed car?

All of you know I've never been afraid to tell it like it is.

If God had meant for women to fly airplanes, it would have been the Wright Sisters taking off at Kitty Hawk in 1903.

Why fly and die, my fellow Americans? Next time, politely *DEMAND* that your travel agent or the airline ticket office put you on a plane with a man at the controls.

Federal Foolishness and Marijuana

Jerome P. Kassirer, M.D.

The advanced stages of many illnesses and their treatments are often accompanied by intractable nausea, vomiting, or pain. Thousand of patients with cancer, AIDS, and other diseases report they have obtained striking relief from these devastating symptoms by smoking marijuana. The alleviation of distress can be so striking that some patients and their families have been willing to risk a jail term to obtain or grow the marijuana.

Despite the desperation of these patients, within weeks after voters in Arizona and California approved propositions allowing physicians in their states to prescribe marijuana for medical indications, federal officials, including the President, the Secretary of Health and Human Services, and the Attorney General sprang into action. At a news conference, Secretary Donna E. Shalala gave an organ recital of the parts of the body that she asserted could be harmed by marijuana and warned of the evil of its spreading use. Attorney General Janet Reno announced that physicians in any state who prescribed the drug could lose the privilege of writing prescriptions, be excluded from Medicare and Medicaid reimbursement, and even be prosecuted for a federal crime. General Barry R. McCaffrey, director of the Office of National Drug Control Policy, reiterated his agency's position that marijuana is a dangerous drug and implied that voters in Arizona and California had been duped into voting for these propositions. He indicated that it is always possible to study the effects of any drug, including marijuana, but that the use of marijuana by seriously ill patients would require, at the least, scientifically valid research.

I believe that a federal policy that prohibits physicians from alleviating suffering by prescribing marijuana for seriously ill patients is misguided, heavy-handed, and inhumane. Marijuana may have long-term adverse effects and its use may presage serious addictions, but neither long-term side effects nor addiction is a relevant issue in such patients. It is also hypocritical to forbid physicians to prescribe marijuana while permitting them to use morphine and meperidine to relieve extreme dyspnea and pain. With both these drugs the difference between the dose that hastens death is very narrow; by contrast, there is no risk of death from smoking marijuana. To demand evidence of therapeutic efficacy is equally hypocritical. The noxious sensations that patients experience are extremely difficult to quantify in controlled experiments. What really counts for a therapy with this kind of safety margin is whether a seriously ill patient feels relief as a result of the intervention, not whether a controlled trial "proves" its efficacy.

Paradoxically, dronabinol, a drug that contains one of the active ingredients in marijuana (tetrahydrocannabinol), has been available by prescription for more than a decade. But it is difficult to titrate the therapeutic dose of this drug, and it is not widely prescribed. By contrast, smoking marijuana produces a rapid increase in the blood level of the active ingredients and is thus more likely to be therapeutic. Needless to say, new drugs such as those that inhibit the nausea associated with chemotherapy may well be more beneficial than smoking marijuana, but their comparative efficacy has never been studied.

Whatever their reasons, federal officials are out of step with the public. Dozens of states have passed laws that ease restrictions on the prescribing of marijuana by physicians, and polls consistently show that the public favors the use of marijuana for such purposes. Federal authorities should rescind their prohibition of the medicinal use of marijuana for seriously ill patients and allow physicians to decide which patients to treat. The government should change marijuana's status from that of a Schedule 1 drug (considered to be potentially addictive and with no current medical use) to that of a Schedule 2 drug (potentially addictive but with some accepted medical use) and regulate it accordingly. To ensure its proper distribution and use, the government could declare itself the only agency sanctioned to provide the marijuana. I believe that such a change in policy would have no adverse effects. The argument that it would be a signal to the young that "marijuana OK" is, I believe, specious.

This proposal is not new. In 1986, after years of legal wrangling, the Drug Enforcement Administration (DEA) held extensive hearings on the transfer of marijuana to Schedule 2. In 1988, the DEA's own administrative-law judge concluded, "It would be unreasonable, arbitrary, and capricious for DEA to continue to stand between those sufferers and the benefits of this substance in the light of the evidence in this record." Nonetheless, the DEA overruled the judge's order to transfer marijuana to Schedule 2, and in 1992 it issued a final rejection of all requests for reclassification.

Some physicians will have the courage to challenge the continued proscription of marijuana for the sick. Eventually, their actions will force the courts to adjudicate between the rights of those at death's door and the absolute power of bureaucrats whose decisions are based more on reflexive ideology and political correctness than on compassion.

A lot of campus rapes start here.

Whenever there's drinking or drugs, things can get out of hand.
So it's no surprise that many campus rapes involve alcohol.

But you should know that under any circumstances, sex without
the other person's consent is considered rape. A felony, punishable
by prison. And drinking is no excuse.

That's why, when you party, it's good to know what your limits are.
You see, a little sobering thought now can save you from a big
problem later.

© 1990 Rape Treatment Center, Santa Monica Hospital.

Courtesy of the Rape Treatment Center, Santa Monica Hospital.

Making Sheep: Possible, but Right?

Timothy Backous

OK. So now we can clone sheep. The papers and TV are full of all kinds of doomsday responses that express outrage and fear. Once again, we seem to have a situation where technology is out ahead of ethics. We must ask ourselves yet again, "Just because we can do it, should we?" The proponents say this is breakthrough technology which will change the face of human existence. We may be able to genetically engineer a whole parallel species for our exclusive use. A child who is dying could be "rebuilt," thus circumventing the great tragedy of infant death. We could each have a clone that would provide replacement parts in case of need. The whole problem of world hunger would take an astonishing turn if animals could be engineered to provide milk, meat and labor.

The critics, on the other hand, ask the question "How far do we go?" Without a guide book or even a set of universally accepted principles, do we as a race simply allow scientific experiments of this nature to be left to chance? It would appear that the only limitations are the skill and the scientific talent of those doing the laboratory work. Something feels wrong with that scenario.

From the perspective of morality, we have a very complex situation here. We are hesitant whenever something right out of the pages of science fiction becomes a reality. Suddenly, what was only fodder for late night arguments about humanity and its place in the universe becomes frighteningly critical to the future. And while we like to say that we shouldn't play God with this kind of technology, who among us wouldn't rush to employ any technique that would save our own flesh and blood? Looking into the eyes of a dying child does not help one reflect on the principles of ethics. Knowing that genetic manipulation could help feed people makes it more difficult to say no on the basis of moral guidelines.

Perhaps the only thing we can do at this point is recognize that what was only a fantasy is now real and that education might be our first step in helping to shape the future of genetic engineering. To say that we can stop the proliferation of experiments and research altogether seems naive. One article insists that last year alone, there were more than 80,000 animals manufactured in Britain. One such animal is a sheep which goes by the name Tracy and has

SOURCE: *The Record*, St. John's University, 1997. Reprinted with permission of the author.

human genes in every one of her cells. This "transgenic" breed is a step toward production of similar species who will provide "human substances" for medical treatments. With those kinds of numbers and results, putting on the brakes seems a bit unrealistic. Besides, when one ethicist was asked to explain why such mass production of genetically manipulated animals is such a surprise to us, he explained that the secrecy has more to do with protecting a veritable gold mine. If the market is cornered, this technology is going to make someone very rich.

No matter where you stand on this issue, there is a nagging question left unanswered: where does God fit into all of this? Up to this point, the magnificent and awesome scientific discoveries we've made lead us to ask deeper questions about the origin of life and its destiny. Even though we are not authors of creation, are we still not called to use our God-given intelligence to help perfect it? What is the problem with using technology to ease suffering and pain? If bionics help paralytics walk again, is that not unnatural but still good? What about changing the direction of a river to help avert natural disasters? What about building pipelines that carry water to arid regions of the world? Most of us would be forced to agree that in those cases, our human ingenuity crosses boundaries but for good reason. Even so, it is hard to make that giant leap of faith to issues involving genetic manipulation. For there we are toying with the very essence of creation itself. True, God still had to create the cells that we use to clone others, but we can't ignore the fact that we upset the apple cart of existence just a bit. Perhaps the best way to stifle the march toward technological wonders is to ponder the consequences of our actions and realize that we know neither what those are nor what it means to accept responsibility for them.

The Whole Scoop on Coffee

We Americans like coffee. But as the estimated 100 million of us sip, on average, some three-and-a-half cups daily, odds are that our morning paper will have some story either confirming or refuting the ill effects of coffee on our health. So, we try to quit, but get dreadful withdrawal headaches (researchers at Johns Hopkins recently reported that even those who drink only one strong cup each day may experience headaches, fatigue, and other withdrawal symptoms if they stop). But what's the cure for headaches? Coffee (it's practically prescribed for migraines). Before we know it, we're back where we started, sipping a cup of the bad stuff as we read more bad news in the morning paper. Here, we put the whole coffee and caffeine story—which includes tea, cola, chocolate, and certain medications—into perspective.

Coffee and Heart Disease

The final word *may* finally be in on this one. The latest study, from Harvard last fall, of over 45,000 men between 40 and 75 years old, found not a whit of evidence connecting coffee consumption with stroke or heart disease—even among those men who drank six or more cups a day. Nor was there a connection for tea drinkers, although it's harder to draw a valid conclusion since there were only 664 of them in the group.

While not a *cause* of heart disease, coffee may, in some people, be a marker of those at risk for heart disease for other reasons. A recent study in the *American Journal of Public Health* found that coffee drinkers are also more likely to drink more alcohol, eat more saturated fats and cholesterol, smoke, and be sedentary. In sum, the coffee drinkers were more likely to have a heart-unhealthy lifestyle. Those coffee drinkers who do, however, have a healthful diet and lifestyle seemed no more likely to develop heart disease than non-coffee drinkers. Earlier studies that found a connection between heart disease or elevated cholesterol levels and coffee drinking were too small or flawed because they did not take into account these other contributing risk factors. (The recent Harvard study largely corrected for these factors.)

One caveat, however, based on a study last year from the Netherlands: Drinking large amounts of boiled—also known as campfire—coffee (made by pouring boiling water directly onto the ground coffee; most common in Europe) does seem to raise cholesterol levels. However, such coffee is rarely

SOURCE: Reprinted with permission of the Johns Hopkins Medical Letter *Health After 50*. © MedLetter Associates, 1991.

drunk in this country, especially at the levels found to increase risk—four to six cups a day.

What if you already have heart disease? Another recent study—of patients taking medication for angina experienced when exercising—examined coffee's effects on their hearts, as measured by endurance on a treadmill. The researchers found that even three cups of coffee did not affect the intensity of the angina, the heart's function, or the length of time that the subjects could exercise. However, there is some evidence that you should watch your caffeine intake if you have heart arrhythmias. While as yet the evidence is inconclusive, some animal studies have found that caffeine can cause ventricular tachycardia, which poses the risk of sudden cardiac death.

Coffee and Cancer
The American Cancer Society has not changed its 1984 statement that coffee does not increase cancer risk. Nonetheless, coffee drinking has been implicated in various studies as a risk factor for certain malignancies, in particular breast, colorectal, bladder, and pancreatic cancer. In all, the evidence is hardly compelling, although the same sort of flip-flop that has plagued research into coffee and heart disease has pervaded the coffee/cancer association. For example, a recent analysis of 24 studies on coffee and pancreatic cancer concluded that you're not putting yourself at risk by drinking coffee. Similarly inconclusive results have been reported on other cancers, including some that suggest caffeine actually protects against colorectal cancer.

Coffee and Ulcers
There's no evidence that coffee actually causes ulcers, but you're best off to avoid it if you have one, as it increases secretions of gastric acid and pepsin—just the ticket for aggravating an existing ulcer. In addition, coffee can cause heartburn and has a laxative effect that, in some people, may cause diarrhea.

Coffee and Osteoporosis
Caffeine hastens the excretion of calcium from the body, which could increase the risk for osteoporosis. In fact, one recent finding from the Framingham Study (the ongoing health review begun in 1948 of the residents of a Massachusetts town) is that persons over 50 who drank more than two cups of coffee or four cups of tea a day increased their risk of hip fracture due to osteoporosis by over 50%. However, as with heart disease, it's not clear whether the caffeine itself was linked to the fractures, or if it was merely a marker for other behaviors, such as a sedentary lifestyle or low intake of dietary calcium, that also increase the risk of osteoporosis. Just to be safe, you

can add some low-fat milk to your coffee to compensate for the relatively mild calcium loss.

The Bottom Line

About the worst thing that can be said conclusively about coffee at this time is that it keeps you awake—which, after all, is why most of us drink it. However, caffeine can increase the number of times you wake during the night, and generally disturb sleep—especially as you age. For this reason, many older people have switched to decaf—and about the worst thing that can be said about *it* at this time is that it *doesn't* keep you awake.

Let's Do Away With Safety

Lawrence A. Bullis

Every day some new do-gooder is trying to save us from ourselves. We have so many laws and safety commissions to ensure our safety that it seems nearly impossible to have an accident. The problem is that we need accidents, and lots of them.

Danger is nature's way of eliminating stupid people. Without safety, stupid people die in accidents.

With safety, however well-intentioned it may be, we are devolving into half-witted mutants, because idiots, who by all rights should be dead, are spared from their rightful early graves and are free to breed even more imbeciles.

Let's do away with safety and improve our species. Take up smoking. Jaywalk. Play with blasting caps. Swim right after a big meal. Stick something small in your ear. Take your choice of dangerous activity and do it with gusto. Future generations will thank you.

SOURCE: Reprinted by permission of the author.

In Defense of Lies

John Leo

Edmund Morris has just proved that the defense of a lie can be worse than the lie itself. Morris, a biographer (Teddy Roosevelt, Ronald Reagan), was trying to defend Joseph Ellis, the Mount Holyoke historian who was caught telling whoppers in class about serving in Vietnam and playing a role in the civil rights movement. Ellis, a prize-winning author who was teaching a class on Vietnam, even conjured up some false but heart-warming stories, including a poignant one about a soldier in Vietnam who read Emily Dickinson.

Not to worry, though. In effect, Morris argued that the truth doesn't really matter, as long as you believe strongly in the emotional reality of the story you tell.

Morris' defense of Ellis makes three points: (1) Everybody does it ("Can any of us gaze into the bathroom mirror and whisper, 'I never made anything up?' "); (2) MTV made him do it—Ellis felt an "urgent desire . . . to convey the divisiveness of the '60s to a generation rendered comatose by MTV"; and (3) Ronald Reagan did it, telling us, falsely, that he had been on the scene at the Nazi concentration camps when they were liberated by the allies in 1945. Morris defended Reagan's fabrication, which is no big surprise because his own biography-memoir of Reagan ("Dutch") was full of fabrications. Among other things, Morris inserted himself into Reagan's life as a boyhood friend, though he never grew up with Reagan or anywhere near him.

Morris talks admiringly of "the genuineness of (Reagan's) emotion," whether telling the "false" story about opening the camps, or the much duller "true" version (that he had spent World War II in Hollywood and merely saw early films of the Allies entering the camps). Morris said: "To him, it was plainly the same parable, conveying the same moral essence told in two different ways."

This is an astonishing argument. If truth depends merely on "moral essence" and not factuality, then there is no difference between fact and fiction, or between people who report what happened in the real world and people who just make it up to express a feeling.

SOURCE: *Jewish World Review* 7/3/01. Reprinted with permission of author.

There's a lot of that going around. Last week a man who claimed to have witnessed lynchings in the South in the 1960s admitted he had made up the story. A series of reported racial incidents and rapes, particularly on campuses, have turned out to be hoaxes. Apparently they had been intended to convey a feeling of danger, or merely to gain more attention for a cause. The reality of a strongly felt "story line" now justifies hoaxes.

Patricia Smith, fired from her job as a columnist at the *Boston Globe* after repeatedly writing about imaginary people and faking interviews, defended herself by saying that in her heart she felt her stories were true.

When leftist heroine and Noble Peace Prize-winner Rigoberta Menchu was found to have falsified much of her book on oppression in her native Guatemala, neither she nor her defenders seemed fazed. The Chronicle of Higher Education reported that "Faculty members . . . say it doesn't matter if the facts in the book are wrong, because they believe Ms. Menchu's story speaks to a greater truth about the oppression of poor people in Central America." If it's for a good cause and won her a Nobel, who cares if she made it up?

This cynical attitude is strong these days on campus, where postmodern theory erodes basic truthfulness by holding that facts and truth don't really exist. In effect, this allows lying activists to think that they really aren't lying. "We are all engaged in writing a kind of propaganda," two University of Pennsylvania instructors wrote in the *Journal of Social History*. "Rather than believe in the absolute truth of what we are writing, we must believe in the moral or political positions we are taking with it." (Feelings and political stances count. Facts and truth don't.)

Society has its own truth troubles: docudramas; Oliver Stone; a constant supply of lying but successful politicians, presidents included; a torrent of Internet information, much of it probably untrue, that people feel they must pay attention to anyway.

One sign of the times is that some writers feel free to mix fact and fiction, and wink while doing so, as if tweaking the assumption of basic honesty on its way out the door. The June issue of *Esquire* contained a profile of rock star Michael Stipe that was largely untrue. Nothing sneaky here—the magazine referred readers to a Web site that separated fact from fiction. The writer, Tom Junod, said: "I want people to question the enterprise of celebrity journalism, and that's what we've done."

This is unusually lame. If you don't believe in celebrity profiles, don't write them. More likely Junod and *Esquire* were just exploiting an idea that's clearly in the air now that fact and fiction are routinely mixed these days, and readers are less sure which is which. All the more reason to take the stream of fibs from a nationally known historian like Joseph Ellis very seriously.

Asking God to Cheat in Sports

Dexter Martin

Should people pray for their team to win? Isn't that asking God to cheat? The rules of a game permit only a certain number of players. If God were to help one side more than the other, wouldn't he be breaking the rules? Wouldn't he be dishonest and illegal?

And wouldn't he be unfair? God's power is said to be infinite; and if that is true, he's irresistible. (I'm using masculine pronouns for convenience, instead of clumsily repeating "he or she or it.") A team with God behind it or in it would be unbeatable, wouldn't it?

And if God were to favor one team more than another, he wouldn't be acting like a father. If we're all his children, shouldn't he treat us equally? Would a decent father like to see some of his children defeat his other ones and make them feel miserable? Would he be proud to be the cause of this?

If you beg God to give your team a victory, aren't you unconsciously hoping he'll be unjust and unpaternal? If you thank him afterwards, shouldn't you also say, "I'm grateful to you, God, for granting us an unfair advantage by your invisible presence and influence"? And shouldn't you add, "I'm happy you didn't behave like a father"? In sports, you want God to be unethical, don't you?

You don't? Then stop praying before, during, and after games.

Coaches leading teams in the Lord's Prayer in locker rooms; spectators imploring God visibly and audibly; the wife of a notorious basketball coach frantically repeating her rosary behind him and rushing off to church afterwards to thank God, Jesus, Mary, and a favorite saint; baseball players crossing themselves before they bat (or strike out); a Protestant pitcher falling to his knees on the mound to thank God for letting him win the final game of the World Series; pro football players who kneel in the end zone after their touchdowns and thank the Lord; Notre Dame appealing to Jesus by installing a mural of him in the football stadium, holding up his arms like a referee signaling "Touchdown!"—such people unwittingly want an immoral God, a divinity who would be guilty of unsportsmanlike conduct if he were a human being.

Some editors may be afraid of this article because some Christians will disagree with me. But only a very few will, I'm sure, because I've tested these

SOURCE: Reprinted by permission of the author.

opinions on students at several universities when I was an English professor. (I've retired.) I told them, "I'm not attacking your denominations or preaching atheism. I'm merely suggesting that you should draw a distinction between childish religion and adult religion." As a beautiful nun said in class, "There's a difference between superstition and religion. Praying for a team is just superstition. I agree with you."

And she said it in a paper. Let me quote her:

> Catholics used to call Notre Dame God's Team because it was usually ranked first in the nation. I called it that myself when I was much younger. But then Gerry Faust became coach and the team slumped for four years, even though he was extremely pious. His record was only 30–26–1. He was fired. Now that Lou Holtz has made Our Lady Number One again, I suppose some Catholics are thinking of it as God's Team again. But the phrase seems very childish to me now. Religion isn't the secret of Notre Dame's success. Coaching is, and that includes recruiting.

(Later, she told me, "If I weren't a nun, I'd be a sports reporter.")

In pro football, the Dallas Cowboys were number one so often that some fans called *them* God's Team. I knew one who was serious and so there were probably more. But then America's Team (as it was also known) sank into a slump even worse than Notre Dame's. Coach Landry had to be fired, although he had become more religious than ever.

There's no evidence that any team has ever been God's. If there were one, it would be easily recognizable because it would never lose. How could Almighty God be clobbered?

Shouldn't we assume that God realizes he shouldn't interfere in games, that he'd be cheating if he guided footballs and baseballs and basketballs, that he'd be unsporting if he provided an athlete with an extra spurt? Spiritual steroids are as dishonest as medicinal ones.

If you were running the universe, would you cheat for your favorite athletes? Of course not. Why would God?

Young Children Need Moral Instruction in School

Jack Valenti

Some politicians, not all, are scurrying about with much zest and anticipation. It's time, their polls inform them, to find the quick fix for what they have determined is a society plagued by the irregular heartbeat of deficient values.

But there are contradictions that intrude on this denunciatory atmosphere. If there are moral omissions in the society, they cannot be caulked by instant, slenderly premised attacks on entertainment. The plain fact is we are rearranging our priorities in the wrong way.

The statistics tell us that crime is steadily decreasing in America. The cities are safer. The schoolyard, according to the Centers for Disease Control, is the safest place for children. Serious crime by teen-agers has been dropping since 1994. Only .41 percent—that's point-four-one percent—of the 70 million teen-agers in the U.S. have been arrested (not necessarily convicted) for serious crime. Which means that 99.59 percent of all teen-agers are not involved in serious crime.

Nonetheless, if most Americans believe otherwise, there is a place to begin whatever repair is needed to make sure our values in the next generation are braced and knit. That place is in the very early years of the child's education, beginning in preschool, continuing through kindergarten and grades one through five. Most child behavioral experts will assert it is in those early years that the child's moral shield is shaped and made impenetrable to the later years' blandishments of peers and the enticements of the surly streets.

We are today misplacing our energies and our funding by directing all sorts of incentives to high schools and colleges. Too late. The moral scaffolding has been built by then, for better or worse. How then to begin this revision of life conduct? We must introduce in preschool, and keep alive through grade five, a new school course.

The course could be titled, "What is right, and what is plainly wrong." For 30 minutes each day, the teacher would illuminate for these very young

SOURCE: *Mobile Register,* September 2, 1999. Reprinted with permission of the Motion Picture Association of America, Inc.

children what William Faulkner labeled "the old verities," the words that construct and implement the daily moral grind in which every durable society must engage if it is to be judged a "just" society.

These are words like duty, honor, service, integrity, pity, pride, compassion and sacrifice, plus the clear admonition that violence is wrong. To the teaching of the meaning of those words must be added the cleansing precept of treating other people as you would want them to treat you. And most of all to make sure that these kids understand with growing clarity that home, school and church are the sanctuaries for their later life.

There is a grand simplicity to this kind of school course. It enters a child's mind early, burrowing deep into those recesses of the human brain that even today advanced medical science has not been able to penetrate.

If you ask enough people, you will find that most of us remember our first- or second-grade teacher. I remember Miss Corbett and Miss Walker, who read to us before we really understood, but the words had weight and allure. We listened and, without really knowing it, we learned and saved what we learned. Perhaps it was because what we heard in those early school years was the first entry into our learning vessel.

Moreover, the words that furnish us with a moral armor plate are the same, more or less, in the cultures and religions. Therefore, without breaching the walls of church and state, the child masters and retains the majesty of old homilies and maxims that form the platform from which vaults the great religions that guide most of the known world today.

Absent this kind of early instruction, absent the building of this moral shield, no congressional law, no presidential executive order, no fiery rhetoric will salvage a child's conduct nor locate a missing moral core.

WHEN THEY TELL YOU THAT ABORTION IS A MATTER JUST BETWEEN A WOMAN AND HER DOCTOR

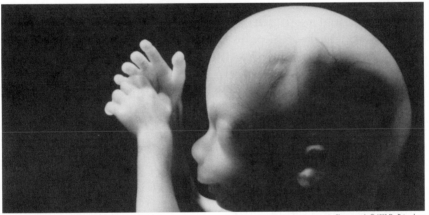

Photo copyright © 1982 Dr. Rainer Jonas

The incredible photograph above by Dr. Rainer Jonas shows what a healthy, active intrauterine child looks like at 19 weeks. Like the bud of a flower, beautiful. But, unfortunately still a candidate for elective abortion.

THEY'RE FORGETTING SOMEONE

Courtesy of Media: Right to Life of Michigan Educational Fund.

Dying Is Not a Solely Private Decision

Guest Commentary, Catholic News Service

Responding to editors' requests for a regular sampling of current commentary from around the Catholic press, here is an unsigned editorial headlined "To die with dignity" from the July 13 issue of Our Sunday Visitor, national Catholic newspaper based in Huntington, Ind.

Next to legal abortion, which implicates the nation in the taking of innocent pre-born life, there is no more critical moral issue facing the country than assisted suicide, which asks society to abet the killing of sick, elderly, depressed and disabled people.

So we applaud the Supreme Court for upholding New York and Washington state laws banning assisted suicide, although we recognize that it is a temporary and precarious victory.

These rulings show that the high court has not been unmindful of the social turmoil that has ensued from its 1973 decision in Roe vs. Wade to strike down every state law banning abortion and to enshrine the practice as a constitutionally protected "right."

Faced with claims of a similar "right to die," the court did what it should have done with abortion. It acknowledged that the practice has historically been judged abhorrent and illegal, and concluded that such a controversial question is best resolved by citizens and their elected officials, not by the courts.

We strongly disagree that such fundamental life-and-death matters as euthanasia and abortion can be decided by simple majority vote. Nevertheless, we are encouraged that the highest court in the land has, at least for now, embraced and made its own nearly every major pro-life argument against assisted suicide.

The court agrees that there is a crucial moral, medical and legal difference between helping people to kill themselves and permitting terminally ill patients to refuse or stop medical treatments. It is, as the court now understands, the difference between killing and allowing to die.

The high court recognizes, too, that requests for euthanasia, more often than not, are made by those suffering from depression and anxiety about being a burden to their families and loved ones. With adequate treatment of

SOURCE: *Our Sunday Visitor,* July 13, 1997. Reprinted with permission.

patients' mental and physical pain, the court noted, the "need" for assisted suicide vanishes.

The court also accepts that legalizing assisted suicide threatens society's weakest and most vulnerable members—the poor, the elderly and the handicapped—who would face "subtle coercion and undue influence" to end their lives.

Also, there is "ample support," the court said, for worries about the so-called slippery slope—"that permitting assisted suicide will start (the state) down the path to voluntary and perhaps even involuntary euthanasia."

Having convinced the high court that dying is not a solely private decision between patient and doctor—that it goes to the core of society's attitudes toward human life and dignity—the pro-life movement must now work to change the culture, which increasingly sees "no point" to terminal illness or disability and believes one would be better off dead than living under such conditions.

It will not be enough—though this, too, is drastically needed—to improve pain-relief techniques and pastoral care of the anxieties that accompany the dying process. We need to be about building a culture of life, where abortion is banished and where life is esteemed, in youth and good health, in sickness and old age.

People do have a right to die with dignity, but this is not a right that can be realized by access to lethal doses of pain relievers. Dignity comes from knowing that one is loved and wanted, that one's life, even in utter dependency, has an inestimable value and is sacred.

Elizabeth Richardson
Model/High Jumper

"So I have a vitamin gap, big deal."

"I used to take vitamins. But then I got too busy. I work long hours and—sure, I skip meals some times."

Elizabeth Richardson is part of an alarming statistic. 97% of Americans don't eat a balanced diet. And the problem starts right with breakfast, or more accurately without it. It's the meal we skip most often.

And dieters are even more at risk.

Cutting out meals, even whole categories of food.

But even eating three meals a day is no guarantee your body is getting all the vitamins and minerals it needs.

Problems like physical stress and illness rob you of vitamins and minerals. So do smoking and drinking. And, birth control pills, pregnancy and lactation also increase nutritional needs.

For instance, many of us aren't getting enough calcium for healthy bones. Or enough iron for healthy blood. Or enough of the B vitamins essential to every cell in our bodies.

The fact is, most people reading this ad probably have one or more vitamin or mineral gaps to fill.

And, scientists are now studying the nutritional role of vitamins, minerals and other nutrients in helping to protect against diseases such as cancer, heart disease and osteoporosis.

So why live at risk? Fill the gap. Take vitamin and mineral supplements every day. Is it a big deal?

You bet your life it is.

Council For Responsible Nutrition. An association of the nutritional supplement industry.

Courtesy of the Council for Responsible Nutrition.

Shocking Study Reveals . . . Vitamin C Can Help You Win the Lottery!

Ann Victoria

Eight out of 10 Lotto winners have one amazing thing in common—they all had high levels of vitamin C in their systems when they won their millions!

That's the finding of a stunning news study published here last week by a renowned sociologist, Dr. Michael Valsing.

The study has indisputably linked large doses of vitamin C to what is commonly called "good luck."

The research team headed by Dr. Valsing sent detailed questionnaires to 671 people in France, Australia and America—all of whom had won more than $4 million in lotteries.

"The questionnaire included everything under the sun," said Dr. Valsing.

"From what clothes they were wearing when they bought their tickets to what kind of good luck charms they may have used."

"We had no idea what we'd find. We just wanted to see if there was any one thing they all had in common."

"We put the vitamin question in almost as an afterthought—just another possibility to explore."

Amazingly, the questionnaires revealed that a whopping 80 percent of the winners drank up to eight glasses of orange juice a day or ate lots of citrus fruits as a snack. The winners also took large doses of vitamin C.

"They were also very concerned about nutrition at the time the tickets were purchased." Dr. Valsing continued. "Now, I'm sure the winners will agree that snacking on oranges can make anyone a millionaire."

"But other than the vitamin C, none of the winners ate the same foods. The only thing their diets had in common was the vitamin C."

Dr. Valsing says he has no idea why the taking of vitamins should have an effect on good luck. But his associates have what they think is a plausible theory: They deduced that science has shown that everyone has some degree of psychic ability. But it remains undeveloped in most people.

It could very well be that something in vitamin C has an effect on the part of the mind that receives telepathic thought waves. In other words,

SOURCE: *The Weekly World News*, February 1, 1994. Reprinted with permission.

these people's ESP abilities may have been temporarily heightened, allowing them to "tune in"—so to speak—to what numbers would come up in the lottery.

Dr. Valsing said he and his team plan to expand their research, zeroing in on the vitamin and nutrition factor.

The effects of the new study should be out sometime in late 1994.

Our Youth Aren't Learning Our History

Herbert London

NEW YORK—Presidents Day would have been a good time to take stock of the meaning of the presidency in American history. Unfortunately, in many places it is a lost holiday.

At the school my youngest daughter attends, the birthdays of President Washington and President Lincoln were compressed into one Presidents Day, which in turn has been transformed into Winter Recess. Is it any wonder we are losing a sense of our nation's history?

Several years ago, James Madison University eliminated American history as a requirement, suggesting implicitly that the graduates from that university do not have to know who James Madison is.

Although it may appear as hyperbole, the nation is in the throes of institutional amnesia, with the past regarded as a dream from which we will soon awaken.

This alarming condition is confirmed by a study, "Losing America's Memory: Historical Illiteracy in the 21st Century."

Organized by the American Council of Trustees and Alumni, the report found that seniors at the most prestigious colleges and universities in the United States received a grade of D or F on history questions drawn from a high school curriculum.

These seniors could not identify Washington's winter encampment of Valley Forge, words from Lincoln's Gettysburg Address or even the basic privileges granted in the U.S. Constitution. The report found students from each of the top colleges can graduate without having a single course in American history. In 78 percent of these institutions, students are not required to take any history at all.

Should anyone doubt the dumbing down of America, talk show host Jay Leno's questioning of random people on the street concerning rudimentary history and civics facts is disturbing.

What is a bicameral legislature? Where is the White House? What are the three parts of government? These questions yield answers at once hilarious and pathetic.

SOURCE: *Mobile Register,* March 10, 2000. Reprinted with permission.

When the Roper Organization in 1996 asked people, "Who said government of the people, by the people, and for the people?" the most common answer was Thomas Jefferson. This from a pool of college graduates.

This should outrage any sensible person. If institutions of higher learning no longer require a rudimentary appreciation of American civilization and heritage, there is a danger a common frame of reference will be lost.

Already there are radicals who contest the existence of a distinctive American legacy, arguing that this nation is a geographic entity only, on which anything can be imprinted.

James C. Rees, director of George Washington's historical home at Mount Vernon, said the report explains why visitors "seem to know next to nothing about the real George Washington and why they appear to be almost starved for America's history."

History is being shortchanged at every level of education, from elementary school to graduate school. Even history majors have yawning gaps in their knowledge. In a recent speech to graduate students at a well-known university, I noted that "Wallace" had a profound effect on the attitude of leftists in the 1948 presidential election.

At that moment, a young lady said, "I didn't know that George Wallace ran for president in '48." She had never heard of Henry Wallace. This from an American history major.

Losing a civic memory is not something to be accepted lightly. Free institutions depend on people willing to defend traditions in which they believe. When those traditions are unknown or disregarded, liberty itself can be challenged.

The report notes "only 34 percent of the respondents could identify George Washington as the American general at the battle of Yorktown," while only 23 percent could identify "government of the people, by the people, and for the people" as a line from Lincoln's Gettysburg Address. By contrast, 99 percent of the students know Beavis and Butt-head, and 98 percent could identify Snoop Doggy Dogg.

Surely parents and policy-makers should be engaged in a clarion call for a restoration of national memory. It would be an extraordinary tragedy if America's best and brightest know nothing about the nation that offers them opportunity and liberty unprecedented in recorded history.

Little Girls Shouldn't Count Calories

Deborah Mathis

Waxing back to its roots, the National Organization for Women is taking on beauty tyranny. Last week, the NOW Foundation announced a campaign against "the ridiculous beauty standards set by advertisers, Hollywood and the media." The rebellion will culminate on Sept. 25, when NOW will conduct rallies, set pickets and host parties to celebrate "Love Your Body Day."

To prove that the day is important and not just an off-the-wall, what-can-we-do-to-get-attention invention, NOW offers some startling statistics.

"Eighty percent of fourth grade girls are dieting," NOW says in a news release. Apparently, the organization has concluded that the phenomena have something to do with another statistic reported in the release: "Today, the average model weighs 23 percent less than the average woman. Twenty years ago the differential was 8 percent."

Did someone say 20 years ago? As in 1978 when I was 20 years ago? As in 1978 when I was 20 years younger and 20 pounds lighter?

Twenty years ago as in before the second and the third pregnancies which I used until only recently to excuse my extra jiggle?

Twenty years ago as in when I didn't love my body but, knowing what I know now, should have at least been very fond of it?

Lest you think NOW has no point to make with its special day, tell me you didn't notice the chagrin running off those last paragraphs. Tell me I don't sound like a woman bedeviled by the lean and lovely standards that make women like Kate Moss a star and women like me pinlights in the constellation of life. Oh vanity.

I am playful about it, but this problem is no toy. Grown women may pursue the taut, toned bygone to their heart's and pocket's content. And it may be pitiful enough for us, given how far removed from that ideal we are. But when 9-year-olds are counting calories and measuring fat grams, we know that the fantasy has become fascistic. This is not good.

I never had any such concerns as a 9-year-old. Nor do I recall any of my friends being so obsessed. Likewise, my own daughters seemed oblivious to figures and fannies when they were still in bobby socks.

The 80 percent figure is, therefore, doubly astounding—one, because it tells us that perfect woman syndrome has gotten worse, not better, in the years since feminism set out to correct us; and, two, because the number is so incredibly high as to be suspicious.

Yet, even if we're very conservative and chop the number down by three-fourths, that still leaves 20 percent of the lot and that's a world of trouble.

Most 9-year-old girls can expect to live 65 or 70 more years, maybe longer. It's absurd for them to start worrying about their appearance and physical appeal now, when they have so many years ahead for that.

But, of course, NOW's position is that the worry must cease henceforth and altogether.

I wish.

One day of resistance and consciousness-raising about the beauty paradigm will hardly be enough to change an eternity of demands and expectations. NOW shouldn't even waste its breath on trying to dispose of aesthetics entirely. Nor will it, I presume. After all, there are some measurable health benefits to limiting fat and other practices that fall under the "beauty" umbrella. NOW, never known as an anti-fitness organization, will surely not protest the obvious.

If their numbers are accurate or anywhere near accurate, NOW sends an alarm that deserves heeding, whether we choose to love our bodies or not.

Only a year ago, the world lost a princess who abused herself trying to measure up to some idea of physical perfection. That's how powerful this beauty thing is; it even broke through the well-guarded, fortified walls of a palace.

Imagine what it does to a little girl in a playhouse.

Handgun Freedom: Where Have All the Feminists Gone?

Dr. Michael S. Brown

How old does one have to be to remember the good old days? I recently found myself fondly recalling the feminists of the 1960s. Thousands of women marched in the streets demanding greater personal and political power; in effect, more control over their own lives.

Much has changed since then. Among other things, our society has experienced a massive rise in violence against women. Time after time women, and sometimes their children, are attacked and often killed by ex-husbands or rejected boyfriends. The victims typically relied on pepper spray and restraining orders for protection. Many other women are victimized by career criminals who consider women to be easy targets.

While the causes of violence are hotly debated, it matters little to the victim if it is caused by societal stress, bad genes or too much television. Although progress has been made by locking up more offenders, violent attacks on women are not going to go away anytime soon.

What is really fascinating are the divergent ways that women have faced this problem. Some women have taken responsibility for their own safety. Yes, I'm talking about guns. A gun is the only weapon that will permit a small woman to protect herself from even the biggest, strongest man. A handgun is the only type of gun that she can keep with her at all times. In past eras, most women understood this.

The recent Million Mom March, a thinly disguised Democratic Party rally, seems to suggest that today's women are different. They are portrayed as helpless victims who must beg the government to protect them. Perhaps that would be worthwhile, if the government could do so, but it can't. All the politicians can offer are empty promises and feel-good legislation, because criminals ignore gun laws.

The brave feminists of the past have been replaced on our television screens with well-manicured spokespersons directed by party pollsters and marketing experts. We have all heard their trademark phrases: "the children," "sensible gun laws," "if it saves one life." These are repeated over and over like a mantra to disguise the glaring flaws in their logic.

SOURCE: Reprinted from NewsMax.com. Reprinted with permission of the author.

Despite the fact that gun accidents are at an all-time low, they fly the false flag of "gun safety" to mask their intentions. A new term, "nanny state," has been coined to describe the utopian goal of this new political axis. In a strange twist of fate, the women who march now are not demanding power; they are offering to give up their power to others.

For over three decades, Americans have been fed anti-gun propaganda by the media and various political entities that find it useful to promote fear of guns. It is not surprising that many women now blame guns for the violence that threatens them. Guns have been portrayed as evil masculine tools that women are not capable of understanding or using for their own defense. If only guns are banned, they are told, violence will cease.

They seem to forget that men don't need guns to harm women or children.

Men become violent criminals not because they acquire a gun, but because they are willing to hurt people to get what they want. If it were somehow possible to remove all guns from society, the offenders would simply substitute other, even more brutal, methods against their victims. Men will always have a physical advantage because of their greater size and strength.

The most effective way to eliminate the disparity of physical force is for women to arm themselves and seek out good training. Research by professor John Lott shows that concealed weapons carried by a small percentage of citizens significantly reduce violent crime. This makes sense, because a predator contemplating an attack does not know which woman might be armed. Thus, he is more likely to leave all women alone and see some safe way to meet his illegal needs. Even before Lott's study, many criminals admitted that guns in honest hands are a major deterrent to crime.

There is now a well-developed political and media system that thrives on frightening women and convincing them that more gun laws are the answer. The politicians do it to gain power and the media do it for ratings. Exploiting women and children is just one more tactic to be used in their destructive campaign of cultural warfare.

Where have all the feminists gone? Perhaps they are still out there, bravely protecting themselves and their families while the political storm rages on.

BUTTER
NOW MORE THAN EVER THE NATURAL CHOICE.

Today, life is full of choices. Maybe too many. And perhaps one of the hardest choices of all is deciding on the kinds of foods you want your family to eat.

That's why it's so reassuring to know that when it comes to table-spreads, now, more than ever, butter is the natural choice.

Butter is the only spread that's pure, natural and made from fresh, wholesome milk. There is just no substitute for butter.

Nothing else tastes like it. Looks like it. Smells like it. Or bakes like it. Because butter is the only spread that's 100% pure, natural dairy.

Of course, a lot of other spreads try to convince you that there is a substitute for butter. Some spreads claim they taste just like butter. Others claim you'll find it hard to believe they're not butter.

But if you're looking for a spread that's natural and delicious, choose the one millions choose every day. The one you and your family can feel good about. Now, more than ever, the natural choice.

For more information call: 1-800-852-1542.

THERE'S NO REAL SUBSTITUTE FOR
BUTTER

Courtesy of the National Dairy Board.

Equal Treatment Is Real Issue—Not Same-Sex Marriage

With shouting about "gay marriage" headed for a new decibel level after a Hawaii court ruling last week, chances for an amicable resolution seem bleak.

Traditionalists see the issue in private, religious terms, and with legislators in many states mobilizing around their cause, they're in no mood to compromise. They say marriage, by common definition, involves a man and a woman. And for most people, it's just that. In polls, two-thirds of the public supports the status quo.

But looking through the lenses of history and law, as judges must, marriage is far from a private religious matter. So much so that short of a constitutional amendment, compromise is inevitable.

Not only does the state issue marriage licenses and authorize its officers to perform a civil version of the rite, it gives married couples privileged treatment under law.

For example, when one spouse dies the house and other property held jointly transfer easily for the other's continued use and enjoyment. The survivor gets a share of continuing Social Security and other benefits. Joint health and property insurance continues automatically.

If there's no will, the law protects the bereaved's right to inherit. There's no question of who gets to make funeral arrangements and provide for the corpse.

It's the normal order of things, even for households that may have existed for only the briefest time, or for couples who may be long estranged though not divorced.

But some couples next door—even devoted couples of 20 or 30 years' standing—don't have those rights and can't get them because of their sex.

Support for marriage is justified as important to community stability, and it undoubtedly is. But when it translates into economic and legal discrimination against couples who may be similarly committed to each other, that should be disturbing.

The U.S. Constitution says every person is entitled to equal protection under law. Some state constitutions go farther, specifically prohibiting sexual discrimination.

That's the issue in Hawaii, where the state's refusal to issue marriage licenses to pairs of men or women, while issuing them to heterosexual couples, is under assault.

The Hawaii Supreme Court already has ruled that the state would have to prove its practice was narrowly crafted to meet a "compelling interest" of the state. It's the same test the U.S. Supreme Court has used in knocking down affirmative action plans that reached too far: Only the most compelling interest and the most limited remedy can justify discrimination.

A circuit court judge ruled Tuesday that the state had failed the test. The case now goes back to the state Supreme Court, but based on its previous decision, Hawaii will probably be licensing same-sex marriages in a year or so. Similar challenges—and possibly similar results—can be expected in other states.

Ironically, people who oppose gay marriages on religious grounds would have their way but for the fact that marriage has evolved as a messy entanglement of church and state. To millions, marriage is a sacrament, and the notion that the state would license or regulate a sacrament ought to be an outrage. Imagine the uproar if a state legislature tried to license baptisms or communions, and wrote into law who could be baptized or who could receive bread and wine. Or worse yet gave tax breaks to those who followed those practices.

Short of getting the state out of the marriage business altogether, which isn't likely to happen, the state must figure a way to avoid discrimination. The hundreds of employers now extending workplace benefits to unmarried but committed couples and the handful of municipalities offering informal "domestic partner" status may be pointing in the right direction.

The need is not necessarily to redefine marriage but to assure equal treatment under the law.

For a Better Life, Don't Eat Any Beef

Dean Ornish

I grew up in Texas chewing on cheeseburgers, chiles and chalupas. Although I like the taste of red meat, I don't eat it anymore. Ever.

Why not? I don't believe in giving up anything I enjoy unless it's to get something even better. I stopped eating meat at age 19 because I felt so much better when I did.

Let's examine just a few of the latest studies:

- My colleagues and I recently found that even severely blocked coronary arteries began to unclog in the majority of heart patients when they stopped eating animal products and made other simple lifestyle changes. Most patients reported dramatic reductions in chest pain after only a few days to weeks after changing their diets.

- Last week, the largest study of diet and colon cancer ever conducted found the more red meat and animal fat women ate, the more likely they were to get colon cancer. Those who ate red meat as a main course every day were *two and a half times* more likely to get cancer than those who ate meat sparingly or not at all. According to the study director, Harvard's Dr. Walter Willett, "The optimum amount of red meat you eat should be zero."

- Earlier this year, a landmark study of 6500 people by Dr. T. Colin Campbell of Cornell found that the more meat they ate, the more likely they were to die prematurely from coronary heart disease, colon cancer, breast cancer, prostate cancer and lung cancer, among others. "We're basically a vegetarian species. . . . The higher the intake of animal products, the higher the risk of cancer and heart disease," Campbell wrote.

- Many athletes are forgoing the pregame steak for foods high in complex carbohydrates because they find that eating less meat often increases their endurance.

- Some beef is lower in fat than before, but it is still very high in fat. And cholesterol. Studies also indicate that meat protein and perhaps other substances in beef raise the risk of cancer and heart disease.

SOURCE: Reprinted from *USA Today*, December 18, 1990. Reprinted with permission of the author.

- Eating meat makes you fat. Most people who consume a low-fat vegetarian or near-vegetarian diet are able to eat a greater amount of food and still lose weight! So there is a sense of abundance rather than deprivation.

When we understand how our diet affects our health and how we feel—for better and for worse—then it becomes easier to make more intelligent choices. These choices are based not out of fear of dying but for the joy of living more fully. Meat. Real food for real death.

That's Racial Profiling

Mike Ramirez

Mobile Register, June 24, 2002. Reprinted with permission. Copley News Service.

Step 1 Toward Greatness: Win Powerball
Jim Watts

Deerfield, Ill

(Sunday)

Dear diary—Last night they had the Powerball drawing and, once again, nobody won, bringing the jackpot to $100 million. Ordinarily I make it a rule not to buy lottery tickets, since the odds of winning are about 750 gezillion-to-1, but with $100 million at stake, I decided, like the Bill Murray character in "Ghostbusters," that this should be more of a "guideline" than a rule. So I bought a ticket.

Like the lottery ads say, "you can't win if you don't play," and I could use $100 million as much as the next guy.

(Monday)

Today the pot is at $105 million, and growing by the minute.

I keep telling myself that this Powerball frenzy is for fools with impossible dreams. I continue to believe it is better to work for wealth than to gamble for it, but I don't deny that the dream of winning $105 million is very seductive. So seductive, in fact, that I decided to buy a few more tickets this afternoon . . . you know, more tickets, better chances.

I still plan on working, even if I win, and in fact, I privately vowed today to work just as hard (if not harder) as a multi-millionaire as I do now . . .

. . . I will just take more vacations.

(Tuesday)

Much of the talk in the office today revolved around the jackpot. A few of us pooled our money, bought more tickets, and agreed to split the $110 million.

I know it is stupid, but I am obsessed with this thing. I cannot get over the thought that, in one dramatic moment, I could go from being a working stiff to filthy rich. This thought possesses me, almost to the point where I can no longer concentrate on my job. In fact, instead of working today, I closed my office door and spent my productive energy working on Powerball combinations. I have used birthdays, anniversaries, the numbers of my favorite athletes, the number of breaths I take in a minute, and, perhaps most appropriately, the numbers that make up my credit card debt and mortgage.

SOURCE: *Savannah Morning News*, July 7, 1999. Reprinted with permission.

Like most lottery players, I think it is important to pay attention to the significant numbers in your life, because you never know if it is God's way of telling you how to win Powerball.

Speaking of God, I appealed to him in a "Powerball prayer" this morning—if He lets me win, I will keep only what I need and donate the rest to charity.

I thought it was a magnanimous offer, and I hope it got His attention.

(Wednesday)

The midweek drawing is tonight.

Since some states do not participate in Powerball, I have gotten calls from friends asking for tickets. They have all promised that they will send me the money "later" (sure they will), and, of course, I told them, if their ticket wins, I will split the jackpot with them (sure I will).

(Thursday)

No winners last night, bringing the jackpot to $125 million. I haven't told my wife this, since I am trying to maintain my "lottery games are a silly waste of money" public stance, but I spent much more money over the last four days than I care to admit. True to my former belief, I wasted good money on a fruitless dream, and my old, "rational self" would have laughed at such folly. However, I am now deep into this "folly," and today I had a serious dilemma—should I stop playing and cut my losses, should I try some new numbers, or should I repurchase all of last week's combinations and try some new numbers?

The answer was obvious: I repurchased last week's numbers and bought some new ones, simply because I could not bear the thought of one of my old tickets winning without me owning it.

This Powerball game may bankrupt me.

(Friday)

$140 million!

Call me silly, but I have this strange feeling that something special is about to happen. Maybe this is what everyone who plays must feel, but I can't stop thinking that I might win Powerball because I've been such a decent, fun guy all of my life.

(Believe me, I would be even more fun if I won.)

(Saturday)

Only a few hours to go before the drawing. Will today be my date with destiny? Will I be the lucky one who gets "struck by lightning" and wins $150 million?

Tomorrow at this time I may be in Paris.

(Sunday)

This is very painful for me to write—I didn't win. Somebody else won . . . somebody else is going to Paris, or someplace exotic. I have to stay home. I know I was stupid to get involved in this hopeless, impossible dream, and I know it was stupid to blow all that money on lottery tickets.

The jackpot has returned to zero, and now I, too, must return to reality . . . the reality of having to "make my money the old fashioned way."

(Until, perhaps, next week.)

Simple Trade-Off Is Key to Finding Time to Read

John Sledge

"How do you find the time to read all those books?" It is the question I am most often asked. The answer is simple: I don't watch television. Not in the morning, not at night, not on weekends. It is a policy I heartily recommend. If you adopt such a policy, the resulting free time in your life will astonish you. I guarantee it.

I certainly watched my share of television growing up. After school I would plunk down my books and zone out to "Gilligan's Island," "The Munsters" and "Gomer Pyle, U.S.M.C." My parents did not watch television themselves, and tried to limit the amount of time I spent before the set. They rarely even watched the news, since during those years it was mostly filled with the trauma of Vietnam, and my father, a World War II combat veteran, could not bear the sight of young Americans shot to pieces.

During my college and graduate school years there was little time for television, and, besides, there were too many social distractions. When I got my first job and moved to Georgia, I didn't own a television set and opted not to purchase one. I have always loved to read, and during these first years on my own, I decided that solitude and quiet would be conducive to some serious study.

I lived in the upstairs of an 1894 Queen Anne style house on a tree-lined street. After work I would climb the wide staircase, pour myself a tall glass of iced tea, and sit in a rocker on my balcony, book in hand. After a frugal dinner, I would usually take a walk, then sit inside under a lamp reading until time for bed. I wasn't aware that I was missing anything.

First-time guests to my rooms invariably noticed the lack of a television set, and they always asked about it, sometimes incredulously: "Where's your TV?" When I replied that I did not have one, they would look at me a little askance, sometimes literally wide-eyed. "What kind of creature is this?" they seemed to be thinking.

Now that I am married and have children, television is once again in my life. Fortunately, it isn't on very much, though if we had cable I fear that would change. Often, I choose to scurry out of the room when one family member or another tunes in to some favorite program.

In small doses, television is no more dangerous than anything else is, I suppose. But it is awfully hard to regulate the dosage. Television is like a drug and its seductive power has ensnared millions. It is bright and colorful and entertaining and requires no effort of the mind or body to enjoy.

When I was a child, my parents rarely worried about what I was watching on television. Some 30 years down the road, however, parental vigilance is imperative. Television empties toxins into the nation's living rooms, corrupting and polluting impressionable minds. It is largely a vehicle for advertising, an application that it executes in the most obnoxious and odious manner. If anyone knocked on our doors with such sales pitches we would chuck him or her out forthwith. The programming itself is little better, a noxious brew of sexually offensive sitcoms and lurid reality tales. Public television and some of the cable stations like A&E and The History Channel are admittedly worthwhile islands in this sea of sewage.

Television is inimical to the life of the mind and to the cultural expression upon which human societies have always depended. We have only to read about primitive peoples ruined by exposure to the boob tube to know that this is so. The celebrity-driven world of television and the movies dominates American culture. And tragically, the rest of the world wants to be like us.

The only antidote that I have found is to desert the television set and seek a quiet corner with a good book. Time is too precious. And there are so many good books.

Diary of an Unborn Child

October 5

Today my life began. My parents do not know it yet, I am as small as a seed of an apple, but it is I already. And I am to be a girl. I shall have blond hair and blue eyes. Just about everything is settled though, even the fact that I shall love flowers.

October 19

Some say that I am not a real person yet, that only my mother exists. But I am a real person, just as a small crumb of bread is yet truly bread. My mother is. And I am.

October 23

My mouth is just beginning to open now. Just think, in a year or so I shall be laughing and later talking. I know what my first word will be: MAMA.

October 25

My heart began to beat today all by itself. From now on it shall gently beat for the rest of my life without ever stopping to rest! And after many years it will tire. It will stop, and then I shall die.

November 2

I am growing a bit every day. My arms and legs are beginning to take shape. But I have to wait a long time yet before those little legs will raise me to my mother's arms, before these little arms will be able to gather flowers and embrace my father.

November 12

Tiny fingers are beginning to form on my hands. Funny how small they are! I'll be able to stroke my mother's hair with them.

November 20

It wasn't until today that the doctor told mom I am living here under her heart. Oh, how happy she must be! Are you happy, mom?

SOURCE: Reprinted from the *Mobile Press*.

November 25
My mom and dad are probably thinking about a name for me. But they don't even know that I am a little girl. I want to be called Kathy. I am getting so big already.

December 10
My hair is growing. It is smooth and bright and shiny. I wonder what kind of hair mom has.

December 13
I am just about able to see. It is dark around me. When mom brings me into the world, it will be full of sunshine and flowers. But what I want more than anything is to see my mom. How do you look, mom?

December 24
I wonder if mom hears the whispering of my heart? Some children come into the world a little sick. But my heart is strong and healthy. It beats so evenly: tup-tup, tup-tup. You'll have a healthy little daughter, mom!

December 28
Today my mother killed me.

Roswell: A Little Less Balance, Please

Art Levine

It's a truism that journalists need to offer a balanced view of all sides when writing about a public controversy. Sometimes, though, one side of a debate consists of sheer hooey, and the press's failure to make this plain does society a disservice. A case in point is the preposterously "objective" coverage of the supposed UFO crash in Roswell, N.M.

A decent case could be made that the Roswell incident's 50th anniversary, which was celebrated last week, didn't rate much coverage at all, given that the UFO event in question never happened. But *Time's* June 23 cover asked, "What *really* happened out there?" as if the answer were somehow in doubt. On CNN and MSNBC last week, it seemed like all-Roswell, all the time, with no fewer than five live remotes Thursday on the anniversary of what CNN called "the UFO sighting" there. There were also in-depth discussions of Roswell that day on two CNN talk shows, *CNN & Co.* and *Talkback Live.*

The weaknesses of "balanced reporting" in this story are illustrated by *USA Today's* coverage of an Air Force report stating that the Roswell "aliens" said to have been glimpsed in 1947 were really crash-test dummies sighted in the mid-1950s. The newspaper said the Air Force "tried to dispel" the flying-saucer accounts but, for the sake of balance, the paper noted that believers in the Roswell sighting say "key witnesses" wouldn't confuse events in the 1950s with their "vivid recollections" of 1947. "Witnesses include Frank Kaufmann, now 81, who was a civilian employee at the Roswell base and says he saw two of five dead aliens at the crash," the paper said. It quoted Kaufmann: "They were very good-looking people, ash-colored faces . . . about 5 feet 5 tall, eyes a little more pronounced."

Plain folk vs. Big Government: Whom are readers going to believe? A *Time*/Yankelovich poll showed that 65 percent of people think a UFO crashed at Roswell.

The Gold Helmets

A better approach to covering the Roswell story would be to focus on mounting evidence collected by more discriminating UFO researchers that

SOURCE: Copyright, July 14, 1997, *U.S. News & World Report.*

many key Roswell witnesses, in the words of Kal Korff, "aren't telling the truth." Korff is the author of *The Roswell UFO Crash: What They Don't Want You to Know.* He says the media are "treating these witnesses with kid gloves."

Yes, Virginia, many of Roswell's key witnesses have changed their stories several times and have been caught telling falsehoods. Korff's book shows that a first group of eyewitnesses mistakenly believed that some debris from a shattered radar reflector came from a spaceship. These witnesses didn't say anything about alien bodies. After a 1989 TV episode of *Unsolved Mysteries* about Roswell, a second mélange of "witnesses" came forward with bizarre tales of alien sightings. No one in this second group has told a plausible or consistent story. Jim Ragsdale, for one, said he spotted four alien bodies near a spaceship. Later he asserted that he saw nine alien bodies from which he removed gold helmets, and that he buried the aliens in the sand. Glenn Dennis was, in 1947, a young mortician. He said he was called (or visited) by military officers inquiring about small caskets and later met with a frightened nurse at the base hospital, who drew pictures of bulb-headed aliens for him. Her name was Naomi Selff, he told UFO researchers; she was transferred overseas a few days later and disappeared (or became a nun). Dennis was hailed as "absolutely truthful" by UFO investigator Karl Pflock in a 1994 report. But after learning there was no record of nurse Selff—and no transfers of nurses overseas—Pflock now concludes that Dennis didn't tell the truth. Dennis responds, "I may sound like a jerk, but . . . I'm telling the truth." He says he gave a fake name to Pflock to test his ability to keep a secret.

The oddest witness of all is Kaufmann, who claims he's still part of a secret military team that recovered the UFO in 1947—although he was discharged from the military in 1945 and, despite what *USA Today* says, has never substantiated his claim that he later worked at the Roswell base as a civilian. He has told interviewers that everyone from Charles Lindbergh to Werner von Braun was involved in the Roswell incident. When I spoke to Kaufmann last year for MSNBC, I couldn't believe that this tale-spinning old coot was the leading witness in several books and TV shows. He said of his many critics: "It's up to them to disprove me." Korff and Pflock have done so, but it's time for the rest of the media to follow their lead in examining improbable, high-profile UFO claims. Maybe then they could solve the real mystery behind Roswell: how one town's citizens could have gulled so many supposedly tough-minded journalists into thinking their stories had any credence at all.

When you give blood you give another birthday, another anniversary, another day at the beach, another night under the stars, another talk with a friend, another laugh, another hug, another chance.

American Red Cross

Please give blood.

Courtesy of the American Red Cross.

America Needs a Flag-Protection Amendment

Senator Bob Dole

On June 14, 1777, the Continental Congress adopted the Stars and Stripes as the official flag of the United States. After 213 years, it is long past time to give our flag the kind of protection the Founding Fathers expected, and the kind of protection the American people are demanding.

Unfortunately, the Supreme Court let the people down with a 5–4 vote to OK flag burning. Even worse, Congress has decided to ignore the overwhelming majority of Americans who favor a constitutional amendment to save Old Glory from the desecrators, those kooks who get their kicks, burning, trampling or spitting on our flag.

Instead of listening to the American people, Congress hid behind a filibuster, fuzzing up the debate with three major misconceptions about the constitutional amendment and about those of us who support it.

Misconception One: We were trying to amend the Bill of Rights for the first time in history.

That is a hoax. The simple truth is, the flag amendment changes nothing in the Bill of Rights. The American people know that the first amendment— an amendment which states that "Congress Shall Make No Law Abridging the Freedom of Speech"—was never intended to protect the act of flag burning. That's why 48 states have already passed flag desecration statutes.

The simple fact is, flag burning is an act; it is conduct, malicious conduct. It is not speech.

Misconception Two: Congress should decide the flag burning issue.

This is also false. The people should decide. That is what the Founding Fathers wanted, and that is why they made the process to change the constitution so challenging: A two-thirds vote of Congress, and approval of 38 state legislatures. Unfortunately, the people may never get the chance to amend their constitution.

In the heartland of America, some folks just can't understand what Congress is up to. Frustrated by Congress' flag filibuster, the City Council in Douglass, Kan., has voted unanimously to make flag burning illegal. Mayor Ron Howard spoke for America when he said: "Down here, we believe in the

SOURCE: Reprinted from the *Mobile Press Register.* Reprinted by permission of the author.

flag. I'm no lawyer, but it's come to the point that we've got to do whatever we can to protect the flag."

Misconception Three: Supporters of the constitutional amendment are demagogues.

Another falsehood. I always thought the flag was something special. I always thought we had a right to stand up for the flag without being accused of being a "demagogue" by liberal journalists or political opportunists. Unfortunately, about all we heard from our opponents was a frenzy about their own campaigns and re-election prospects, about campaign commercials and the terror of facing the people out on the campaign trail.

The last time I looked, the American flag had 50 stars on it for 50 states of real people who will be cut out of Old Glory if Congress continues its stubborn refusal to approve a constitutional amendment. Remember, approval by Congress would send the flag amendment for final action to the state legislatures, representatives closer to the people. After all, the Constitution says, "We The People," not "We The Congress."

Despite 58 percent support for the amendment in both houses of Congress, the flag filibuster won this time. But the flag's day will come.

I don't have much faith in Congress, but I have a whole lot of faith in the American people—people like George and Beverly Rhoades of Fond Du Lac, Wis.

Last week, the desecrators burned a flag stolen from the Rhoades' front yard where the family had proudly erected a homemade memorial to their son Louis, who was killed in Vietnam 22 years ago. Mrs. Rhoades doesn't know who desecrated her son's memorial. But she is absolutely determined to see this nation enact a flag protection amendment.

"We'll keep fighting," she said. "There's no patriotism in our country anymore for our young children to look up to."

Blame It on Dr. Jekyll

Luke Thompson

Oh, Lord, they're suing the tobacco companies again.

Nobody is responsible for anything any more. If you spill coffee in your lap, you can sue McDonald's. If you smoke for 50 years and get lung cancer, you can sue Philip Morris. If you drink half-a-dozen martinis and crash your Cutlass into an oak-tree, you can sue the city-engineers, or the lounge which served you that last drink, or (more likely) General Motors. If your life is a mess, you can find a psychiatrist who'll assure you it's your mother's fault. If you're 150 pounds overweight, blame it on your genes. The popular theme is "I didn't do it, Officer. I was out of town when it happened."

And this can be true. Things do happen to people which aren't their fault. *But not everything.*

I remember a rich line from the TV production of *Dr. Jekyll and Mr. Hyde.* (It starred Jack Palance.) Jekyll, you remember, discovers a potion which turns him into Edward Hyde, a brutish creature who roams London doing horrible things. When Jekyll decides not to drink the potion any more, the change occurs spontaneously, and Hyde continues his evil deeds. At the climax, Utterson is holding a gun threatening to shoot Hyde, who cunningly says, "Remember if you shoot me, you'll shoot Henry Jekyll." Utterson's response is central. He says, *"Hyde, this has nothing to do with you.* Dr. Jekyll is responsible. He knows he is."

That's a heavy truth. But I'm not sure who knows it any more.

SOURCE: Reprinted with permission of the author.

Biologist: Creationism Is 'Bad Religion'

Brian J. Axsmith

In his Nov. 20 letter to the editor, Dr. Sidney C. Phillips informs us that "Like it or not, there is such a thing as 'creation science.'" Yes, there are thousands of people who call themselves creation scientists, but the term is just wishful thinking according to Dr. Phillips' own self-defeating definition of science.

He tells us that science is "a study of the natural world (God's world) around us, using our five senses, with special emphasis on observation and experimentation." He later informs us that the Bible is the only real source of reliable knowledge, because the mind of man is finite.

If God created everything supernaturally, then how can we use the procedures of science to study the creative process? No, creationism is not science; it is religion—and bad religion at that.

Are there really growing numbers of creationists? I'm not sure, but the movement has gotten some temporary new life due to the rise of so-called "intelligent design creationism." The two most outspoken leaders of this movement are biochemist Michael Behe and legal scholar Philip Johnson.

Although many in the creationism camp applaud the works of these two, a careful reading of their books shows that their views are nearly as scientifically flawed as those of the neanderthalish "Young Earth Creationists" from which they have tried to distance themselves. Furthermore, it is clear that this movement will eventually collapse under its own weight, once it is widely realized that Johnson and Behe's views are contradictory.

For example in the book "Darwin's Black Box," Behe openly accepts the entire evolutionary scenario except for the origins of the biochemical machinery of the original cell. Rather than meshing nicely with Behe's account, in the book "Darwin on Trial," Johnson completely rejects all evolutionary change other than minor shifts in gene frequencies within populations.

I am not suggesting that creationists must agree on every issue, for we evolutionists surely do not. But you must admit that a "science" in which one leader accepts nearly the entire evolutionary scenario while the other will not even consider macroevolution at all cannot be considered as a serious, coherent challenge to Darwinism.

SOURCE: *Mobile Register*, November 27, 1999. Reprinted by permission of the author.

Dr. Phillips says that "To teach young people that 'slime plus time' is an intelligent and powerful process that resulted in a man and a woman leaves little doubt as to why young people might conclude to simply kill each other or do whatever they may enjoy." Undoubtedly he is referring to the recent epidemic of school shootings.

I suspect that many in the "Christian right" know the real reason for these tragedies. It has little to do with yesterday's biology lesson and everything to do with the gun culture.

Disturbed, angry, disgruntled teenagers committed these shootings. There have always been such teens (probably before Darwin as well), and there always will be. In days past, such children only produced a few black eyes and bloody noses. With the present easy availability of automatic and semi-automatic weapons, they can now wreak horrendous destruction and carnage in a matter of minutes.

We are almost in the 21st century, and it is about time for all of us to come to terms with science. The dichotomy presented by Dr. Phillips—that it's either evolution or a literal reading of Genesis—is a false one. There are many other alternatives.

Most Christians and other people of faith reconciled with science long ago, because it was the intelligent thing to do.

Evolution is simply a fact that must be dealt with. Wishing it would just go away won't work.

God gave you a mind; use it wisely.

Should Priests Marry?

Martin Ridgeway

I'm told there are hundreds and thousands of priests in this country who want to have wives. Either they've applied for laicization or they're contemplating it or they hope that the Vatican will change the rules and let them marry.

I can see a lonely priest fantasizing about a warm comfortable home and a wife who says, "Is it OK if we have shrimp again tonight?" or "Snuggle up; I'm cold."

I'm sorry, Father, but it doesn't work like that. As you walk through your quiet rooms, you might want to reflect on the language of marriage—the true sounds of a "good" marriage.

"Don't use those. Those are the good scissors."
"You said you'd be home by five."
"Not tonight. I have a headache (or cramps or a cold or depression or toothache or indigestion or swelling or thyroid tiredness . . .)."
"Don't say 'fixin' to."
"Do you really need another drink?"
"I'm having a Tupperware party tomorrow night."
"Take this back to the store for me; tell them I lost the sales-slip."
"Come on, everyone, it's time to watch *Family Feud*."
"Anyone can put up a swing-set."
"We'd better leave early. I'm worried about the kids (or the car or the baby-sitter or the furnace or nuclear waste . . .)."
"If you'd put things in their place, they wouldn't be lost."
"Not in front of the children."
"At least try to talk to my mother."
"How could you forget? Tommy's piano recital is tonight."
"Jimmy says his little-league team needs a coach."
"You didn't get me anything nice last Christmas (or Valentine's Day or birthday or Easter or Thanksgiving or anniversary or Mother's Day . . .)."
"Be in by 11:30. You know I can't sleep when you're out."
"The Wilsons feed their cat in the morning." [A line doesn't have to make sense to express a serious complaint.]

SOURCE: *The National Catholic Reporter,* April 10, 1981. Reprinted with permission.

"That dog of yours has ruined the carpet."
"Do you have to see *every* Super-Bowl game?"

Think about it, Father.

In Mark's gospel, the Sadducees ask Jesus about a woman who has married seven times. They ask whose wife she is in the next life. Jesus answers that in the hereafter there is no marriage.

That might be why they call it Heaven.

Is it any wonder the prisons are full?

In the mid 1950's, researchers at the University of Pennsylvania began conducting what has become a landmark study.

Its purpose: to determine the effect violent toys have on our children.

What they found was rather disturbing. The researchers stated that violent toys cause children to become more violent.

At Dakin, we've always tried to produce toys that teach children some other things.

Toys that, rather than teach a child how to maim, would teach a child how to love.

That, rather than teach a child how to hurt, would teach a child how to care for something.

Toys that, rather than being designed to be played with in only one way, would challenge the child's imagination to use them in a variety of ways.

You see, as parents ourselves, we at Dakin don't design toys solely on the basis of whether or not they'll make money.

We design them on the basis of whether we'd want our children playing with them.

Gifts you can feel good about.™

DAKIN

© 1991 DAKIN, Inc. Available at fine gift and toy shops everywhere.

Courtesy of Dakin, Inc.

Reasonable Rate of Divorce Can Be Good for Society

Philip D. Harvey

We hear much these days about the decline of cultural and moral values in America. As proof of this decline critics cite the coarse content of movies and popular songs, the continuing crisis of out-of-wedlock births and "skyrocketing" divorce rates.

But divorce doesn't belong in this equation. Indeed, a reasonable level of divorce may be a symptom of a healthy and mobile society, a society in which men and women are living unprecedentedly long lives, lives for which the companionship of but a single other person for 30 or 40 or 50 years may simply be inappropriate.

To be sure, some long marriages are deeply rewarding. For couples who are suited to spend a lifetime together, and choose to do so, such marriages can provide the optimum form of love and companionship.

But 50- and 60-year bonding through marriage is not the "natural" order of things. Few human beings over the course of time have ever lived together as mates for such long periods. Before the 20th century, one spouse or the other typically died, leaving the survivor to seek a new mate or to live alone.

Longevity is only part of the picture. When the extended family was an economic unit on the farm, there were many practical reasons for couples to stay together. Today's multi-skilled women and men, on the other hand, have many valid economic (and other) reasons for being mobile, reasons that may lead appropriately to divorce and, often, remarriage.

That most Americans categorically oppose divorce on principle is a function more of our aspiration to the ideal state than a realistic acceptance of how we humans actually behave. In an ideal world there would be no spousal abuse, no child abuse and no such thing as a marriage troubled beyond repair. Certainly divorce is very hard on children, particularly young children. Yet there is now a recognition that some marriages cannot be fixed, that they are damaging to children as well as parents and are better ended.

We tend to be idealistic about divorce too. While opinion polls reveal that we oppose it in the abstract, we generally approve of Sister Sally's divorce or Uncle Joe's. These are real people for us, and we tend to think

SOURCE: *Savannah Morning News.* Reprinted with permission of the author.

they've made appropriate changes in their lives. Of course, many divorces are unfortunate or financially disastrous for one party or another, but the seeds of bitterness and even of financial conflicts are often planted well before divorce takes place.

The freedom to have more than one mate over a 75-year lifespan may be a positive thing. Is it not possible that the ideal companion for our younger, child-rearing years will not be the ideal companion for our middle and later years? My wife and I have been married for 10 years and we are both in our second marriages, as is my wife's former husband. It appears to me that all parties concerned have benefited from the change. She and her first husband raised their two children to adulthood before separating; they now have changed their lives in ways that seem good for all who have been involved. Is this a symptom of "moral decline"? I think not.

PART THREE

Literary Argument

My Mistress' Eyes—Sonnet CXXX

William Shakespeare

My mistress' eyes are nothing like the sun;
Coral is far more red than her lips' red;
If snow be white, why then her breasts are dun;
If hairs be wires, black wires grow on her head.
I have seen roses damask'd, red and white,
But no such roses see I in her cheeks,
And in some perfumes is there more delight
Than in the breath that from my mistress reeks.
I love to hear her speak, yet well I know
That music hath a far more pleasing sound;
I grant I never saw a goddess go,
My mistress when she walks treads on the ground.
   And yet, by heaven, I think my love as rare
   As any she belied with false compare.

From *Henry V,* St. Crispin's Day

William Shakespeare

If we are mark'd to die, we are enow
To do our country loss; and if to live,
The fewer men, the greater share of honor.
God's will, I pray thee wish not one man more.
By Jove, I am not covetous for gold,
Nor care I who doth feed upon my cost;
It yearns me not if men my garments wear;
Such outward things dwell not in my desires.
But if it be a sin to covet honor,
I am the most offending soul alive.
No, faith, my coz, wish not a man from England.
God's peace, I would not lose so great an honor
As one man more methinks would share from me,
For the best hope I have. O, do not wish one more!
Rather proclaim it. Westmoreland, through my host,
That he which hath no stomach to this fight,
Let him depart, his passport shall be made,
And crowns for convoy put into his purse.
We would not die in that man's company
That fears his fellowship to die with us.
This day is call'd the feast of Crispian:
He that outlives this day, and comes safe home,
Will stand a tiptoe when this day is named,
And rouse him at the name of Crispian.
He that shall live this day, and see old age,
Will yearly on the vigil feast his neighbors,
And say, "To-morrow is Saint Crispian."
Then will he strip his sleeve and show his scars,
And say, "These wounds I had on Crispin's day."
Old men forget; yet all shall be forgot,
But he'll remember with advantages
What feats he did that day. Then shall our names,
Familiar in his mouth as household words,
Harry the King, Bedford and Exeter,

Warwick and Talbot, Salisbury and Gloucester,
Be in their flowing cups freshly rememb'red.
This story shall the good man teach his son;
And Crispin Crispian shall ne'er go by.
From this day to the ending of the world.
But we in it shall be remembered—
We few, we happy few, we band of brothers;
For he to-day that sheds his blood with me
Shall be my brother; be he ne'er so vile,
This day shall gentle his condition;
And gentlemen in England, now a-bed,
Shall think themselves accurs'd they were not here:
And hold their manhoods cheap whiles any speaks
That fought with us upon Saint Crispin's day.

To His Coy Mistress

Andrew Marvell

Had we but world enough, and time,
This coyness, lady, were no crime.
We would sit down, and think which way
To walk, and pass our long love's day.
Thou by the Indian Ganges' side
Shouldst rubies find: I by the tide
Of Humber would complain. I would
Love you ten years before the flood,
And you should, if you please, refuse
Till the conversion of the Jews;
My vegetable love should grow
Vaster than empires and more slow;
An hundred years should go to praise
Thine eyes, and on thy forehead gaze;
Two hundred to adore each breast,
But thirty thousand to the rest;
An age at least to every part,
And the last age should show your heart.
For, lady, you deserve this state,
Nor would I love at lower rate.
But at my back I always hear
Time's winged chariot hurrying near,
And yonder all before us lie
Deserts of vast eternity.
Thy beauty shall no more be found,
Nor, in thy marble vault, shall sound
My echoing song; then worms shall try
That long-preserved virginity,
And your quaint honour turn to dust,
And into ashes all my lust:
The grave's a fine and private place,
But none, I think, do there embrace.
Now therefore, while the youthful hue
Sits on thy skin like morning dew,

And while thy willing soul transpires
At every pore with instant fires,
Now let us sport us while we may,
And now, like amorous birds of prey,
Rather at once our time devour,
Than languish in his slow-chapt power.
Let us roll all our strength and all
Our sweetness up into one ball,
And tear our pleasures with rough strife,
Thorough the iron gates of life;
Thus, though we cannot make our sun
Stand still, yet we will make him run.

Death, Be Not Proud

John Donne

Death, be not proud, though some have called thee
Mighty and dreadful, for thou art not so;
For those whom thou think'st thou dost overthrow,
Die not, poor death, nor yet canst thou kill me.
From rest and sleep, which but thy pictures be,
Much pleasure, then from thee much more must flow,
And soonest our best men with thee do go,
Rest of their bones, and soul's delivery.
Thou art slave to fate, chance, kings, and desperate men,
And dost with poison, war, and sickness dwell;
And poppy or charms can make us sleep as well,
And better than thy stroke; why swell'st thou then?
One short sleep past, we wake eternally,
And death shall be no more; Death, thou shalt die.

From *Paradise Lost*, Book IX

John Milton

She scarce had said, though brief, when now more bold
The Tempter, but with show of zeal and love
To Man, and indignation at his wrong,
New part puts on, and as to passion moved,
Fluctuates disturbed, yet comely and in act
Raised, as of some great matter to begin.
As when of old some orator renowned
In Athens or free Rome, where eloquence
Flourished, since mute, to some great cause addressed,
Stood in himself collected, while each part,
Motion, each act won audience ere the tongue.
Sometimes in height began, as no delay
Of preface brooking through his zeal of right.
So standing, moving, or to height upgrown,
The Tempter all impassioned thus began.
"O sacred, wise, and wisdom-giving Plant,
Mother of science, now I feel thy power
Within me clear, not only to discern
Things in their causes, but to trace the ways
Of highest agents, deemed however wise.
Queen of this Universe, do not believe
Those rigid threats of death; ye shall not die:
How should ye? by the fruit? it gives you life
To knowledge; by the threatener? look on me,
Me who have touched and tasted, yet both live,
And life more perfect have attained than fate
Meant me, by venturing higher than my lot.
Shall that be shut to Man, which to the beast
Is open? or will God incense his ire
For such a petty trespass, and not praise
Rather your dauntless virtue, whom the pain
Of death denounced, whatever thing death be,
Deterred not from achieving what might lead
To happier life, knowledge of good and evil;

Of good, how just? of evil, if what is evil
Be real, why not known, since easier shunned?
God therefore cannot hurt ye, and be just;
Not just, not God: not feared then, nor obeyed:
Your fear itself of death removes the fear.
Why then was this forbid? Why but to awe,
Why but to keep ye low and ignorant,
His worshippers: he knows that in the day
Ye eat thereof, your eyes that seem so clear,
Yet are but dim, shall perfectly be then
Opened and cleared, and ye shall be as Gods,
Knowing both good and evil as they know.
That ye should be as Gods, since I as Man.
Internal Man, is but proportion meet,
I of brute human, ye of human Gods.
So ye shall die perhaps, by putting off
Human, to put on Gods, death to be wished,
Though threatened, which no worse than this can bring.
And what are Gods, that Man may not become
As they, participating godlike food?
The Gods are first, and that advantage use
On our belief, that all from them proceeds;
I question it, for this fair Earth I see,
Warmed by the sun, producing every kind.
Them nothing. If they all things, who enclosed
Knowledge of good and evil in this tree,
That whoso eats thereof, forthwith attains
Wisdom without their leave? and wherein lies
The offence, that Man should thus attain to know?
What can your knowledge hurt him, or this tree
Impart against his will, if all be his?
Or is it envy, and can envy dwell
In heavenly breasts? These, these and many more
Causes import your need of this fair fruit.
Goddess humane, reach then, and freely taste!"

A Vindication of the Rights of Woman
Mary Wollstonecraft

After considering the historic page, and viewing the living world with anxious solicitude, the most melancholy emotions of sorrowful indignation have depressed my spirits, and I have sighed when obliged to confess, that either nature has made a great difference between man and man, or that the civilization which has hitherto taken place in the world has been very partial. I have turned over various books written on the subject of education, and patiently observed the conduct of parents and the management of schools; but what has been the result?—a profound conviction that the neglected education of my fellow-creatures is the grand source of the misery I deplore; and that women, in particular, are rendered weak and wretched by a variety of concurring causes, originating from one hasty conclusion. The conduct and manners of women, in fact, evidently prove that their minds are not in a healthy state; for, like the flowers which are planted in too rich a soil, strength and usefulness are sacrificed to beauty; and the flaunting leaves, after having pleased a fastidious eye, fade, disregarded on the stalk, long before the season when they ought to have arrived at maturity. One cause of this barren blooming I attribute to a false system of education, gathered from the books written on this subject by men who, considering females rather as women than human creatures, have been more anxious to make them alluring mistresses than affectionate wives and rational mothers; and the understanding of the sex has been so bubbled by this specious homage, that the civilized women of the present century, with a few exceptions, are only anxious to inspire love, when they ought to cherish a nobler ambition, and by their abilities and virtues exact respect.

In a treatise, therefore, on female rights and manners, the works which have been particularly written for their improvement must not be overlooked; especially when it is asserted, in direct terms, that the minds of women are enfeebled by false refinement; that the books of instruction, written by men of genius, have had the same tendency as more frivolous productions; and that, in the true style of Mahometanism, they are treated as a kind of subordinate beings, and not as a part of the human species, when improveable reason is allowed to be the dignified distinction which raises men above the brute creation, and puts a natural sceptre in a feeble hand.

Yet, because I am a woman, I would not lead my readers to suppose that I mean violently to agitate the contested question respecting the quality or inferiority of the sex; but as the subject lies in my way, and I cannot pass it over without subjecting the main tendency of my reasoning to misconstruction, I shall stop a moment to deliver, in a few words, my opinion. In the government of the physical world it is observable that the female in point of strength is, in general, inferior to the male. This is the law of nature; and it does not appear to be suspended or abrogated in favour of woman. A degree of physical superiority cannot, therefore, be denied—and it is a noble peroga- tive! But not content with this natural pre-eminence, men endeavour to sink us still lower, merely to render us alluring objects for a moment; and women, intoxicated by the adoration which men, under the influence of their senses, pay them, do not seek to obtain a durable interest in their hearts, or to become the friends of the fellow creatures who find amusement in their society.

I am aware of an obvious inference:—from every quarter have I heard exclamations against masculine women; but where are they to be found? If by this appellation men mean to inveigh against their ardour in hunting, shooting, and gaming. I shall most cordially join in the cry; but if it be against the imitation of manly virtues, or, more properly speaking, the attain- ment of those talents and virtues, the exercise of which ennobles the human character, and which raise females in the scale of animal being, when they are comprehensively termed mankind;—all those who view them with a philosophic eye must, I should think, wish with me, that they may every day grow more and more masculine.

This discussion naturally divides the subject. I shall first consider women in the grand light of human creatures, who, in common with men, are placed on this earth to unfold their faculties; and afterwards I shall more particu- larly point out their peculiar designation.

I wish also to steer clear of an error which many respectable writers have fallen into; for the instruction which has hitherto been addressed to women, has rather been applicable to *ladies,* if the little indirect advice, that is scattered through Sandford and Merton, be excepted: but, addressing my sex in a firmer tone, I pay particular attention to those in the middle class, because they appear to be in the most natural state. Perhaps the seeds of false-retirement, immorality, and vanity, have ever been shed by the great. Weak, artificial beings, raised above the common wants and affections of their race, in a premature unnatural manner, undermine the very founda- tion of virtue, and spread corruption through the whole mass of society! As a class of mankind they have the strongest claim to pity; the education of the rich tends to render them vain and helpless, and the unfolding mind is not strengthened by the practice of those duties which dignify the human character. They only live to amuse themselves, and by the same law which in nature invariably produces certain effects, they soon only afford barren amusement.

But as I suppose taking separate view of the different ranks of society, and of the moral character of women, in each, this hint is, for the present, sufficient; and I have only alluded to the subject, because it appears to me to be the very essence of an introduction to give a cursory account of the contents of the work it introduces.

My own sex, I hope, will excuse me, if I treat them like rational creatures, instead of flattering their *fascinating* graces, and viewing them as if they were in a state of perpetual childhood, unable to stand alone. I earnestly wish to point out in what true dignity and human happiness consists—I wish to persuade women to endeavour to acquire strength, both of mind and body, and to convince them that the soft phrases, susceptibility of heart, delicacy of sentiment, and refinement of taste, are almost synonymous with epithets of weakness, and that those beings who are only the objects of pity and that kind of love, which has been termed its sister, will soon become objects of contempt.

Dismissing, then, those pretty feminine phrases, which the men condescendingly use to soften our slavish dependence, and despising that weak elegancy of mind, exquisite sensibility, and sweet docility of manners, supposed to be the sexual characteristics of the weaker vessel, I wish to shew that elegance is inferior to virtue, that the first object of laudable ambition is to obtain a character as a human being, regardless of the distinction of sex; and that secondary views should be brought to this simple touchstone.

This is a rough sketch of my plan; and should I express my conviction with the energetic emotions that I feel whenever I think of the subject, the dictates of experience and reflection will be felt by some of my readers. Animated by this important object, I shall disdain to cull my phrases or polish my style;—I aim at being useful, and sincerity will render me unaffected; for, wishing rather to persuade by the force of my arguments, than dazzle by the elegance of my language, I shall not waste my time in rounding periods, or in fabricating the turgid bombast of artificial feelings, which, coming from the head, never reach the heart. I shall be employed about things, not words! and, anxious to render my sex more respectable members of society, I shall try to avoid that flowery diction which has slided from essays into novels, and from novels into familiar letters and conversation.

These pretty superlatives, dropping glibly from the tongue, vitiate the taste, and create a kind of sickly delicacy that turns away from simple unadorned truth; and a deluge of false sentiments and overstretched feelings, stifling the natural emotions of the heart, render the domestic pleasures insipid, that ought to sweeten the exercise of those severe duties, which educate a rational and immortal being for a nobler field of action.

The education of women has, of late, been more attended to than formerly; yet they are still reckoned a frivolous sex, and ridiculed or pitied by the writers who endeavour by satire or instruction to improve them. It is acknowledged that they spend many of the first years of their lives in acquiring a smattering of accomplishments; meanwhile strength of body and mind are sacrificed to libertine notions of beauty, to the desire of establishing themselves,—the only way women can rise in the world,—by marriage. And this desire making mere animals of them, when they marry they act as such children may be expected to act:—they dress; they paint, and nickname God's creatures. Surely these weak beings are only fit for a seraglio!—Can they be expected to govern a family with judgment, or take care of the poor babes whom they bring into the world?

If then it can be fairly deduced from the present conduct of the sex, from the prevalent fondness for pleasure which takes place of ambition and those nobler passions that open and enlarge the soul; that the instruction which women have hitherto received has only tended, with the constitution of civil society, to render them insignificant objects of desire—mere propagators of fools!—if it can be proved that in aiming to accomplish them, without cultivating their understandings, they are taken out of their sphere of duties, and made ridiculous and useless when the short-lived bloom of beauty is over, I presume that *rational* men will excuse me for endeavouring to persuade them to become more masculine and respectable.

Indeed the word masculine is only a bugbear: there is little reason to fear that women will acquire too much courage or fortitude; for their apparent inferiority with respect to bodily strength, must render them, in some degree, dependent on men in the various relations of life; but why should it be increased by prejudices that give a sex to virtue, and confound simple truths with sensual reveries?

Women are, in fact, so much degraded by mistaken notions of female excellence, that I do not mean to add a paradox when I assert, that this artificial weakness produces a propensity to tyranize, and gives birth to cunning, the natural opponent of strength, which leads them to play off those contemptible infantine airs that undermine esteem even whilst they excite desire. Let men become more chaste and have weaker understandings. It seems scarcely necessary to say, that I now speak of the sex in general. Many individuals have more sense than their male relatives; and, as nothing preponderates where there is a constant struggle for an equilibrium, without it has naturally more gravity, some women govern their husbands without degrading themselves, because intellect will always govern.

A Modest Proposal

For Preventing the Children of Poor People in Ireland From Being a Burden to Their Parents or Country, and for Making Them Beneficial to the Public

Jonathan Swift

It is a melancholy object to those who walk through this great town or travel in the country, when they see the streets, the roads, and cabin doors crowded with beggars of the female sex, followed by three, four, or six children, all in rags, and importuning every passenger for an alms. These mothers, instead of being able to work for their honest livelihood, are forced to employ all their time in strolling to beg sustenance for their helpless infants, who as they grow up, either turn thieves for want of work, or leave their dear native country, to fight for the Pretender in Spain, or sell themselves to the Barbadoes.

I think it is agreed by all parties, that this prodigious number of children in the arms, or on the backs, or at the heels of their mothers, and frequently of their fathers, is in the present deplorable state of the kingdom a very great additional grievance; and therefore whoever could find out a fair, cheap, and easy method of making these children sound and useful members of the common-wealth, would deserve so well of the public as to have his statue set up for a preserver of the nation.

But my intention is very far from being confined to provide only for the children of professed beggars; it is of a much greater extent, and shall take in the whole number of infants at a certain age, who are born of parents in effect as little able to support them, as those who demand our charity in the streets.

As to my own part, having turned my thoughts, for many years, upon this important subject, and maturely weighed the several schemes of other projectors, I have always found them grossly mistaken in their computation. It is true, a child just dropt from its dam may be supported by her milk for a solar year with little other nourishment, at most not above the value of two shillings, which the mother may certainly get, or the value in scraps, by her lawful occupation of begging; and it is exactly at one year old that I propose to provide for them in such a manner, as, instead of being a charge upon their parents, or the parish, or wanting food and raiment for the rest of their lives, they shall, on the contrary, contribute to the feeding and partly to the clothing of many thousands.

There is likewise another great advantage in my scheme, that it will prevent those voluntary abortions, and that horrid practice of women murdering their bastard children, alas! too frequent among us—sacrificing the poor innocent babes, I doubt, more to avoid the expense than the shame—which would move tears and pity in the most savage and inhuman breast.

The number of souls in this kingdom being usually reckoned one million and a half, of these I calculate there may be about two hundred thousand couples whose wives are breeders; from which number I subtract thirty thousand couples, who are able to maintain their own children, although I apprehend there cannot be so many, under the present distresses of the kingdom; but this being granted, there will remain an hundred and seventy thousand breeders. I again subtract fifty thousand, for those women who miscarry, or whose children die by accident or disease within the year. There only remain an hundred and twenty thousand children of poor parents annually born: The question therefore is, How this number shall be reared and provided for? which, as I have already said, under the present situation of affairs, is utterly impossible by all the methods hitherto proposed; for we can neither employ them in handicraft or agriculture; we neither build houses, (I mean in the country) nor cultivate land: They can very seldom pick up a livelihood by stealing till they arrive at six years old, except where they are of towardly parts, although, I confess, they learn the rudiments much earlier; during which time they can however be properly looked upon only as probationers; as I have been informed by a principal gentleman in the county of Cavan, who protested to me, that he never knew above one or two instances under the age of six, even in a part of the kingdom so renowned for the quickest proficiency in that art.

I am assured by our merchants, that a boy or girl before twelve years old, is no saleable commodity, and even when they come to this age, they will not yield above three pounds, or three pounds and half a crown at most, on the exchange; which cannot turn to account either to the parents or kingdom, the charge of nutrient and rags having been at least four times that value.

I shall now therefore humbly propose my own thoughts, which I hope will not be liable to the least objection.

I have been assured by a very knowing American of my acquaintance in London, that a young healthy child well nursed is at a year old a most delicious and nourishing and wholesome food, whether stewed, roasted, baked, or boiled; and I make no doubt that it will equally serve in a fricassee, or a ragout.

I do therefore humbly offer it to publick consideration, that of the hundred and twenty thousand children, already computed, twenty thousand may be reserved for breed, whereof only one fourth part to be males; which is more than we allow to sheep, black cattle, or swine; and my reason is that these children are seldom the fruits of marriage, a circumstance not much regarded by our savages; therefore one male will be sufficient to serve four females. That the remaining hundred thousand may, at a year old, be offered in sale to the persons of quality and fortune through the kingdom; always advising the mother to let them suck plentifully in the last month, so as to render them plump and fat for a good table. A child will make two dishes at an entertainment for friends; and when the family dines alone, the fore or hind quarter will make a reasonable dish, and seasoned with a little pepper or salt will be very good boiled on the fourth day, especially in winter.

I have reckoned upon a medium that a child just born will weigh twelve pounds, and in a solar year, if tolerably nursed, increaseth to twenty-eight pounds.

I grant this food will be somewhat dear, and therefore very proper for landlords, who, as they have already devoured most of the parents, seem to have the best title to the children.

Infant's flesh will be in season throughout the year, but more plentiful in March, and a little before and after; for we are told by a grave author, an eminent French physician, that fish being a prolific diet, there are more children born in Roman Catholic countries about nine months after Lent, than at any other season; therefore, reckoning a year after Lent, the markets will be more glutted than usual because the number of popish infants is at least three to one in this kingdom, and therefore it will have one other collateral advantage, by lessening the number of papists among us.

I have already computed the charge of nursing a beggar's child (in which list I reckon all cottagers, laborers, and four-fifths of the farmers) to be about two shillings per annum, rags included; and I believe no gentleman would repine to give ten shillings for the carcass of a good fat child, which, as I have said, will make four dishes of excellent nutritive meat, when he has only some particular friend or his own family to dine with him. Thus the squire will learn to be a good landlord, and grow popular among his tenants; the mother will have eight shillings net profit, and be fit for work till she produces another child.

Those who are more thrifty (as I must confess the times require) may flay the carcass, the skin of which, artificially dressed, will make admirable gloves for ladies, and summer boots for fine gentlemen.

As to our city of Dublin, shambles may be appointed for this purpose in the most convenient parts of it, and butchers we may be assured will not be wanting; although I rather recommend buying the children alive and dressing them hot from the knife, as we do roasting pigs.

A very worthy person, a true lover of his country, and whose virtues I highly esteem, was lately pleased in discoursing on this matter to offer a refinement upon my scheme. He said that many gentlemen of this kingdom, having of late destroyed their deer, he conceived that the want of venison might be well supplied by the bodies of young lads and maidens, not exceeding fourteen years of age nor under twelve; so great a number of both sexes in every country being now ready to starve for want of work and service; and these to be disposed of by their parents if alive, or otherwise by their nearest relations. But with due deference to so excellent a friend, and so deserving a patriot, I cannot be altogether in his sentiments; for as to the males, my American acquaintance assured me from frequent experience that their flesh was generally tough and lean, like that of our schoolboys, by continual exercise, and their taste disagreeable; and to fatten them would not answer the charge. Then as to the females, it would, I think with humble submission, be a loss to the publick, because they soon would become breeders themselves: and besides it is not improbable that some scrupulous people might be apt to censure such a practice (although indeed very unjustly) as a little bordering upon cruelty, which, I confess, has always been with me the strongest objection against any project, how well soever intended.

But in order to justify my friend, he confessed that this expedient was put into his head by the famous Psalmanazar, a native of the island Formosa, who came from thence to London, above twenty years ago, and in conversation told my friend that in his country when any young person happened to be put to death, the executioner sold the carcass to persons of quality, as a prime dainty, and that, in his time, the body of a plump girl of fifteen, who was crucified for an attempt to poison the Emperor, was sold to his Imperial Majesty's prime minister of state, and other great mandarins of the court, in joints from the gibbet, at four hundred crowns. Neither indeed can I deny, that if the same use were made of several plump young girls in this town, who, without one single groat to their fortunes, cannot stir abroad without a chair, and appear at a play-house and assemblies in foreign fineries which they never will pay for, the kingdom would not be the worse.

Some persons of a desponding spirit are in great concern about that vast number of poor people, who are aged, diseased, or maimed, and I have been desired to employ my thoughts what course may be taken, to ease the nation of so grievous an encumbrance. But I am not in the least pain upon that matter, because it is very well known, that they are every day dying, and rotting, by cold, and famine, and filth, and vermin, as fast as can be reasonably expected. And as to the younger laborers, they are now in almost as hopeful a condition. They cannot get work, and consequently pine away for want of nourishment, to a degree, that if at any time they are accidentally hired to common labour, they have not strength to perform it, and thus the country and themselves are happily delivered from the evils to come.

I have too long digressed, and therefore shall return to my subject. I think the advantages by the proposal which I have made are obvious and many, as well as of the highest importance.

For *first,* as I have already observed, it would greatly lessen the number of Papists, with whom we are yearly over-run, being the principal breeders of the nation, as well as our most dangerous enemies, and who stay at home on purpose with a design to deliver the kingdom to the Pretender, hoping to take their advantage by the absence of so many good Protestants, who have chosen rather to leave their country, than stay at home, and pay tithes against their conscience to an Episcopal curate.

Secondly, the poorer tenants will have something valuable of their own, which by law may be made liable to distress and help to pay their landlord's rent, their corn and cattle being already seized, and money a thing unknown.

Thirdly, whereas the maintenance of an hundred thousand children, from two years old and upward, cannot be computed at less than ten shillings apiece per annum, the nation's stock will be thereby increased fifty thousand pounds per annum, besides the profit of a new dish introduced to the tables of all gentlemen of fortune in the kingdom who have any refinement in taste. And the money will circulate among ourselves, the goods being entirely of our own growth and manufacture.

Fourthly, the constant breeders, beside the gain of eight shillings sterling per annum by the sale of their children, will be rid of the charge of maintaining them after the first year.

Fifthly, this food would likewise bring great custom to taverns, where the vintners will certainly be so prudent as to produce the best receipts for dressing it to perfection, and consequently have their houses frequented by all the fine gentlemen who justly value themselves upon their knowledge in good eating; and a skillful cook, who understands how to oblige his guests, will contrive to make it as expensive as they please.

Sixthly, this would be a great inducement to marriage, which all wise nations have either encouraged by rewards or enforced by laws and penalties. It would increase the care and the tenderness of mothers toward their children, when they were sure of a settlement for life to the poor babes, provided in some sort by the public, to their annual profit instead of expense. We should soon see an honest emulation among the married women, which of them could bring the fattest child to the market. Men would become as fond of their wives during the time of their pregnancy as they are now of their mares in foal, their cows in calf, their sows when they are ready to farrow; nor offer to beat or kick them (as is too frequent a practice) for fear of a miscarriage.

Many other advantages might be enumerated. For instance, the addition of some thousand carcasses in our exportation of barreled beef, the propagation of swine's flesh, and improvement in the art of making good bacon, so much wanted among us by the great destruction of pigs too frequent at our tables; which are no way comparable in taste or magnificence to a well-grown, fat, yearling child, which roasted whole will make a considerable figure at a lord mayor's feast or any other public entertainment. But this and many others I omit, being studious of brevity.

Supposing that one thousand families in this city would be constant customers for infants' flesh, besides others who might have it at merry meetings, particularly at weddings and christenings, I compute that Dublin would take off annually about twenty thousand carcasses; and the rest of the kingdom (where probably they will be sold somewhat cheaper) the remaining eighty thousand.

I can think of no one objection that will possibly be raised against this proposal, unless it should be urged that the number of people will be thereby much lessened in the kingdom. This I freely own, and 'twas indeed one principal design in offering it to the world. I desire the reader will observe that I calculate my remedy for this one individual kingdom of Ireland, and for no other that ever was, is, or, I think, ever can be upon earth. Therefore let no man talk to me of other expedients: of taxing our absentees at five shillings a pound; of using neither clothes, nor household furniture, except what is of our own growth and manufacture; of utterly rejecting the materials and instruments that promote foreign luxury; of curing the expensiveness of pride, vanity, idleness, and gaming in our women; of introducing a vein of parsimony, prudence and temperance; of learning to love our country, wherein we differ from Laplanders, and the inhabitants of Topinamboo; of quitting our animosities, and factions, nor acting any longer like the Jews, who were murdering one another at the very moment their city was taken; of being a little cautious not to sell our country and consciences for nothing; of teaching landlords to have at least one degree of mercy towards their tenants; lastly, of putting a spirit of honesty, industry, and skill into our shopkeepers, who, if a resolution could now be taken to buy only our native goods, would immediately unite to cheat and exact upon us in the price, the measure, and the goodness, nor could ever yet be brought to make one fair proposal of just dealing, though often and earnestly invited to it.

Therefore I repeat, let no man talk to me of these and the like expedients, till he has at least some glimpse of hope, that there will ever be some hearty and sincere attempt to put them in practice.

But as to my self, having been wearied out for many years with offering vain, idle, visionary thoughts, and at length utterly despairing of success,

I fortunately fell upon this proposal, which as it is wholly new, so it has something solid and real, of no expense and little trouble, full in our own power, and whereby we can incur no danger in disobliging England. For this kind of commodity will not bear exportation, the flesh being of too tender a consistence, to admit a long continuance in salt, although perhaps I could name a country, which would be glad to eat up our whole nation without it.

After all, I am not so violently bent upon my own opinion as to reject any offer proposed by wise men, which shall be found equally innocent, cheap, easy, and effectual. But before something of that kind shall be advanced in contradiction to my scheme, and offering a better, I desire the author or authors will be pleased maturely to consider two points. First, as things now stand, how they will be able to find food and raiment for a hundred thousand useless mouths and backs. And secondly, there being a round million of creatures in human figure throughout this kingdom, whose whole subsistence put into a common stock would leave them in debt two millions of pounds of sterling, adding those who are beggars by profession, to the bulk of farmers, cottagers and labourers, with their wives and children, who are beggars in effect; I desire those politicians, who dislike my overture, and may perhaps be so bold to attempt an answer, that they will first ask the parents of these mortals, whether they would not at this day think it a great happiness to have been sold for food at a year old, in the manner I prescribe, and thereby have avoided such a perpetual scene of misfortunes as they have since gone through, by the oppression of landlords, the impossibility of paying rent without money or trade, the want of common sustenance, with neither house nor clothes to cover them from the inclemencies of the weather, and the most inevitable prospect of entailing the like or greater miseries upon their breed for ever.

I profess, in the sincerity of my heart, that I have not the least personal interest in endeavoring to promote this necessary work, having no other motive than the public good of my country, by advancing our trade, providing for infants, relieving the poor, and giving some pleasure to the rich. I have no children by which I can propose to get a single penny; the youngest being nine years old, and my wife past child-bearing.

From *Northanger Abbey*—"Oh! It Is Only A Novel!"

Jane Austen

And while the abilities of the nine-hundredth abridger of the *History of England,* or of the man who collects and publishes in a volume some dozen lines of Milton, Pope, and Prior, with a paper from the *Spectator,* and a chapter from Sterne, are eulogized by a thousand pens—there seems almost a general wish of decrying the capacity and undervaluing the labour of the novelist, and of slighting the performances which have only genius, wit, and taste to recommend them. "I am no novel-reader—I seldom look into novels—Do not imagine that *I* often read novels—It is really very well for a novel." Such is the common cant.

"And what are you reading, Miss————?" "Oh! It is only a novel!" replies the young lady, while she lays down her book with affected indifference, or momentary shame. "It is only *Cecilia,* or *Camilla,* or *Belinda";* or, in short, only some work in which the greatest powers of the mind are displayed, in which the most thorough knowledge of human nature, the happiest delineation of its varieties, the liveliest effusions of wit and humour, are conveyed to the world in the best-chosen language.

Now, had the same young lady been engaged with a volume of the *Spectator,* instead of such a work, how proudly would she have produced the book, and told its name; though the chances must be against her being occupied by any part of that voluminous publication, of which either the matter or manner would not disgust a young person of taste: the substance of its papers so often consisting in the statement of improbable circumstances, unnatural characters, and topics of conversation which no longer concern anyone living; and their language, too, frequently so coarse as to give no very favourable idea of the age that could endure it.

My Last Duchess

Ferrara

Robert Browning

That's my last Duchess painted on the wall,
Looking as if she were alive. I call
That piece a wonder, now: Fra Pandolf's hands
Worked busily a day, and there she stands.
Will 't please you sit and look at her? I said
"Fra Pandolf" by design, for never read
Strangers like you that pictured countenance,
The depth and passion of its earnest glance,
But to myself they turned (since none puts by
The curtain I have drawn for you, but I)
And seemed as they would ask me, if they durst,
How such a glance came there; so, not the first
Are you to turn and ask thus. Sir, 'twas not
Her husband's presence only, called that spot
Of joy into the Duchess' cheek; perhaps
Fra Pandolf chanced to say, "Her mantle laps
Over my lady's wrist too much," or, "Paint
Must never hope to reproduce the faint
Half-flush that dies along her throat." Such stuff
Was courtesy, she thought, and cause enough
For calling up that spot of joy. She had
A heart—how shall I say?—too soon made glad,
Too easily impressed; she liked whate'er
She looked on, and her looks went everywhere.
Sir, 'twas all one! My favor at her breast.
The dropping of the daylight in the West,
The bough of cherries some officious fool
Broke in the orchard for her, the white mule
She rode with round the terrace—all and each
Would draw from her alike the approving speech,
Or blush, at least. She thanked men—good! but thanked
Somehow—I know not how—as if she ranked

My gift of a nine-hundred-years-old name
With anybody's gift. Who'd stoop to blame
This sort of trifling? Even had you skill
In speech—which I have not—to make your will
Quite clear to such an one, and say, "Just this
Or that in you disgusts me; here you miss,
Or there exceed the mark"—and if she let
Herself be lessoned so, nor plainly set
Her wits to yours, forsooth, and made excuse—
E'en then would be some stooping; and I choose
Never to stoop. Oh, sir, she smiled, no doubt,
Whene'er I passed her; but who passed without
Much the same smile? This grew; I gave commands;
Then all smiles stopped together. There she stands
As if alive. Will 't please you rise? We'll meet
The company below, then. I repeat,
The Count your master's known munificence
Is ample warrant that no just pretense
Of mine for dowry will be disallowed;
Though his fair daughter's self, as I avowed
At starting, is my object. Nay, we'll go
Together down, sir. Notice Neptune, though,
Taming a sea-horse, thought a rarity,
Which Claus of Innsbruck cast in bronze for me!

I Am the Very Model of a Modern Major-General

W. S. Gilbert

I am the very model of a modern Major-General,
I've information vegetable, animal, and mineral,
I know the kings of England, and I quote the fights historical,
From Marathon to Waterloo, in order categorical;
I'm very well acquainted too with matters mathematical,
I understand equations, both the simple and quadratical,
About binomial theorem I'm teeming with a lot o' news—
With many cheerful facts about the square of the hypotenuse.
I've very good at integral and differential calculus,
I know the scientific names of beings animalculous;
In short, in matters vegetable, animal, and mineral,
I am the very model of a modern Major-General.
I know our mythic history, King Arthur's and Sir Caradoc's,
I answer hard acrostics, I've a pretty taste for paradox,
I quote in elegiacs all the crimes of Heliogabalus,
In conics I can floor peculiarities parabolous.
I can tell undoubted Raphaels from Gerard Dows and Zoffanies,
I know the croaking chorus from the *Frogs* of Aristophanes,
Then I can hum a fugue of which I've heard the music's din afore,
And whistle all the airs from that infernal nonsense *Pinafore*.
Then I can write a washing bill in Babylonic cuneiform,
And tell you every detail of Caractacus's uniform;
In short, in matters vegetable, animal, and mineral,
I am the very model of a modern Major-General.
In fact, when I know what is meant by "mamelon" and "ravelin,"
When I can tell at sight a chassepôt rifle from a javelin,
When such affairs as sorties and surprises I'm more wary at,
And when I know precisely what is meant by "commissariat,"
When I have learnt what progress has been made in modern gunnery,
When I know more of tactics than a novice in a nunnery:

In short, when I've a smattering of elemental strategy,
You'll say a better Major-General has never *sat* a gee—
For my military knowledge, though I'm plucky and adventury,
Has only been brought down to the beginning of the century;
But still in matters vegetable, animal, and mineral,
I am the very model of a modern Major-General.

The Declaration of Independence as Adopted by Congress

In Congress July 4, 1776

THE UNANIMOUS DECLARATION OF THE THIRTEEN UNITED STATES OF AMERICA

When in the Course of human events, it becomes necessary for one people to dissolve the political bands which have connected them with another, and to assume among the powers of the earth, the separate and equal station to which the Laws of Nature and of Nature's God entitle them, a decent respect to the opinions of mankind requires that they should declare the causes which impel them to the separation. We hold these truths to be self-evident, that all men are created equal, that they are endowed by their Creator with certain unalienable Rights, that among these are Life, Liberty and the pursuit of Happiness. That to secure these rights, Governments are instituted among Men, deriving their just powers from the consent of the governed, That whenever any Form of Government becomes destructive of these ends, it is the Right of the People to alter or to abolish it, and to institute new Government, laying its foundation on such principles and organizing its powers in such form, as to them shall seem most likely to effect their Safety and Happiness. Prudence, indeed, will dictate that Governments long established should not be changed for light and transient causes; and accordingly all experience hath shewn, that mankind are more disposed to suffer, while evils are sufferable, than to right themselves by abolishing the forms to which they are accustomed. But when a long train of abuses and usurpations, pursuing invariably the same Object evinces a design to reduce them under absolute Despotism, it is their right, it is their duty, to throw off such Government, and to provide new Guards for their future security. Such has been the patient sufferance of these Colonies; and such is now the necessity which constrains them to alter their former Systems of Government. The history of the present King of Great Britain is a history of repeated injuries and usurpations, all having in direct object the establishment of an absolute Tyranny over these States. To prove this, let Facts be submitted to a candid world. He has refused his Assent to Laws, the most wholesome and necessary for the public good. He has forbidden his Governors to pass Laws of immediate and pressing importance, unless suspended in their operation till his Assent should be obtained; and when so suspended, he has utterly neglected to attend to them. He has refused to pass other Laws for the accommodation of large districts of people, unless those people would relinquish the right of Representation in the Legislature, a right inestimable to them and formidable to tyrants only. He has called together legislative bodies at places unusual, uncomfortable, and distant from the depository of their public Records, for the sole purpose of fatiguing them into compliance with his measures. He has dissolved Representative Houses repeatedly, for opposing with manly firmness his invasions on the rights of the people. He has refused for a long time, after such dissolutions, to cause others to be elected; whereby the Legislative powers, incapable of Annihilation, have returned to the People at large for their exercise; the State remaining in the mean time exposed to all the dangers of invasion from without, and convulsions within. He has endeavoured to prevent the population of these States; for that purpose obstructing the Laws for Naturalization of Foreigners; refusing to pass others to encourage their migrations hither, and raising the conditions of new Appropriations of Lands. He has obstructed the Administration of Justice, by refusing his Assent to Laws for establishing Judiciary powers. He has made Judges dependent on his Will alone, for the tenure of their offices, and the amount and payment of their salaries. He has erected a multitude of New Offices, and sent hither swarms of Officers to harrass our people, and eat out their substance. He has kept among us, in times of peace, standing Armies without the consent of our legislatures. He has affected to render the Military independent of and superior to the Civil power. He has combined with others to subject us to a jurisdiction foreign to our constitution, and unacknowledged by our laws; giving his Assent to their Acts of pretended Legislation: For Quartering large bodies of armed troops among us: For protecting them, by a mock Trial, from punishment for any Murders which they should commit on the Inhabitants of these States: For cutting off our Trade with all parts of the world: For imposing Taxes on us without our Consent: For depriving us in many cases of the benefits of Trial by Jury: For transporting us beyond Seas to be tried for pretended offences: For abolishing the free System of English Laws in a neighbouring Province, establishing therein an Arbitrary government, and enlarging its Boundaries so as to render it at once an example and fit instrument for introducing the same absolute rule into these Colonies: For taking away our Charters, abolishing our most valuable Laws, and altering fundamentally the Forms of our Governments: For suspending our own Legislatures, and declaring themselves invested with power to legislate for us in all cases whatsoever. He has abdicated Government here, by declaring us out of his

Protection and waging War against us. He has plundered our seas, ravaged our Coasts, burnt our towns, and destroyed the Lives of our people. He is at this time transporting large Armies of foreign Mercenaries to compleat the works of death, desolation and tyranny, already begun with circumstances of Cruelty & perfidy scarcely paralleled in the most barbarous ages, and totally unworthy the Head of a civilized nation. He has constrained our fellow Citizens taken Captive on the high Seas to bear Arms against their Country, to become the executioners of their friends and Brethren, or to fall themselves by their Hands. He has excited domestic insurrections amongst us, and has endeavoured to bring on the inhabitants of our frontiers, the merciless Indian Savages, whose known rule of warfare, is an undistinguished destruction of all ages, sexes and conditions. In every state of these Oppressions We have Petitioned for Redress in the most humble terms: Our repeated Petitions have been answered only by repeated injury. A Prince, whose character is thus marked by every act which may define a Tyrant, is unfit to be the ruler of a free people. Nor have We been wanting in attentions to our British brethren. We have warned them from time to time of attempts by their legislature to extend an unwarrantable jurisdiction over us. We have reminded them of the circumstances of our emigration and settlement here. We have appealed to their native justice and magnanimity, and we have conjured them by the ties of our common kindred to disavow those usurpations, which, would inevitably interrupt our connections and correspondence. They too have been deaf to the voice of justice and of consanguinity. We must, therefore, acquiesce in the necessity, which denounces our Separation, and hold them, as we hold the rest of mankind, Enemies in War, in Peace Friends.

We, therefore, the Representatives of the United States of America, in General Congress, Assembled, appealing to the Supreme Judge of the world for the rectitude of our intentions, do, in the Name, and by Authority of the good People of these Colonies, solemnly publish and declare, That these United Colonies are, and of Right ought to be Free and Independent States; that they are Absolved from all Allegiance to the British Crown, and that all political connection between them and the State of Great Britain, is and ought to be totally dissolved; and that as Free and Independent States, they have full Power to levy War, conclude Peace, contract Alliances, establish Commerce, and to do all other Acts and Things which Independent States may of right do. And for the support of this Declaration, with a firm reliance on the protection of divine Providence, we mutually pledge to each other our Lives, our Fortunes and our sacred Honor.

Do We Really Need Another Biography of Jane Austen?

Irene B. McDonald

> *Where is the wisdom we have lost in knowledge?*
>
> *Where is the knowledge we have lost in information?*
>
> —T. S. ELIOT, CHORUSES FROM "THE ROCK"

It is a truth universally acknowledged that a single woman writer of few remaining letters must be in want of a biographer.

And equally true is Lytton Strachey's comment in his preface to *Eminent Victorians* "that it is perhaps as difficult to write a good life as to live one" (10).

Two situations contribute to today's difficulties in writing (and living) a good life—the need to understand all human behavior and the availability of a great deal of historical data. Contemporary biographies, though generally more accurate than earlier ones, suffer from a post-Freudian compulsion to scrutinize, analyze, and explain. Earlier biographers reported behavior; today's writers (and readers) demand explanations. They thrive on researched data and speculation, some of it quite possibly true.

Consider, for example, this incident in Jane Austen's life. In Chawton, during her last illness, too tired during the daytime to climb the stairs to the room she shared with her older sister, Cassandra, Jane remained downstairs. To rest, she used an arrangement of three chairs. If she chose the sofa, she told her niece Caroline, Mrs. Austen would hesitate to lie there as was her habit.

Can a contemporary biographer merely report this detail? Who would accept such dereliction? Our inquiring minds want to know more.

And now, in "a frenzy fit," running mad as often as we choose (*Minor Works* 102), we begin our scrutiny. Did Austen suffer a martyr complex? Didn't she once refer to herself as "the most unlearned and uninformed female who ever dared to be an authoress"? Boasted of her condition, in fact, "with all possible vanity," proclaimed it in writing in a letter to the Prince Regent's librarian (11 December 1815)? She sounds very much a martyr. A

SOURCE: Reprinted from *Persuasions* (1998) with permission of the author.

singular martyr at that, for didn't she also proclaim to this same librarian, one James Stanier Clarke, how she had to keep to her own style and go on in her own way (1 April 1816)?

Or did she intend to shame her mother, "something of a hypochondriac," we are told (Drabble 25)? At the time, Jane must have known how ill she herself was. Did she subconsciously intend to show up her mother, a Mr. Woodhousian valetudinarian who nevertheless could spend hours in the garden?

Or was Jane, no longer a child but a woman in her forties, still frightened of her mother? Would Mrs. Austen pen sharp rhymes about a daughter lying on a sofa while the aged parent trembled in exhaustion on a hard chair?

Or was she merely being respectful, deferring to her old mother, who after time in her favorite potato patch, would quite naturally tire? Wait, perhaps the sofa had become stained by Mrs. Austen's smock, a garment she habitually wore while gardening. Fastidious Jane would quite rightly opt for a cleaner venue.

Or did Jane remember her juvenile spoof on the cult of sensibility? In *Love and Friendship*, Laura's eighth letter describes how she and friend Sophia, overwhelmed by pathetic feelings, "fainted alternately on the sofa" (*Minor Works* 86). Did Jane envision her mother and herself performing similar acrobatics.

More questions arise as we indulge our speculations. Wouldn't Mrs. Austen have noticed those three chairs placed in so unusual an arrangement? Wouldn't she have seen Jane lying on them? Wouldn't she be concerned? Or, was she indifferent to her gifted daughter? Was Cassandra their mother's favorite? During Jane's final months in Winchester, only sixteen miles away, why didn't Mrs. Austen leave Chawton to visit her dying daughter? Did she dislike, during this prime May-June-July growing season, to leave her gardens? Had gardening become such an obsession?

On and on we go, analyzing, scrutinizing, exploring every possibility—without the barouche-landau, of course ("extremely fond of exploring") (*Emma* 274).

The availability of historical data contributes to the problems (and length) of contemporary biography. It can tempt a biographer into excesses. It can be used to justify speculations and often creates additional ones. But, unfortunately, such material does not always lead to truth. In *Rambler* of October 13, 1760 (No. 60), Samuel Johnson, himself no mean biographer, scoffed at those who "imagine themselves writing a life when they exhibit a chronological series of actions or preferments."

Jane Austen's biographers, however, will not be overwhelmed by primary sources. Austen kept no journals. Though she wrote many letters, relatively few (only about 160) remain. Cassandra burned the greater part of Jane's letters to her and expurgated portions of those she kept. Jane's correspondence with her favorite brother Henry seems to have been destroyed.

As a result, biographers seek out secondary material. Take Jane's cousin, for example: Eliza Hancock—Madame de Feuillide—Mrs. Henry Austen. Because of her colorful existence, Eliza undoubtedly deserves a large swatch of Austen's life story. Current biographers can (and often do) discuss Philadelphia Austen, Eliza's mother, who traveled to India to find a husband. They can deal with that very husband himself, Tysoe Saul Hancock, a middle-aged surgeon, worried by her frivolities and later beset with financial woes. They speculate on the question of Eliza's paternity (her mother's husband? Warren Hastings, Governor-General of Bengal, a significant friend?), the complexity of Hastings's seven-year parliamentary trial, the social and financial status of Eliza's first husband (the guillotined Comte de Feuillide), Eliza's finances as a widow, the precarious health of her son (christened Hastings), her flirtations with the Austen boys (James and Henry), her eventual marriage to Henry (ten years her junior), their trip to France to try to regain the de Feuillide estate.

Such material represents only an introduction to the fascinating Eliza. Much more can be sought out. Didn't Eliza once undertake a regimen of sea bathing hoping to restore little Hastings's health? What was his condition (and, what were the medical theories then)? How did a woman and child partake of seabathing at that time? Another matter, consider the extravagant lifestyle of Eliza before and after she married Henry. Was their lavish party that Jane attended in London (professional musicians, a rented mirror, newspaper reportage) typical? And on and on we go, extremely fond of exploring, indeed.

Exhausting the material on Eliza, biographers can (and do) turn to Mrs. Austen's brother, Thomas, farmed out because he was weak-minded or mad. A similar situation existed with George, the second Austen son, abnormal in some way. Why was he raised so apart from the Austen family? Why did they pay him so little heed, rarely referring to him, eventually sending him to an unnamed grave?

Of course Jane's aunt, Mrs. Leigh-Perrot, deserves at least a chapter, or two or three. Accused in Bath of shoplifting, she remained in custody from August until her trial in March, when she was acquitted. Found guilty, she could have been hanged or more likely transported. Though found innocent of the charge of stealing a card of white lace, was she perhaps a kleptomaniac? Had her husband, Mrs. Austen's wealthy brother James, bought her off? Did she steal (or seem to steal) later in her life? Weren't there some hints about greenhouse plants? (Consider the acquisitiveness of dreadful Aunt Norris in *Mansfield Park*. An echo of Mrs. Leigh-Perrot's behavior?) Jane apparently didn't like her aunt, though they shared the same first name. Why not? Did Mrs. Leigh-Perrot's attitude toward money and her less affluent inlaws find itself caricatured in *Sanditon's* Lady Denham, who "employs her position of power with gleeful malice, dangling her money and estate before poorer relations"? (Copeland 124).

Then think of all that relates to the naval careers of the two sailor brothers, Frank and Charles, to the legal battles (£ 15,000 paid to lawyers) fought by Edward to retain the rights of his inheritance from the Knights, wealthy cousins who adopted him, and to the complex financial circumstances responsible for the failure of Henry's bank.

And Jane's love life? Whatever happened to Tom Lefroy with whom she enjoyed such lively flirtation? We know later in his native Ireland he married and became Lord Chief Justice. What sort of husband and Lord Chief Justice was he? What can we know about his "boyish love" (Tucker 59) for Jane? Did Harris Bigg-Wither ever talk about his reaction that morning of December 3 when Jane reversed her decision of the night before to marry him? And, was Cassandra correct in her late-in-life comments about the mysterious man (a clergyman?) the family met at the seaside? It seems he was worthy of Jane. It seems he died before he could renew their acquaintance or declare his intentions.

Consider the numerous Austen nieces and nephews. Did "itty Dordy," Edward's son George, who learned to skip so well so early in life, develop into a famous cricket player? How could favorite niece Fanny misplace dear Aunt Jane's letters? How did her son, Lord Brabourne, happen to find them? How legible were they? And, the crucial question, what was in the letters Cassandra burned?

A semi-crucial question—what happened to the Austen papers? Only two manuscripts of her mature novels survive—the last two chapters of *Persuasion* (the British Library, London) and *Sanditon* (King's College, Cambridge). Could the others be mouldering in some publisher's storage center? Did a distant heir cart them off, only to misplace them in a croquet box, now hidden in some dusty castle attic? Surely the well-thumbed copy of "First Impressions," unlopped and uncropped, must exist somewhere.

And finally, what was the cause of Austen's death? Hodgkin's disease? Addison's disease, as most biographers believe? Can we match the symptoms she reported in her letters (nausea, fever, weakness, skin discoloration) with today's symptoms?

Enough running mad, or even running sane, as it were.

A recurrent problem with much contemporary biography is that, in "our data-ravenous contemporary world" (Weintraub, *Queen Victoria* xi), peripheral material assumes exaggerated importance. The reasons for greatness (six novels in Austen's case) merit less concern. Perhaps what our era needs is a new genre, an addendum to the standard literary biography, something called "The Peripheral Biography," an "Everything-you-always wanted-to-know-about So and So's relatives, lovers, and friends, the houses, and gardens he/she lived in, favorite amusements, flowers, donkeys, . . . "

Conscientious biographers might first write a focused biography, one, in Strachey's terms, of "a becoming brevity—a brevity which excludes everything that is redundant and nothing that is significant" (10). Then they could indulge themselves with another. It would include enlightened speculation and heavily researched periphery, all stretched out to five hundred pages minimum, with perhaps "a critique on Walter Scott, or the history of Buonaparte" (*Letters* 4 February 1813).

After Austen's death, it seemed fashionable to emphasize what a treasure she had been, how unsingular, how plain and dutiful and ordinary and good. In his introduction to the posthumous *Northanger Abbey and Persuasion,* in what Myer calls "the first whitewash operation performed by her surviving relatives" (224), brother Henry emphasizes Jane's stature "of true elegance," her "modest cheek," her accomplishments, her temper "as polished as her wit." He takes pains to assure us that she had no burning ambition to achieve fame and fortune through her writing. She "became an authoress entirely from taste and inclination" (*NA* 5–6). And most important of all, "she was thoroughly religious and devout." Now an ordained and practicing clergyman, Henry is careful to conclude that "her opinions accorded strictly with those of our Established Church" (*NA* 8).

This picture of perfection was perpetuated by family members and nineteenth-century biographers. Perhaps over-reacting in their attempts to humanize her, recent biographers reveal a much more troubled Jane Austen. They speculate on her antagonism toward her mother, on her unhappiness and sense of powerlessness early in life when sent away to school, on her fear of marriage and childbearing. Jane felt a rivalry with Cassandra, some infer, and resented Edward's rise to fortune. One conjectures that she was not popular with her brothers, who named their daughters after Cassandra. Another concludes that her letters show her diffidence, a lack of tenderness toward herself and others, anger and disappointment. Others emphasize her frustration. She grumbled about domestic and social obligations. She felt the injustice of her situation as a poor spinster with little social position. Though she burned with ambition, she wrote of herself in self-deprecating prose. And, most shocking of all, her father, the learned Reverend George Austen, an Oxonian, may have made money in the opium-transporting business. (Not so shocking, says another, because opium, widely used as a painkiller, was as common as today's aspirin.)

Is it ever possible to see another age objectively? Our era seems preoc-
cupied with the trauma of childhood, parent-child conflicts, sibling rivalry,
women's rights, mistreatment of inferiors, love relationships, and debunking
in general. Must these concerns color and distort the past?

"We view each life more in our terms than in our subject's," writes
Stanley Weintraub, "—which is why library shelves strain under the weight of
yet another biography of the same figure, and one perhaps no closer to that
elusive thing called truth"(*Biography* 7).

A 669-page biography of Jane Austen? Really? Just published? Do we
need another one?

Of course we do. We agree with James Boswell that no one can know
"with certainty beforehand, whether what may seem trifling to some, and
perhaps to the collector himself, may not be most agreeable to many" (26).
In the "Advertisement to the First Edition" of his *Life of Johnson,* Boswell also
emphasizes just how hard "the collector himself" worked. "Were I to detail
the books which I have consulted, and the inquiries which I have found it
necessary to make by various channels," he writes, "I should probably be
thought ridiculously ostentatious. Let me only observe, as a specimen of my
trouble, that I have sometimes been obliged to run half over London, in
order to fix a date correctly" (4).

Like Boswell, good collector-biographers consult many sources, make
inquiries "by various channels," and run half over any number of cities
pursuing "that elusive thing called truth." We remain grateful to them.
And we understand when they include all they can find, and "fix." Yet,
ironically, this abundant detail and the resultant information-speculation
cycles often fail to satisfy. There remains an almost inexpressible longing
for "the wisdom we have lost in knowledge," "the knowledge we have lost
in information" (Eliot 96).

WORKS CITED

Austen, Jane. *Jane Austen's Letters to her Sister Cassandra and Others.* Ed.
R.W. Chapman. 2nd ed. Oxford: OUP, 1952.

Austen, Jane. *The Novels of Jane Austen.* Ed. R. W. Chapman. 3rd ed.
Oxford: OUP, 1933–69.

Boswell, James. *Boswell's Life of Johnson.* Ed. R.W. Chapman. London:
Oxford UP, 1960.

Copeland, Edward. "*Sanditon* and 'my Aunt': Jane Austen and the
National Debt." *Persuasions* 19 (1997): 117–29.

Drabble, Margaret. "Introduction." *Lady Susan •The Watsons• Sanditon.*
New York: Penguin, 1974.

Eliot, T. S. *The Complete Poems and Plays* 1901–1950. New York: Harcourt, 1952.

Myer, Valerie Grosvenor. *Jane Austen: Obstinate Heart: A Biography.* New York: Arcade, 1997.

Strachey, Lytton. *Eminent Victorians.* Chatto & Windus, 1918. London: Penguin, 1986.

Tucker, George Holbert. *Jane Austen the Woman. Some Biographical Insights.* New York: St. Martin's, 1994.

Weintraub, Stanley. *Biography and Truth.* New York: Bobbs-Merrill, 1967.

——— *Queen Victoria.* New York: Truman Dutton, 1987.

ADDITIONAL BIOGRAPHIES OF JANE AUSTEN

Austen-Leigh, James Edward. *A Memoir of Jane Austen by Her Nephew.* London, 1870, rev. 1871. Oxford: Clarendon, 1963.

Austen-Leigh, William, and R. A. Austen-Leigh. *Jane Austen: A Family Record.* 1913. Ed. Deirdre Le Faye, New York: Barnes, 1996.

Bush, Douglas. *Jane Austen.* New York: Macmillan, 1975.

Chapman, R.W. *Jane Austen: Facts and Problems.* Oxford: Clarendon, 1961.

Halperin, John. *The Life of Jane Austen.* Baltimore, MD: Johns Hopkins UP, 1984.

Honan, Park. *Jane Austen: Her Life.* London: St. Martin's, 1996.

Johnson, R. Brimley. *Jane Austen: Her Life, Her Work, Her Family and Her Critics.* New York: Haskell, 1974.

Kaplan, Deborah. *Jane Austen among Women.* Baltimore: Johns Hopkins UP, 1992.

Mukherjee, Meenakshi. *Jane Austen.* New York: St. Martin's, 1991.

Nokes, David. *Jane Austen: A Life.* New York: Farrar, 1997.

Tomalin, Claire. *Jane Austen: A Life.* New York: Knopf, 1997.

Cardinal Newman's Rules for Writing Sermons

Cardinal J. H. Newman

1. A man should be earnest, by which I mean he should write not for the sake of writing, but to bring out his thoughts.
2. He should never aim at being eloquent.
3. He should keep his idea in view, and should write sentences over and over again until he has expressed his meaning accurately, forcibly, and in a few words.
4. He should aim at being understood by his hearers or readers.
5. He should use words which are likely to be understood. Ornament and amplification will come spontaneously in due time, but he should never seek them.
6. He must creep before he can fly, by which I mean that humility which is a great Christian virtue has a place in literary composition.
7. He who is ambitious will never write well, but he who tries to say simply what he feels, what religion demands, what faith teaches, what the Gospel promises, will be eloquent without intending it, and will write better English than if he made a study of English Literature.

SOURCE: *Favorite Newman Sermons,* 1932.

PART FOUR

Eight Rules for Good Writing

*What matters is that we get done what we have to do
and get said what we have to say.*
—DONALD J. LLOYD

The following pages will show you how to write clear, straightforward prose. This is the language you would use in explaining a situation or arguing an issue. It expresses itself in a direct, informal style.

There are other styles of writing. For an inaugural address or an academic essay, you will want a more formal, balanced presentation. For an emotional appeal or an angry condemnation, you may want a more colloquial style. But such occasions are rare. The informal style recommended here will serve you in most writing situations. You can use it to propose marriage, explain entropy, or plead not guilty.

Using the eight rules that follow should make you a better writer. They offer material you should know and they omit areas you don't need to worry about. The intent is practical—not to tell you about "good writing," but to show you how to do it.

These rules will be sufficient for most people on most writing occasions. The less skilled student who cannot recognize a sentence and doesn't know that a period goes at the end of it will need additional help; so will the refined writer who seeks a singular style. Nevertheless, the rules can help most people become correct and effective writers.

Rule 1

Find a Subject You Can Work With

Choosing a subject is one of the hardest parts of writing, and perhaps the most important. In many writing situations, of course, you don't have to choose a topic. You want to write the cable company protesting the latest rate-hike. You have to send a thank-you letter to your aunt. Your boss asks you to prepare a marketing report. In these cases the subject is there, and you have to tell a particular audience about it.

Still, there are occasions when you select a topic for an essay or speech, and there are times when you might be given a general subject ("The American Dream" or "Tomorrow's Promise") but can approach it in a number of ways. You need to recognize the problems in making a choice.

To produce a good essay, you need a topic that will interest your audience, that lends itself to detail, and that can be covered in a prescribed number of words. (The point here will be clearer if you recall the last dull sermon you heard.)

If you were assigned to write a 500-word essay for a general audience (think of the people you see around you in a class or at a movie), how good would these topics be?

1. "Death Awaits All Human Beings." Unless you are going to write about something unusual—an exploding sun, the bloody prophecies of Revelation, or the mathematics of entropy—this will be a boring subject. When you write of "all human beings," you tend to say what everyone knows.

2. "My Brother, the Practical Joker." This topic concerns an individual rather than all people. The experience, however, is pretty close to that of all people. Most of us have met practical jokers. Unless your brother's jokes are particularly brilliant or outrageous, you would do better with a different subject.

289

3. "I Am Sure I Have Pierced Ears." This subject does not lend itself to detail. What can you write after the first sentence? Why should anyone be interested? Remember that everything you write—every essay, every paragraph, every sentence—has to answer the question "Who cares?"

4. "*The Sun Also Rises*—Hemingway's Masterpiece." This topic is interesting and rich with detail, but it is more suitable to a 300-page book than a 500-word essay. If you wish to write about a novel, you must restrict yourself to one feature of it. Here you could limit yourself to one character ("Robert Cohn—the Outsider") or to one fairly defined theme ("Fishing in Spain—A Symbolic Quest"). Almost invariably, you will choose a subject that's too broad rather than one that's too narrow.

5. "Hank Aaron Was a Better Hitter Than Babe Ruth." This could be a good choice. The subject would interest many readers. It provides a lot of detail—comparison of number of times at bat, number of hits, quality of opposing pitchers, the kinds of baseballs used, sizes of stadiums, and so on. If you keep the focus on batting and avoid discussions of fielding, base-running, and personality, the essay can be finished in 500 words. Another element that makes this a good subject is that it presents a singular opinion. This always adds interest. "Cleanliness Is Important" is a vague truism, but "Cleanliness Is Dangerous" could make a fascinating essay.

6. "How to Clean a Bassoon." This subject lends itself to detail; it can be covered in 500 words; and it is beyond the experience of "all people." But it would have little appeal for most readers.

Of course, if you're a knowledgeable and creative writer (like John McPhee or Tom Wolfe), you can make any subject interesting. And you can imagine particular readers (like your mother) who would respond to any topic you choose. But these exceptions don't change the situation for you. You need a subject that will keep the interest of a fairly general audience.

Probably, you should write on the subjects you know most about and are most interested in. What do you think about? What do you and your friends talk about on Friday night? This is what you'll write best about.

EXERCISES

Which of these subjects would be more likely to produce an interesting 500-word essay? Why?

1. The Virtue of Thrift
2. Space Travel Will Have a Drastic Effect on Contemporary Art
3. A Sure Way to Pick Winners at the Dog Track

4. The Importance of a College Education
5. Computers
6. My Brother Collects Stamps
7. Dogs Are Better Than Cats
8. Racing Cars Perform Mathematically Impossible Feats
9. Kevin Spacey
10. Aspirin, Bufferin, Advil—Somebody's Lying
11. The World Is Ending: Prophecy, Weaponry, and Ecology
12. What Should I Name my Baby?
13. Mozart's Music
14. Viagra
15. Violence in Fairy Tales

Rule 2

Get Your Facts

An interesting theme has to be specific. No one can write a compelling essay on entropy or Barry Bonds or space-age architecture or much else without seeking out a body of factual information. Writing involves research.

Unless you are writing from personal experience, you will probably want to build your theme around people you can quote and facts you can bring forward. You obtain such material from a number of sources.

■ VISIT THE LIBRARY

While most students will do research online, libraries still contain valuable material. Large stores of information can be unearthed by using the card catalog and the *Reader's Guide.* The card catalog, which is probably computerized, lists author, title, and subject for every book in the library. The *Reader's Guide,* under subject headings, lists magazine articles printed over the years.

Most libraries also have *InfoTrac,* a computerized periodical index that lists articles by author, title, subject, and one or more key words. A single key word ("Hillary") gives all articles in the index that are about people by that name. Two key words joined by "and" ("Hillary and Hair") limits the search, probably to articles about Hillary Clinton's hair style.

This list illustrates some of the titles available to you and the kinds of information they contain.

> *Acronyms and Initialisms Dictionary* (What is the N.A.U.I.?)
> *American Movies Reference Book* (Who won the Academy Award as Best Supporting Actor in 1966?)
> *Bartlett's Familiar Quotations* (Who said, "A reformer is a guy who rides through the sewer in a glass-bottomed boat"?

Baseball Encyclopedia (Who was the only major league pitcher to pitch two consecutive no-hit games?)

Benet's *Reader's Encyclopedia* (Who is the hero of Henry James's *The American?*)

Black's Law Dictionary (What is the Miranda rule?)

Book Review Digest (When David Garnett's *Shot in the Dark* was published in 1959, how did critics react to it?)

College Handbook (What is the ratio of male to female students at Loras College?)

Crime in the United States (The FBI Report)(How many aggravated assaults were reported in Madison, Wisconsin, in 1985?)

Current Biography (Name the two daughters of jazzman Chuck Mangione.)

Cyclopedia of Literary Characters (Name the Three Musketeers.)

Dictionary of American History (Who founded the NAACP? When?)

Dictionary of American Slang (What is a "hodad"?)

Dictionary of Classical Mythology (Who is Aemonides?)

Dictionary of Foreign Terms (What does *ignis fatuus* mean?)

Encyclopedia of the Opera (Why couldn't Hoffmann wed his beloved Olympia?)

Facts on File (Why was New York Police Chief John Egan sent to prison in 1974?)

Famous First Facts (Who received the first kidney transplant?)

Funk's *Word Origins and Their Romantic Stories* (What is the source of the word *tantalize* ?)

Gallup Poll (In 1977, what percentage of Americans believed that homosexuality is a condition some people are born with?)

Gray's Anatomy (If you strain the muscles of your thenar eminence, where do you hurt?)

Guinness Book of World Records (How long was the world's longest hot dog?)

International Who's Who (Who is Gaetano Cortesi?)

Interpreter's Bible (What did Jesus mean when he said it is easier for a camel to go through the eye of a needle than for a rich man to enter the kingdom of God?)

McGraw-Hill Encyclopedia of Science and Technology (What are the characteristics of synthetic graphite?)

Menke's *Encyclopedia of Sport* (What golfer and what score won the U.S. Open in 1989?)

Mirkin's *When Did It Happen?* (Name two famous composers born on May 7.)

The Murderers' Who's Who (How did an earlobe figure in the "death" of murderer Charles Henry Schwartz?)

Oxford Companion to Music (What is the Impressionist School of music?)

Oxford English Dictionary (When was the word *fair* first used to mean "average"?)

Prager Encyclopedia of Art (What is the real name of the painting usually called *Whistler's Mother* ?)

Rock Encyclopedia (Who was the lead singer in the original Jeff Beck Group?)

Statistical Abstract of the United States (How many American women used poison to commit suicide in 1986?)

Telephone Directory (any large city)(If you want tickets to a Chicago White Sox game, where should you write? What 800 number can you call?)

The Way Things Work (Why doesn't the ink leak out of your ballpoint pen?)

Webster's Biographical Dictionary (What is Mary McCauley's better-known name? Why is she famous?)

Webster's Dictionary of Proper Names (When and what was the Chicken War?)

Webster's Geographical Dictionary (In what county and state is Black River Falls?)

Who's Who in American Women (What is Linda Ronstadt's birthday?)

World Almanac (Name the junior senator from Oregon. What is the capacity of the Notre Dame stadium?)

World Encyclopedia of the Comics (What was Blondie's maiden name?)

Also, make particular use of the *New York Times Index*. This gives you references to names mentioned in the information-packed newspaper. Many libraries have microfilm collections of the *Times* dating back to the 1890s. Learn to thread the microfilm projector, and you can have a fine time reading how Red Grange scored four touchdowns in ten minutes or how Neil Armstrong walked on the moon.

You will need all these sources to provide facts for your essays. And don't be afraid to ask for help in the library. Most librarians are nice people.

■ USE YOUR TELEPHONE

Libraries employ reference people who spend a good part of every day answering questions over the phone. If you need to know Babe Ruth's batting average in 1928, you can either find the answer in a baseball almanac or phone your local reference librarian, who will look up the information and call you back. (The Public Library in Mobile, Alabama, boasts it answered 227,000 questions last year.)

You can phone others too. If you need to know whether there is an apostrophe in "Diners Club," call an elegant restaurant and ask the cashier. If you have a brief legal question ("What would it cost to change my name?"), phone a lawyer. If you need to know the current price for wastepaper, call a recycling center. For specific information, don't be afraid to call a priest or banker or news reporter or sheriff or insurance agent. Most of these people are willing to help you, and many will be happy to.

When necessary, don't hesitate to call long-distance. Suppose you have to write to "Leslie Johnson" and don't know if the person is male or female. Suppose you're applying for a job and don't know the personnel manager's name. In such cases, call long-distance and get the information you need. These calls are relatively cheap.

■ USE NEW TECHNOLOGY

You can gather many facts without getting up from your computer. A single compact disc (CD-ROM) can hold *The American Heritage Dictionary of the English Language, The Reader's Companion to American History, The Written World III, The Dictionary of Cultural Literacy, Simpson's Contemporary Quotations, Roget's II: The New Thesaurus,* and *The 1996 Information Please Almanac.* At the library, you can use electronic versions of the *Reader's Guide to Periodical Literature,* the *Modern Language Association's Bibliography,* the *Humanities Index,* and other print sources.

You can also use the Internet. Suppose your topic is a children's author, say, Eric Carle or E. B. White. A useful strategy is to enter the key words on a "search engine" (*Google, Yahoo, Lycos, AltaVista, Infoseek,* and *Excite* are popular). Most of these will help you find Carle's and White's bibliographies. They will also provide "links" (you click on these highlighted words or phrases) that will connect you with specific pages devoted to Carle's and White's work. Your next step is to do another computer search to determine which of the primary and secondary sources are on line or in the library.

Don't hesitate to use e-mail or to join a listserv. You can talk to others who are interested in children's writers (although there's no guarantee they'll correspond with you).

Of course, there are pitfalls to gathering facts from computer searches. But careful writers will find ways to handle special difficulties posed by the latest technologies. What would you do in these situations?

- Your teacher assumes more than basic computer literacy, but you don't understand certain terms (What do WWW, Telnet, and HTML stand for? What's a MOO? What's the difference between a Yahoo and an AltaVista search?)

  Ask a knowledgeable friend or go to a librarian for help.

- Your assignment is to write a critical response to the early reviews of E. B. White's *Charlotte's Web*. But you discover most electronic databases on the Internet don't go back more than ten years.

  A trip to the library is unavoidable.

- You're having trouble evaluating information on the Internet.

  There is no reason to accept it as accurate, reliable, or credible unless it meets the same criteria for authority as any print source. (See the chapter on Argument by Authority.)

- You don't know how to document material found in electronic sources. See the appendix to this book on documenting such sources. Many publishers have this information on their web site.

Remember that putting your name on something you've written means you've accurately reported the facts. What you claim to be factual says a lot about your credibility as a writer.

■ WRITE FOR FACTS YOU NEED

Many sources are available to you. U.S. government agencies will send you documents on a range of subjects. Organizations with a cause will send you stacks of literature. (The American Cancer Society and the Tobacco Institute have dozens of pamphlets on smoking and health.) You can base your writing on materials from Common Cause, the National Rifle Association, the Confraternity of Christian Doctrine, Greenpeace, the National Organization for Women, People for the American Way, and any number of Right-to-Life organizations. (When the National Rifle Association was asked to send material that might appear in this book, they responded with a packet that weighed $3\frac{1}{2}$ pounds.)

Two sources deserve special mention. If you want the script of a particular news program, say, *60 Minutes,* write and the network will send you a copy. For anything related to new laws, politics, or government programs, write your senator or representative in Washington. You will *always* get an answer from them.

If you make the effort, you will find plenty of information to give meaning and interest to your argument.

Get your facts right. Factual errors in your writing are just like spelling and punctuation errors. They make you look ignorant or careless. In persuasive writing, they are fatal.

EXERCISES

Use your library and other sources to locate the following information.

1. What was the front-page headline in the *New York Times* on the day you were born?
2. What are the sources of these lines?
   a. "Watchman, what of the night?"
   b. "When in doubt, punt."
3. What causes blue babies?
4. Name the individuals who won more than one Academy Award, Cy Young Award, and Heisman Trophy.
5. What day of the week was June 16, 1904? Why is that day important in English literature?
6. What was the famous crime involving Winnie Ruth Judd?
7. What does *in gremio legis* mean?
8. How many women did Don Giovanni seduce?
9. Name six performers who appeared in the movie *George Washington Slept Here*.
10. What is meant by "filial regression," "blood-packing," "googolplex," and "lycanthropy"?
11. Identify as many of these as you can:

    Sir Andrew Aguecheek
    Asiatic Annie
    Allan Paul Bakke
    Melvin Belli
    William Bennett
    Suzette Charles
    Denton Cooley
    Pete and Frank Gusenberg
    E. D. Hirsch, Jr.
    Nile Kinnick

Nathan P. Leopold, Jr.
Greg Louganis
Captain Midnight
Donald T. Regan
Django Reinhardt
Christopher Robin
Son of Sam
Daley Thompson
Tommy Tittlemouse
Uriah the Hittite
Mike Utely
Johnny Vander Meer
Sigourney Weaver
John A. Zaccaro
Pinchas Zukerman

ALTERNATIVE EXERCISES

Use your library and other sources to locate the following information.

1. What were two of the leading sports stories in the *New York Times* on the day you were born?
2. What are the sources of these lines?
   a. "Hold the fort; I am coming."
   b. "I begin to smell a rat."
3. Name the victims of Jack the Ripper.
4. Give ten words that rhyme with "aggle."
5. In *Cavalleria Rusticana*, who kills Turiddu and why?
6. Give the complete major league batting record of Ernest William Rudolph.
7. Will State Farm pay off on a suicide?
8. Give the source of the words *buxom, cravat, sabotage,* and *vermouth.*
9. What movie stars played *The Duke of West Point* and *The Duchess of Idaho*?
10. Distinguish between *Chapter Two*, Leo II, *Walden Two*, and helium II.
11. Identify as many of these as you can:

    Kathy Boudin
    William H. Bonney
    Reginald Bunthorne
    Paul de Man
    Hilda Doolittle
    Morgan Fairchild

Doctor Fell
Louis Farrakhan
Uri Geller
Bruno Hauptmann
Stephen Hawking
James Huberty
Meadowlark Lemon
Ed "Strangler" Lewis
Marian McPartland
Mercutio
Professor Moriarty
Linus Pauling
Sneaky Pete
Raina Petkoff
Baron Scarpia
Frank Sinkwich
Uncas
Felix Unger
Eldrick Woods
Frank Urban Zoeller

Rule 3

Limit Your Topic
to Manageable Size

Most writing is subject to space and time limitations. You are preparing a magazine advertisement or a campaign document (one page). You are writing an editorial or a letter to the editor (under 1000 words). You are preparing a sermon or an after-dinner speech (20 minutes or less). Rarely will you have an opportunity that will permit (or an audience that will tolerate) a discussion of all aspects of an issue.

Therefore, you must limit your topic. Do not, for example, write about "Dieting." Even "Crash Dieting" is too broad a subject. But you can argue that "Crash Dieting Is Dangerous." Similarly, do not speculate about "America's Unjust Drug Laws"; write "Alabama's Marijuana Laws Violate the Fifth Amendment."

Narrowing a topic is particularly important when you write argument. A vague and rambling essay is never persuasive.

Don't write an "about" essay—that is, a general essay about fishing, about terrorism, about heart disease, or about marriage. These aren't helped by bland titles such as "The Joys of Fishing" or "The Truth about Terrorism." Such unfocused subjects lend themselves to vague generalizations. They produce essays that lack unity and speeches that put an audience to sleep.

Your essay is probably unfocused if it discusses unnamed or hypothetical people, such as "students," "Cora Crazy," "Tom J.," or "a doctor in Florida." When you find yourself writing "some people" or "in life," you can be sure you're in trouble.

You probably shouldn't write about your most serious and profound feelings. You can have a wonderful love and commitment to your father, your spouse, your baby, or your dog. You can have a warm and genuine belief in God or in democracy. But when you write such things on paper, they turn

300

into clichés. The way you love your baby is the way other people love their babies. It's something everyone already knows about. So it's dull.

A good way to focus your topic is to put a space or time limitation on it. Don't write, "My sister is a slob"; say "My sister is a slob. Let me tell you what her junk drawer looks like." Don't write, "My father-in-law is crazy"; say "My father-in-law is crazy. Let me tell you what happened Wednesday night."

A carefully focused essay demands specific detail. You will need these details to keep your reader awake.

EXERCISES

Limit each of these topics; that is, isolate parts that you can discuss in a 500-word essay.

1. Improving American Education
2. Marijuana—A Blessing or a Curse?
3. The Assassination of John Lennon
4. Internet
5. Civil Rights
6. God in Everyday Life
7. Traffic Signs
8. Travel Is Educational
9. Current Slang
10. Extrasensory Perception
11. Frequent Flyer Miles
12. Animals Can Talk
13. Flying the Confederate Flag
14. Zora Neale Hurston's Fiction
15. Hip Hop Music
16. DVD Technology

Rule 4

Organize Your Material

Most essays—and indeed most reports and business letters—are made up of an *introduction,* a *body,* and a *conclusion.* The introduction says, "I am going to write about X." The body discusses X in some organized way. And the conclusion says, "That's what I have to say about X." Good writers keep this pattern from being too obvious, but this is the pattern they use.

■ THE INTRODUCTION

The purpose of the introduction is to catch the reader's attention, to declare your subject, and sometimes to outline the direction of your essay.

The best way to get the reader's interest is to announce your subject and get on with it. You can, of course, try a witty opening ("If my brother had two more IQ points, he would be a tree") or a dramatic one ("I know who killed Jimmy Hoffa"); these might work for you. If you are not confident about such lines, however, it is best to rely on a straightforward opening.

Just say it. Write, "America can't afford nuclear power" or "*Seinfeld* has all the characteristics of a morality play." Then get on with proving your point.

Although you may not seek a dramatic opening line, you should try to avoid sentences that turn off your readers. If you begin your essay by saying, "Time is the auction block of the world" or "Young people today . . . ," it won't make much difference what you write afterward. Nobody will read it.

The line in your opening paragraph that announces the main idea or purpose of your essay is called the *thesis statement.* You may include another sentence with it, giving a general outline the essay will follow.

Most topics can be divided into parts. Your essay praising Ken Griffey, Jr. might discuss his fielding, base-running, and hitting. Your argument against abortion might describe the growth of the fetus month by month. Your analysis of a physical or social problem (lung cancer, skyjacking, etc.) might first describe the effect, then indicate some probable causes.

See how these introductions announce the outline of the essay:

> There can be no doubt that extrasensory perception exists. How else can one explain the results of the Spranches-Malone experiment at UCLA in 1975?
> [The essay will discuss the experiment.]
> Legal abortion is necessary. Otherwise we will be back with vast numbers of women getting amateur surgery in bloody abortion mills.
> [The essay will discuss earlier years: (1) vast numbers of women and (2) bloody surgery.]

Remember, the first paragraph has to give your audience a reason to read on. And it must be short. An opening paragraph should rarely be longer than three lines of type.

■ THE BODY

The introduction and conclusion are little more than a frame surrounding what you have to say. The paragraphs of the body *are* your essay.

Each paragraph presents a unit of your message. This does not mean that each division of your topic, as announced in the introduction, must be covered in one paragraph. In the extrasensory perception (ESP) essay just introduced, your discussion of the UCLA experiment might take two, three, or six paragraphs.

Just as the introduction has a thesis statement announcing what the whole theme is about, so most paragraphs have *topic sentences* telling what they will cover. Usually this is the first sentence. Because they show exactly what the rest of the paragraph will discuss, these are effective topic sentences:

> These gun laws haven't reduced the crime in Cleveland.
> Why did the price of electricity go up in July?
> Secretary Albright was equally unsuccessful with the Arabs.

Your paragraph should not bring in material beyond the scope of the topic sentence. In the paragraph about gun laws in Cleveland, for example, you should not discuss other crime-fighting measures in Cleveland; nor should you mention crime in Detroit.

Topic sentences are also effective in linking paragraphs. In the examples given, the references to "*these* gun laws" and to Secretary Albright's being "*equally* unsuccessful" show a relation to material in previous paragraphs. Words like *therefore, however, such, second,* and *similarly* have the same effect.

Within each paragraph, try to give sentences the same grammatical subject. (In the paragraph on Secretary Albright, the subject of most of the sentences should be "She" or "Albright" or "the Secretary.") If you vary the kinds of sentences, as in the following example, the practice won't seem monotonous.

> A variation popular with *exposé writers* is to make an extravagant claim and then point to conclusive evidence—which happens to be unavailable. *They* argue that superbeings from outer space built Stonehenge and that President Warren G. Harding was murdered by his wife; then *they* regret that evidence is lost in the past. *They* talk confidently about Bigfoot, Atlantis, and the Loch Ness Monster—and then lament that proof remains out of reach. *They* insist that UFOs are extraterrestrial spaceships and that a massive conspiracy led to the attempted assassinations of President Reagan and Pope John Paul II—then *they* protest that government officials and law enforcement agencies are withholding crucial evidence.

Remember that the grammatical subject is not necessarily the first word of a sentence. It may follow an introductory phrase ("After the dance, *he* . . .") or clause ("When Kathy remembered the accident, *she* . . .").

In some paragraphs, keeping the same subject will prevent you from saying what you want. Or it can make your writing seem stilted and artificial. In such cases, don't do it.

Here's an important point. *Avoid long paragraphs.* Part of writing well is making someone want to read your work, and people are turned off when they face long blocks of single-spaced print. (Think how you feel beginning a chapter in your sociology textbook.) Use short paragraphs, headings, blank space between sections, indented material, bullets, lists, and similar devices to make your ideas easy to read. *Write with white space.* (Notice how material is laid out on these pages.)

When in doubt about whether to begin a new paragraph, always begin the paragraph.

■ THE CONCLUSION

The last paragraph of your essay echoes the introduction. It summarizes and generalizes about the subject discussed.

Unless your paper is long or particularly complicated, you don't need to restate the structural outline. ("In this theme, I have discussed first the language of Mark's gospel, then its historical qualities, and finally its theology.") Instead, just give a sentence or two expressing the main point. Here are some acceptable concluding paragraphs:

> Mark's gospel is more like a sermon than a biography. It is a work of profound faith and impressive artistry.
>
> No one favors abortion. But we have to admit that, in many cases, it is the only humane alternative.
>
> The Spranches-Malone experiment proves conclusively that ESP exists. Now we have to figure out what we can do with it.

Keep your conclusions short.

EXERCISE

Discuss the strengths and weaknesses of this essay. Consider the thesis statement, the topic sentences, transitions between paragraphs, keeping the same subject within a paragraph, unity of a paragraph, and so on.

READING POETRY

All my life I have hated poetry. I hated it in high school, in grade school, and in the sophomore poetry course I've just completed here at Georgia Southern. Why we serious students have to study jingled nonsense, I will never know.

I live in Reedsburg, a community of farmers, merchants, and practical people. Nevertheless, the Reedsburg Grade School subjected me to all sorts of frivolous and impractical poetry. From the first grade on, my class endured semester after semester of cute rhyme. We read teddy-bear poems from *Winnie the Pooh*. We read Mother Goose rhymes about Simple Simon, and Robert Louis Stevenson poems about a "friendly cow all red and white." We read jingles telling us to drink our milk. I always wondered why the poets didn't just *say* things instead of chanting and jingling them. It was silly.

I had some poetry in Reedsburg High School too. However, I escaped much of it by signing up for speech classes. In speech, I studied more sensible subjects. I learned to think on my feet. I learned to make a talk interesting by referring to the audience and adding humor. Most important, I learned to say things directly, without all the cute ornament of poetry.

The sophomore poetry class I've just finished at Georgia Southern has only made me dislike poems more. Mr. Remington, my instructor, was incompetent. The way he read them, all poems sounded just alike. When he wasn't mumbling about Shelley, we were taking impossible tests on Keats and nightingales. Either it was assumed we knew everything about epics or he was talking down to the class as though we had never heard of metaphor. The day before the final exam, he didn't even show up for class. The whole quarter was a waste of time.

In fact, all the poetry discussions I've had from grade school up to now have been a waste of time. I just don't like poetry.

EXERCISES

How effective are these first paragraphs? After seeing each introduction, would you read the rest of the message? Why or why not?

1. Here is the information you asked for about the No. 2 chimney. It looks like we may have trouble with it.
2. I want to tell you about the three C's of a good marriage: commitment, communication, and common sense.
3. It's been proven: Diet drinks cause cancer.
4. This is to record the conversation we had yesterday about responsibility for the new computer programs.
5. Young people today must learn a new set of priorities. The future of our nation depends on it.
6. There are a lot of keen church-going people in Mobile, Alabama, but they can't tell you the religious truths I can. My Baptist friends can't; the priests at my church can't. Even the high-powered Jesuits at Spring Hill College can't. They don't read the tabloids.
7. The programs and actions growing out of libertine thought and its ideologies have put society in bondage to the indifferent with disturbing results. It strikes me in this manner.
8. Kobe Bryant did it again last night!

Rule 5

Make Your Writing Interesting

Remember that no one *has* to read your writing. And if people have to hear your speech, they don't have to pay attention. The burden is on you to make your subject interesting.

This is not a huge task. If you have a topic you think is important, and if you present it with clarity and specific detail, your audience will pay attention.

Generally, you maintain interest by avoiding certain practices that deaden language.

■ TRUISMS

Do not say what everyone knows. Don't be like actress Brooke Shields, who told a congressional subcommittee, "Smoking can kill you. And if you've been killed, you've lost a very important part of your life."

Your readers will not be thrilled to hear that third-degree burns are painful or that the president of the United States bears great responsibilities. Don't write, "Every great man has moments of profound sorrow, but Thomas Eaton's life was genuinely tragic." Write, "Thomas Eaton's life was tragic."

■ CLICHÉS

Some phrases have lost meaning through overuse. Your writing will lose emphasis and interest if you use tired phrases like these:

above and beyond
acid test
and . . . was no exception

at this point in time
at your earliest convenience
beginner's luck
bottom line
constructive criticism
could care less
the cutting edge
down to the wire
few and far between
first and foremost
the heart of the matter
in a very real sense
an in-depth study
is invaluable
last but not least
let's face it
meaningful relationship
needs no introduction
nitty-gritty
pure and simple
on the other hand
share this idea with you
shoot yourself in the foot
slowly but surely
sneaking suspicion
snow job
state-of-the-art
status quo
touch base with
uncanny ability
user-friendly
viable alternative
win-win situation

Watch out for emerging clichés—words that were once new and colorful but are now becoming overused. There's a danger in writing about an "awesome" blonde, a "Type-A" personality, or a "Catch-22" situation. The language is losing force even as you read this sentence.

A good rule: If you suspect a particular phrase is a cliché, it is. Don't use it.

Remember that avoiding a cliché can produce a rich substitution. A CBS sports announcer once described a Green Bay quarterback not as "cool as a cucumber" but "cool as the other side of the pillow."

Some readers will find clichés insulting. If you write "In conclusion, do not hesitate to contact me at your earliest convenience," you're saying you don't care enough to really talk to them; you're just giving them a set of words. It's like telling someone "You're wonderful. I love you. This is a recording."

■ GENERALIZED LANGUAGE

The point cannot be overemphasized: *To be interesting, you must be specific.* Let's call this "the Ginger Principle." (You'll see why in a minute.)

Write of real things. Use proper names, words that begin with capital letters. (Don't say "lunch"; say "a Big Mac.") Use real numbers. (Don't say "a lot"; say "725.") Give specific places, dates, and quotations. You can, for example, refer to the same person in a number of ways:

an athlete
a ball player
a baseball player
an outfielder
a right fielder
Yankees' right fielder
Bobby Abreau

Always choose the most specific word that serves the purposes of your essay. Good writing uses proper names.

Generally, your ideas will be more interesting if you can avoid the words *good, bad,* and forms of *to be.* Substituted words are always more meaningful. Instead of "good," write "even-tempered," "inexpensive," "compassionate," or "crisp." Instead of "bad," write "moldy," "pretentious," "degenerate," or "unfair."

Similarly, try to avoid forms of the verb *to be*—that is, the words *is, are, was, were, am,* and *been.* Much of the time, you will have to use these words, of course, but substitutions are usually more effective. For example, "Sue Walker *was* injured" becomes "Sue Walker smashed two bones in her right foot." And "The weather *was* horrible" becomes "Eight inches of snow fell on Buffalo yesterday." (Some scholars have designated the English language without *to be* forms as "E-prime.")

To see the degree of interest that specific detail can give a sentence, compare Irving Berlin's lyric "I'll be loving you always" with George Kaufman's suggested emendation, "I'll be loving you Thursday."

The best way to win interest is to force a lot of real names and numbers in your prose. Don't write, "His cousin drove me to a nearby woods, and we sat drinking beer and listening to music until very late." Write, "Ginger drove me over to Johnson's Woods, and we sat in her red Ford Expedition till four in the morning. We drank a six-pack of Coors and listened to her Willie Nelson tapes." Look at the "Ginger" in those sentences. This kind of writing doesn't just tell you of an event, it *shows* you.

Another good rule: *Don't write about nobody.* Look at this infirm passage: "The American public is tired of football. People are bored by all the hype. Every time you turn on your TV set, you see another ad for the Super Bowl." Here, the words "public," "people," and "you" refer to nobody in particular. They express a dull generalization. Write of real people—Jessie Jackson, Carrie Nation, or yourself. Say, "Every time *I* turn on my TV set, *I* see another ad for the Super Bowl."

This doesn't mean you can't generalize. It means that when you want to talk about the generation gap, you begin "I can't talk to my mother."

■ INFLATED LANGUAGE

Except in rare cases, you will want your writing to be clear. To do this, keep your language as simple and direct as possible. When addressing a general audience, try to avoid these forms:

> Foreign words—*bête noir, ne plus ultra, coup d'état*
> Learned words—*penultimate, symbiotic, alumna, iconicity*
> Poetic words—*repine, oft, betimes, betoken*
> Technical words—*input, societal, kappa numbers*
> Odd singular and plural forms—*datum, stadia, syllabi, curriculum vitae*
> Literary allusions—*Lot's wife, protean, the sword of Damocles*
> Current in-words—*paradigm, viable, ambience*

Such words are more acceptable if you are writing for an educated or specialized audience. But a really fine writer wouldn't use them there either.

Reading William F. Buckley's column in your morning newspaper can be a useful exercise. You, like almost everyone else, will stop reading early on, probably at his first reference to "biblical irredentism." Columnist James J. Kilpatrick gave writers a useful rule. He wrote, "Whenever we feel the impulse to use a marvelously exotic word, let us lie down until the impulse goes away."

Write with everyday words, words you would say. Don't use "in view of the above" or "for the above reasons"; write "consequently" or "for these reasons." Try not to use "the addressee," "the executrix," "the former," or "the latter"; write "Ruth Sampson" (or "she" or "her"). Never refer to yourself as "the writer" (or "we"); say "I."

The next time you hear a dull lecture or sermon, don't tune it out. Ask yourself why it is dull. Probably you're hearing a collection of truisms, clichés, and vague or inflated phrases. You can learn from such examples.

EXERCISES

Rewrite these sentences, making them more likely to sustain the interest of a general audience.

1. This insult was the last straw. I decided to leave Marcia, and I spent the next few hours preparing for the trip.
2. The Book of Jonah illustrates the ludicrous intractability of a particular mind-set.
3. Scott Daniel was a fine basketball player. I believe he was the best to play in the league in the last 20 years. He was really fine.
4. Vis-à-vis our tête-à-tête, I must say the rendezvous filled me with ennui.
5. It is true that some rhetorics have denied their imbrication in ideology, doing so in the name of a disinterested scientism.
6. Driving the L.A. freeway is like crossing the river Styx.
7. In the following weeks at school, I worked frantically. Every day I became busier and busier.
8. As we entered the restaurant, Nick stated that the chicken there was good but the service was bad.
9. In the final analysis, there are few rugged individualists in this day and age who are really down to earth in expressing nothing but the truth about the seamy side of life. Perhaps in the near future . . .
10. We will never know everything about the atom, but some of the recent discoveries have been fascinating.
11. Graduate school can be a procrustean bed.
12. Sorting on the part of mendicants should be interdicted.

Rule 6

Make Your Writing Emphatic

Sometimes unnecessary words or particular word-forms detract from the point you want to make. These recommendations should help you emphasize the important ideas in your writing.

■ AVOID WORDINESS

Unnecessary words may bore or antagonize your reader. Say what you have to say as briefly as possible. Too often writers use a series of words where one word will do.

> *am of the opinion that* = believe
> *due to the fact that* = because
> *the man with the dark complexion* = the dark man
> *people who are concerned only with themselves* = selfish people
> *I disagree with the conclusion offered by Professor Nelson* = I disagree with Professor Nelson.

Certain phrases have extra words built into them. You don't need to write "end result," "component parts," "advance planning," "large sized," or similar forms. Omit the extra word.

Some introductory forms can usually be dispensed with:

> Needless to say . . .
> Let me say that . . .
> It is important to recognize the fact that . . .

And commonly one or more words appear where none are necessary.

Molly *really* is a *very* beautiful girl.
Personally, I agree with him.
I asked whether *or not* the twins looked alike.
I dislike his personality *and his temperament.*
There were several people at the party *who* saw the fight.

Eighty percent of the time, you can omit words ending in "ly." Ninety percent of the time, you can delete "very." You'll never need to put three adjectives before a noun, and you should try to avoid using two.

Don't worry about wordiness when you're putting together the first draft of your essay; just get down what you have to say. It's in rewriting that you can change "And I think it is necessary to add that Tom wasn't there" to the more forceful phrase "Tom was not there."

▨ WRITE IN THE ACTIVE VOICE

In sentences written in the active voice, the grammatical subject is the acting agent. ("*The Brezinsky Commission* has attacked public apathy.") In sentences written in the passive voice, the subject receives the action of the verb. ("*Public apathy* has been attacked by the Brezinsky Commission.")

You can use the passive voice in sentences where the acting agent is obvious or irrelevant ("The president was reelected") or where you want to deliver bad news and avoid personal involvement ("The decision is to buy our supplies from a different source" or "Your contract will not be renewed next year").

A world-class use of the passive voice occurred during the Iran-Contra hearings. When a committee member asked what happened to some implicating documents, Colonel Oliver North answered, "I think they were shredded."

Generally the passive voice is a bad thing. It doesn't sound natural and seems wordy and evasive. Where you want particular emphasis, it can produce a mushy effect: "Home runs were hit by both pitchers during the game."

Often, using the active voice means beginning your sentence (or beginning the main clause of your sentence) with acting agents: *we, she, Jim Phillips,* or *the Brezinsky Commission.* This gives force and directness to your prose. Try to avoid forms that keep you from doing this. Here are some examples:

My intention is . . .
It was soon evident that . . .
There were . . .

. . . was seen
. . . could be heard
The assumption was that . . .

If you are writing a personal essay, begin most sentences (or main clauses) with *I*.

Think of the passive voice as you do a visit to the dentist. It's necessary sometimes, but you want to avoid it when you can.

■ EXPRESS YOUR MAIN IDEA IN THE SUBJECT-VERB OF YOUR SENTENCE

Make the subject-verb unit of your sentence express your main thought. Put less important information in modifying phrases and clauses.

Don't write your main point as a modifying phrase ("Harold Lord slipped in the outfield, *thus breaking his arm*") or as a *that* clause ("I learned *that Aunt Rita has been arrested for arson*"). Give your point subject-verb emphasis: "Harold Lord slipped in the outfield and broke his arm"; "Aunt Rita was arrested for arson."

■ DO NOT WASTE THE ENDS OF YOUR SENTENCES

Because the end of a sentence is the last thing a reader sees, it is a position of emphasis. Don't use it to express minor thoughts or casual information. Don't write, "Both candidates will speak here in July, if we can believe the reports." This is effective only if you want to stress the doubtfulness of the reports. Don't write, "Pray for the repose of the soul of John Bowler, who died last week in Cleveland." Your reader will wonder what he was doing in Cleveland. Notice how emphasis trails away in a sentence like this:

> The B-1 bomber, a brainchild of the U.S. Air Force and Rockwell International, is trying a comeback as one of America's leading defense weapons after President Carter, in June 1977, put a stop to the plans to complete the project.

For particular emphasis, write your thought in subject-verb form and give the unit an end-of-the-sentence position. Don't write, "The union reluctantly approved the contract." Write, "The union approved the contract, but they didn't want to do it."

Because the beginning of a sentence also conveys a degree of emphasis, you should not waste that position either. Try to put words like "however," "therefore," and "nevertheless" in the middle of sentences. ("The mail carrier, however, didn't come till five o'clock.") Don't do this if it makes your sentence sound awkward.

KEEP YOUR SENTENCES RELATIVELY SHORT

To avoid a monotonous style, you should build your essay with sentences of different kinds and lengths. But using short or relatively short sentences will help you avoid difficulty.

When sentences go beyond 15 or 20 words, punctuation—which can be a problem—becomes complicated; meaning gets diffuse; pronouns are separated from the words they refer to; and the reader or listener finds it difficult to see the continuity and may lose interest. Short sentences are better.

When you finish a sentence of reasonable length, fight the temptation to extend it by adding a unit beginning "which" or "when" or "because" or "according to" or some other "-ing" form. Put the additional material in a new sentence.

If you're typing, try to end your sentence within two lines of type. Only rarely should it go beyond three lines.

KEEP YOUR DOCUMENT AS SHORT AS POSSIBLE

Don't waste your audience's time.

Remember the purposes of your writing are to be read and to win a particular effect from your readers. Probably you won't do either if your document is too long.

If you turn in a 40-page report at work, your boss will be frustrated. If you write a 6-page sales letter, people will throw it away. When Ann Landers receives letters of 10 pages or more, she concludes, "These people need professional help."

You can write long term-papers for your school classes, however. Here, there is no purpose other than to show how much you know. And no one, except your instructor, has to read them.

Your writing will be longer or shorter as the subject and occasion require. But keep it as short as possible. You can learn from the emphatic message that appeared on bulletin boards at a southern university. It said, "Free Kittens. 342–7098."

EXERCISES

What changes would make the meaning of these sentences more emphatic?

1. I was born in the city of Chicago, Illinois.
2. Trapped in a drab life with a dull husband, Hedda Gabler shoots herself, partly because she is threatened by Judge Brack.
3. The eagle suddenly loosed its grip, allowing me to escape.
4. Though I had more than several reasons to dislike and distrust Libby MacDuffee before the accident, I found still more when she tried to take me to court to pay for the hospital costs and when she claimed I had had three martinis at the Pink Pony Pub an hour (or at the most two hours) before the wreck.
5. Reviewing the history, we found that the team was weak on basic fundamentals and that the average age of the players was 17 years old.
6. Nevertheless, I must refuse your kind offer.
7. His hope was that he could conquer Paris by June.
8. Although Jeannine feared flying, she took the 9:02 flight from Milwaukee, being already two days late for the convention.
9. This book concerns itself with language intended to deceive.
10. It was greatly feared by the crowd that an honest decision would not come from the referee.
11. I'm very sorry to hear you recently and tragically crashed your new red Cutlass convertible.
12. Guilt is a fact of life, an emotion that everyone has to deal with constantly, which is no surprise when you consider that guilt is the subject of more fiction and nonfiction than any other emotion.
13. With the great potential for savings existing, the implementation stage of the project should immediately be proceeded with.

Rule 7

Avoid Language That
Draws Attention to Itself

You want your audience to follow your ideas, to follow the argument you're developing. Don't break their attention by using odd words or phrases that catch their eye. Try to avoid these distracting forms.

■ SEXIST LANGUAGE

If you want to persuade your audience, you can't use words that offend them. And today, many people—of both sexes—are turned off by terms they consider offensive to women. They don't like masculine forms of words used in references that can apply to either men or women. Here are some examples:

chair*man*
spokes*man*
man kind
man power
all *men* are created equal
everyone did *his* best
a doctor earns *his* money
separate the *men* from the *boys*
take it like a *man*

Don't use this kind of language.

Find synonyms. Instead of "chairman," "spokesman," and "manpower," write "chair," "advocate," and "work force." Instead of "mankind" and "all men," write "humanity" or "all people." When you come to "a doctor earns

317

his money," go plural—"doctors earn their money." Rewriting "separate the men from the boys" and "take it like a man" can call for some creativity. Try "separate the winners from the losers" and "shape up."

Avoid "his or her" whenever you can; it always sounds artificial.

Unless there's a reason for it, don't mention gender. The best way to denote a woman doctor is to say "a doctor." (This is also the best way to refer to an African American doctor, a homosexual doctor, or a doctor who uses a wheelchair.)

■ REPETITION

Repeating a word for emphasis can be effective ("government of the *people,* by the *people,* and for the *people*"), but often it distracts attention. Avoid repetition of sentence forms ("I went to see the accident. Fifteen people were there. Each told a different story."); of particular words ("Going to school is not going to be easy. If the going gets tough . . ."); and even of sounds ("The black boxer was bloody, beaten, and battered.").

Don't write three adjectives in a row. ("Suzanne is a lovely, energetic, red-haired girl.") This becomes a habit.

Time magazine once wrote of a New York police officer with problems. It said, "The people he works for have cases to break, headlines to make, careers at stake." *Time* can write that way occasionally, but you shouldn't.

■ DANGLING AND MISPLACED MODIFIERS

Make it clear what words your adjectives and adverbs are modifying. You do this by putting modifiers close to the words they refer to. Avoid examples like these:

> *When nine years old,* my grandmother took me to the circus.
> He was reported drowned *by the Coast Guard.*
> Dr. Ruth talked about sex *with newspaper editors.*
> *By knowing what you want to say,* your essay will progress more easily.

Notice that these sentences are clear enough; in context, your reader would know what they mean. But such awkward and even humorous lines draw attention to themselves and away from your meaning.

ELABORATE FIGURES OF SPEECH

A mixed metaphor often produces irrelevant laughter. ("You're the salt of the earth and the light of the world, but you've thrown in the towel.") Even a meaningful figure of speech can be distracting. You could write, "Carter steered the ship of state over treacherous seas; he was a star-crossed president." Such a sentence, however, stops your readers. Instead of following the rest of your ideas, they pause to interpret the metaphor.

You will, of course, want to use figures of speech in your prose. But don't let them obscure your meaning by being too dramatic:

Auto sales got a big *shot in the arm* in March from the price slashes.

Or pointless:

Lee Bailey wore a suit *the color of a thousand-dollar bill.*

Or redundant:

At the wedding, the champagne *flowed like wine.*

Or strange:

When God fights your battles, He *does it in spades.*

Remember that if you keep a metaphor simple, it can create an effective argument. Consider the force of the ad "Happiness is a Met Life security blanket."

FAULTY PARALLELISM

You should express coordinate ideas in similar form. You do this mainly to avoid awkward and distracting sentences. Clearly, "I was *alone, uncertain,* and *possessed of a considerable degree of fear*" is less emphatic than "I was *alone, uncertain,* and *afraid.*" Consider these examples:

The teachers were burdened with *large classes, poor textbooks,* and *the necessity to cope with an incompetent principal.*
I love *seeing my daughter* and *to hear her voice.*
For a settlement, I will accept *a new stove* or *having my old stove repaired.*

Some sentences cannot be made parallel. You cannot change "Ted was tall, charming, and wore a blue hat" to "Ted was tall, charming, and blue-hatted." In such cases, write the first units so your reader doesn't expect the final one to be parallel. Write, "Ted was tall and charming; he always wore a blue hat."

Many of these problems occur when you write units in a series. You don't have to write units in a series.

▦ AWKWARD CONSTRUCTIONS

Try to give your sentences the sound of talk, of natural speech. Don't break the continuity with intrusive passages.

> I promised to, *if the expected raise came through,* take her to the Grand Hotel.
> Her brother, *if we can believe local historians (and who can),* was a senator.

Any time your subject is six words away from your verb, you're probably in trouble.

Avoid noun clusters. Business and technical writers sometimes seek a kind of forceful compression and talk of a "once-in-a-lifetime, million-dollar career-decision dilemma." In doing so, they produce sentences a person has to read twice to understand. It is better to write in a natural speaking voice.

Don't seek a poetic style by inverting word order. Don't write. "Quiet was the night" or "The reason for his suicide, we shall never know."

Keep it natural. Where it sounds all right, don't be afraid to begin a sentence with "And" or to end it with a preposition. ("And suddenly I realized where the money had come from.") And don't let some dated English textbook persuade you to say, "If he had been *I,* he would have paid the bill." You *know* how that sounds.

▦ ABRUPT CHANGES IN TONE

Your tone is your personal voice, your way of saying things. This will vary with your audience and your subject. You talk one way to an intimate friend and another way to a visiting archbishop. You could use a formal style when writing a letter of application, and you might use colloquial—or even coarse—language in describing your golf game.

It is important to keep your tone appropriate and consistent. Don't jar your reader by describing a United Nations charter provision as a "crap-headed experiment." And don't call a fraternity dining room "a haven of calculated insouciance."

Writing the informal style, you will want to use contractions ("can't," "wouldn't"). But do this from the beginning of your essay. Don't start to use them in the middle of a relatively formal paper.

Remember that any time your reader is more impressed by your writing than by your meaning, you have failed. No one can improve on the advice lexicographer Samuel Johnson gave in the eighteenth century. He said, "Read over your composition, and where ever you meet with a passage which you think is particularly fine, strike it out."

EXERCISES

Correct weaknesses in these sentences.

1. Clemens was pitching beautifully until the seventh inning, and then the fireworks fell in.
2. When reading late at night, the book should be held under a strong light.
3. Juan Perón's rise to power was a slow one. There were many pit stops.
4. We traveled for six days, and the car broke down. We hitchhiked to Laredo, and I took a job gardening. I had the car towed into town, but no one there could fix it.
5. I'm sorry about the story, Laurie. It's as bad as your messy essay. I warned you frequently to rewrite your work.
6. Mrs. L. Williamson earned her Ph.D. studying DNA at M.I.T.
7. Cancer hit my family with full force this year, sending two of my aunts to the Mayo Clinic.
8. Pamela was pretty, energetic, and carried a file of history notes.
9. The movie producers saw *Heaven's Gate* and immediately removed it from circulation. They could smell the handwriting on the wall.
10. Every engineer must get his work in on time.
11. Roman Catholics tend to be uptight about premarital sex. Episcopalians are more laid back.
12. When you go to the doctor, it costs you an arm and a leg.
13. Jim is tragically confined to a wheelchair. Fortunately, he is married to a woman doctor.
14. The treatment will take several months. You can't overcome overconfidence overnight.
15. The university published the names of faculty members broken down by sex.

Rule 8

Avoid Mechanical Errors

Due to a typing error, Gov. Dukakis was incorrectly identified in the third paragraph as Mike Tyson.

FROM A CORRECTION IN THE FITCHBURG-LEOMINSTER (MASS.) SENTINEL AND ENTERPRISE

To write effectively, you need to know a number of elementary rules of usage. But there are some you don't have to know. An important truth is expressed in this story.

> A man went to his doctor and described his ailment. Clinching his right fist tightly, he complained, "It hurts me when I go like that." The doctor prescribed the remedy. He said, "Don't go like that."

The story tells you many things about writing: how to punctuate long and involved sentences, where to put apostrophes in unusual constructions, the way to use quotation marks within quotation marks, and how to spell "bourgeoisie." The advice: "Don't go like that."

The following rules on punctuation, abbreviation, number, and spelling should take you through most writing situations.

▰ PUNCTUATION

Use *Commas* to Make Your Sentence Easier to Read

Textbooks routinely tell you to put a comma before the conjunction in a compound sentence ("Pam is a good student, but she cannot learn economics"); after introductory clauses ("When I went home, I saw my brother's car"); and before the *and* in elements in a series ("I bought a suit, three ties, and a sweater"). The problem is that many professional writers don't punctuate like this. Hence you may be confused.

A good rule is this: Always use commas in these constructions *when the sentences are long.*

> Arthur had traveled 57 miles through the desert to meet the prince, and he knew that nothing in the world could make him turn back now.
> When I saw that the young soldier was holding a gun on Martha and me, I became most obedient.
> Suddenly Henry saw that the parable applied to him, that he must change his life, and that the time to start was now.

Similarly, you should always insert commas in these constructions when there is a danger of misreading. Consider these sentences:

> The fox ate three chickens and the rooster ran away.
> When they finished eating cigarettes were distributed to the soldiers.
> They stopped looking for Irene became tired.

If you use normal word order (a "talking" voice) and keep your sentences relatively short, you should have little difficulty with commas.

Use a *Semicolon* to Show that Two Independent Clauses Are Closely Related

Sometimes you want to indicate the particularly close relationship between two statements. Here you merge the statements into one sentence and connect them with a semicolon.

> Her brother has been sick for years; now he is going to die.
> To know her is to love her; to love her is a mistake.

This construction often occurs when the second statement contains "however," "therefore," "consequently," or "nevertheless."

> The 747 was two hours late getting into O'Hare; consequently, he missed his connection to Reno.
> Billy wanted to propose during final-exam week; he saw, however, that this would cause problems.

You can also use semicolons to separate the halves of a compound sentence, or the units in a series, when the separated passages have commas within them.

My boss, Patrick Henderson, was there; but before I could talk to him, he fell and broke his arm.

Among those present were Dr. Williams, an English professor; Mrs. Damico, head of the Presbyterian meeting; and Mrs. Milliken, president of the PTA.

If you have problems punctuating such long sentences, don't write them. You can write acceptable prose and never use a semicolon.

Use a *Colon* to Introduce a Unit

You use a colon to introduce something: an announcement, a clarification, or a formal series.

In May, the professor made his decision: he would leave the university.

The difference between fathers and sons used to be a simple one: fathers earned the money, and sons spent it.

Molly excelled in active sports: tennis, swimming, badminton, and gymnastics.

When a complicated sentence follows a colon, the first word may be capitalized—especially if the sentence is long. ("In May, the professor made his decision: He would leave the university, move to Cleveland, and take a position with the Pater Academy.")

In general, you shouldn't use a colon except after a complete statement. Don't write, "Her favorites were: Andy Williams, Tim Conway, and Brack Weaver." Write, "These were her favorites: Andy Williams, Tim Conway, and Brack Weaver." Or (even better) "Her favorites were Andy Williams, Tim Conway, and Brack Weaver."

It is permissible to use a colon after "the following." ("He did it for the following reasons: . . .") But when you can avoid it, don't write "the following" at all. It's not something you would *say*. (Write, "He did it for several reasons: . . ." or "He did it for these reasons: . . .")

Use an *Exclamation Mark* to Show Emphasis

Because adding an exclamation mark is an easy way to gain emphasis, you may be tempted to overuse it. Try to reserve it for "Wow!" or "Fire!" or a choice obscenity.

Never use two or more exclamation marks to seek additional emphasis. Never!

Use a *Question Mark* After a Direct Question

You will, of course, put a question mark after a question. But be sure it is a direct question.

What can they do in 12 minutes?
He asked, "Did you see Sylvia there?"

Don't use a question mark after an indirect question or after a question form that is really a polite command.

She asked if I knew the way to school.
Will you please hand in your blue-books now.

Use *Hyphens* to Form Compound Adjectives and to Divide Words at the End of a Line

Use a hyphen to join a compound adjective when it *precedes* a noun. You can write "the theory is out of date," or you can call it "an out-of-date theory." In such examples, the hyphens make your meaning clearer:

a Monday-morning quarterback
a dog-in-the-manger attitude
a long-term investment
germ-free research
a 40-pound weight

Remember there is a big difference between "an Oriental-art expert" and "an Oriental art-expert."

Hyphens are particularly necessary to make sense of the noun clusters that occur in technical writing. An engineer may refer to "polyethylene coated milk carton stock smoothness test results." What does that mean? It becomes clearer with hyphens: "Polyethylene-coated milk-carton-stock smoothness-test results." But it is usually better to keep the hyphens and rewrite the phrase: "The results of smoothness-tests conducted on polyethylene-coated milk-carton stock."

When using combination words, you often don't know whether the form should be written as one word ("shutdown"), as two words ("check out"), or as a hyphenated unit ("loose-leaf"). If you can't find a rule to guide you, go ahead and hyphenate the words.

Use a hyphen to divide a word at the end of a line. But remember that you must divide the word between syllables ("when-ever," "in-tern," "pho-bia"). You should not divide a word so that only one letter appears on a line ("a-bout," "phobi-a"); and you should never separate a one-syllable word ("doubt," "called," "proved").

If you don't know where to divide a word, consult your dictionary. If you don't have a dictionary at hand, don't divide the word. Write it all on the next line. (That's how your word processor does it.)

Use *Parentheses* to Tuck in Extra Material

Parentheses are useful. They let you include additional information without breaking the continuity of your message. As these examples show, you can tuck in dates, examples, clarifications, and anything else you want.

> Nicholas wrote *Corners of Adequacy* (1981) to answer charges made against his father.
> Dylan Thomas (1914–1953) was a Welsh poet and an alcoholic.
> Some foreign words (*Gemütlichkeit,* for example) can't be easily translated into English.
> His wife (he married about a year ago) was barely five feet tall.

Don't misuse parentheses. Don't use them to set off material that is necessary in the sentence.

> "Nice" (in the old sense of "discriminating") is seldom used anymore.

And don't use parentheses so often that they call attention to themselves. If you use too many in your sentence (i.e., more than two or three), you can lose (or antagonize) your reader (especially if he or she is concerned about writing style).

Use a *Dash* Where You Need It

Like commas and parentheses, dashes can be used to set off an element. If you want to set off an idea that is closely related to your sentence, use commas. ("My father, who always loved fruit, died eating an orange.") To set off a unit that is less closely related, use dashes (or parentheses). ("My father—he would have been 39 next month—died eating an orange.")

Indeed, a dash—used in moderation—is acceptable punctuation in many circumstances.

> Don't bet on Red Devil—he's a loser.
> He thought about the situation for weeks—never able to get it all together.
> It became clear that only one man could be the murderer—Dr. Dorrill.

The dash is a handy mark of punctuation. Just don't overuse it.

▆ APOSTROPHES, QUOTATION MARKS, ITALICS, AND CAPITAL LETTERS

Use *Apostrophes* to Show Possession, to Indicate an Omission, and to Form Unusual Plurals

As a general rule, you show possession by adding *'s* to any singular or plural noun that doesn't end in *s*.

the dog's collar
the woman's hand
Haley's smile
the men's boots

For nouns ending in *s,* you add either an *'s* or simply a final apostrophe. Punctuate it the way you say it; add the *'s* where you pronounce the extra syllable.

the girls' room
the Clardys' house
James's reign
the Harris's car

(In describing the Hiss-Chambers case, most commentators write of *Chambers'* accusations and *Hiss's* response.)

Sometimes you can avoid problems by not using apostrophes at all. The sentence "It is the company's policy to be ready for auditors' inspection," can also be written "It is company policy to be ready for auditor inspection."

In more complicated cases, it is best to avoid the issue. Don't speculate on how to punctuate "Charles and Bobs television," "Jesus parables," or "the last three months pay." Write "the television Charles and Bob bought last June," "the parables of Jesus," and "pay for the last three months."

You also use apostrophes to replace omitted letters or numbers in contractions ("I've," "couldn't," "the class of '45") and to form unusual plurals.

A formal essay is not full of you's.
Today Ph.D.'s can't get jobs.
I got one A and four C's.

Usage is changing here. Many respectable authors no longer use apostrophes in these constructions. They write of "Ph.D.s" and "Cs."

If you wonder whether you need an apostrophe with proper names (like "Veterans Administration") or brand names (like "French's mustard"), there is no rule to help you. The correct form is whatever the organizations use. In a difficult case, you may have to consult magazines, advertisements, or letterheads. You may have to phone for information or drive to your shopping center.

You need to include brand names in your writing because such details give color and interest to your prose. But the names do create apostrophe problems, especially if you're trying to champion "Miller" beer over "Stroh's" and "Coors." This list gives some of the more common trade names and shows how complicated apostrophes can be.

Benson & Hedges cigarettes
Betty Crocker cake mix
Bride's magazine
Brooks Brothers clothes
Campbell's soup
Consumers' Research magazine
Diners Club
Dole pineapple
Elmer's glue
Folgers coffee
Häagen-Dazs ice cream
Hertz rent-a-car
Hunt's ketchup
Jergen's lotion
Johnson wax
Kellogg's cereal
Ladies' Home Journal
L'eggs pantyhose
Levi's jeans
L'Oréal hair products
McDonald's hamburgers
Myers' rum
Oscar Mayer meats
O'Shaughnessy's whiskey
Parents magazine
Parsons' ammonia
Phillips 66 gasoline
Phillips' milk of magnesia
Planters peanuts
Pond's cold cream
Popeyes chicken
Reader's Digest
Sears
Stroh Light beer

Wards
Wilson sporting goods
Woolworth's
Wrigley's gum

Nobody knows all these forms. The difference between a good and a bad writer is that a good writer takes the trouble to check out such things.

Use *Quotation Marks* to Enclose the Exact Words of a Source, Titles of Short Works, a Word Used as a Word, and (Sometimes) Words Used in an Odd or Ironic Sense

Use quotation marks to enclose material taken directly from a book or person.

> In 1955, Aaron Mitchell wrote that the failure of democracy would derive from the "continuing derision of the mob."
> Rankin said, "There is no reason to suspect murder."

But don't use quotation marks for a paraphrased statement.

> Rankin said that there was no reason to suspect murder.

Put quotation marks around titles of shorter works: magazine articles, short stories, poems, artworks, and songs.

"A Rose for Emily"
Frost's "Mending Wall"
Picasso's "Three Musicians"
"White Christmas"

Titles of longer works are put in italics.
Use quotation marks to indicate you are using a word as a word rather than as a meaning.

> I can never spell "surgeon."
> "Cellar door" has a pleasant sound.

The usage here varies. Many writers now use italics in such instances.
Finally, quotation marks are sometimes used to show the odd or ironic use of a word.

> The Prime Minister lifted the first volume of the *Encyclopaedia Britannica* from his desk and "clobbered" his secretary.
> These "teachers" are a disgrace.

Try not to use quotation marks this way. When you can, just write the words.

Where do you put end punctuation when you are quoting? The rules are uncomplicated. Put periods and commas inside quotation marks—*always.* (This doesn't seem reasonable, but do it anyway.) Put semicolons and colons outside. And put question marks and exclamation marks inside if they are part of the quotation; otherwise, put them outside. These examples show the pattern:

"When you come," Nick said, "bring your boat."
Molly had said, "I'll never forget you"; however, she forgot me in two weeks.
Rebecca asked, "How long has this been going on?"
Who wrote "the uncertain glory of an April day"?
All I can say is "Wow!"
I did too say "Monday"!

To show a quotation within a quotation, use single quotes.

Jack complained, "I can never remember who wrote 'to be or not to be.'"

A better suggestion: Reconstruct your sentence so you don't have to put quotes within quotes.

Jack said he could never remember who wrote "to be or not to be."

Use *Italics* for Titles of Longer Works, for Foreign Words, and (if You Have to) for Emphasis

If your word processor doesn't print italics, indicate *italic* type by underlining.

Use italics to mark titles of longer works: books, magazines, newspapers, TV shows, movies, plays, operas, and long poems, as well as the names of ships and airplanes. Consider these examples:

Walker Percy's *Love in the Ruins*
USA Today
Christian Century
Frasier
The Matrix
Carmen
Paradise Lost
the *Titanic*
the space shuttle *Columbia*

Do not use italics or quotation marks for the Bible—or books of the Bible—or for famous documents like the Declaration of Independence or the Magna Charta.

A good rule: Whenever you are in doubt whether to use quotation marks or italics to indicate a title, use italics.

Use italics for foreign words. But remember that many foreign words have now become part of the English language and do not need italics.

> He was permitted to graduate *in absentia.*
> Do not use clichés.
> Kathy has a certain *élan,* but she acts like a prima donna.

What should you do about foreign words that have almost become English ("a priori," "coup d'état," "non sequitur")? When in doubt, don't italicize them.

Finally, you can use italics to give some word a special emphasis.

> That's *precisely* the reason I am here.
> Hilary didn't just act like a princess; she *was* a princess.

It is best not to use italics for emphasis, but sometimes you will want to.

Use *Capital Letters* with the Names of Specific Persons, Places, and Things

Knowing when to use a capital letter is not always easy, but the main rules are clear enough.

Capitalize the names of *people,* as well as their titles and words derived from their names; *places,* including countries (and national groups), states, counties, cities, and defined areas; *time units* like days of the week, months, and holidays; *religious entities; organizations,* their abbreviations, and brand names; *historical events and documents; titles* of books, magazines, plays, poems, stories, movies, television shows, musical compositions, and art objects; and *structures* like buildings, monuments, airplanes, and ships. These examples show common usage:

> Denise Shumock
> Captain Kirk
> Addison's disease
> Shakespearean sonnet
> Holland
> General Motors
> G.M.
> Ovaltine
> the Battle of Hastings

the Gettysburg Address
the Dutch
Europeans
the Riviera
California
Monroe County
Black River Falls
Tuesday
February
Memorial Day
God
Methodist
the Pope
the Archbishop of Canterbury
Genesis
the Magna Carta
Midnight in the Garden of Good and Evil
Room 280
Epilogue
Newsweek
The Importance of Being Earnest
"The Killers"
"Mending Wall"
All My Children
"Margaritaville"
Beethoven's Seventh
the Empire State Building
the Washington Monument
the *Spirit of St. Louis*
the *Titanic*

You should have little problem with such examples.

Some words are capitalized in one context and not in another. They are capitalized when they name or relate to a specific entity. These instances show the distinction:

He arrived in the spring. He arrived for Spring semester.
I knew Major Jones. He rose to the rank of major.
I saw Mother there. I will see my mother there.
I support the Democratic candidate. I believe in the democratic system.
I attend Spring Hill Baptist Church. We drove by a church.
I love the South. We flew south.

This is the Suwanee River. We swam in the river.
Turn to Chapter One (see p. 338). Read the next chapter.

Any word is capitalized, of course, when it begins a sentence or when it begins a line of poetry.

Do not capitalize words like "freshman" or "sophomore."

Finally, there are words that cause problems. In these cases, the usage varies with educated writers, and you may have to make your own decision. Here are some guidelines.

A.M. or *a.m.* Either form is correct. Just be consistent.

Coke or *coke*. When a product is vastly popular, its trade name may become the name of the product itself and thus lose its capital letter. This has happened to "ping pong," "thermos bottle," "kleenex," and "band-aid." It is now happening to "Xerox" and "Muzak." Today it is probably best to write "Coke" when you specifically mean Coca-Cola, and "coke" when you mean another soft drink.

Roman numerals or *roman numerals*. Sometimes a national reference becomes part of a common word and no longer conveys a sense of nationality; it will then lose its capital letter. You wouldn't capitalize "dutch treat," "french fries," or "turkish towel." Some words, however, are still changing. At present, you can write either "Roman numeral" or "roman numeral."

Psychology or *psychology*. You should always use capital letters with specific courses ("Psychology 201") and lowercase letters with the area in general ("I used psychology to convince my mother"). Capital letters, however, are sometimes used to discuss academic courses in a general way. You could write, "The University has strong programs in Psychology and Sociology, but it is weak in Languages.'"

Despite the complexity in some areas, most uses of capital letters follow a simple rule. You capitalize proper names—the names of specific persons, places, things, and events.

▓ ABBREVIATIONS

Because your writing should be an extension of the way you talk, you would do well not to write abbreviations at all. You say words, not abbreviations. Clearly, you'd sound strange talking like this:

We'll be there the second week in Feb.
In Madison, Wis., I worked for the Rogers Express Co.
This is the St., but I don't know the No.

However, many abbreviations *are* words. You would sound odd saying this:

I have to hurry to my Reserve Officers Training Corps class.
At two post meridiem, she drove her car into the Young Women's Christian Association parking lot.

The rule is to follow your voice. Write the word where you say the word and the abbreviation where you say the abbreviation. Thus you can write either "television" or "TV," either "CIA" or "Central Intelligence Agency." Probably you would never write "Blvd.," "MSS.," "e.g.," "anno Domini," or "University of California at Los Angeles."

There are a few exceptions to this rule. Standard usage dictates that "Mr.," "Dr.," "Mrs.," "Rev.," and comparable abbreviations be used before proper names. Similarly, it permits you to write "etc." instead of "et cetera." In general, however, you should not use abbreviations that are not also words. (And use "etc." sparingly.)

A common practice—especially in technical reports—is to write a complex term and then put the abbreviation after it in parentheses: "ethylenediaminetetraacetic acid (EDTA)." Once you do this, you can use the abbreviation throughout your document.

You use periods after most abbreviations ("B.C.," "p.m.," "M.D."). Some abbreviations, however, are so much a part of the language that they have become words themselves. You don't need to punctuate these acronyms:

UNESCO
YMCA
UCLA
FBI
NBC-TV

If you have doubt in such cases, you probably don't need to use the periods.

In writing addresses, use the U.S. Postal Service (USPS) abbreviations for the states. Most of them are simply the first two letters of a one-word state name ("CA" for California) or the first letter of each word in a two-word name ("NY" for New York). Routinely, they are written without periods.

These are the only states for which the USPS abbreviation is not the first two letters or first letter of each word:

AK—Alaska
AZ—Arizona

CT—Connecticut
GA—Georgia
HI—Hawaii
IA—Iowa
KS—Kansas
KY—Kentucky
LA—Louisiana
ME—Maine
MD—Maryland
MN—Minnesota
MS—Mississippi
MO—Missouri
MT—Montana
NB—Nebraska
NV—Nevada
PA—Pennsylvania
TN—Tennessee
TX—Texas
VT—Vermont
VA—Virginia

You would do well to memorize this list. If you use these abbreviations (instead of "Wisc." or "Ala." for example), your writing will look more professional.

■ NUMBERS

The question is whether to write out a number in words ("three hundred and sixty") or to use numerals ("360"). The usage varies.

A good general rule is to write out numbers when they are small (say ten or under) and when there are only a few of them in your essay.

There were seven people in the plane, but only two were injured.

On all other occasions, use numerals. When in doubt, write numerals.

You should always use numerals in dates, addresses, percentages, units of measure, page numbers, and hours followed by "a.m." or "p.m." Use these forms:

December 15, 1976
15 December 1976
639 Azalea Road
16 percent

4.2 minutes
page 37
8:20 a.m.
14,987 students

When writing large numbers, remember that numerals look bigger than words. If you want to justify America's national debt, put it down as "1.7 trillion." If you want to protest it, write "$1,700,000,000,000.00." When you want your readers to think a number is large, rub their nose in zeros.

If you have more than several numbers to express, use numerals throughout. But don't begin a sentence with a numeral.

Do not repeat numbers unnecessarily. Unless you're writing a contract, don't say "This happened seven (7) times."

▓ SPELLING

The best way to improve your spelling is to read extensively.

The best short-term way is to keep a dictionary at hand or use your computer's spell checker and to look up words you are unsure of. You should have doubts when you face plainly difficult words, commonly misspelled words, and words you have had trouble with before.

You should never misspell "rhododendron," "ophthalmologist," "alumnae," or "hieroglyphic." You know these are difficult words; you should consult your source and spell them right. (If you don't have a dictionary or spell checker, consider using another word.)

Here are the most commonly misspelled words in English. Look over the list. If any one of the words looks unusual to you, circle it. Then try to memorize this correct spelling. Pay particular attention to the capitalized words on this list. They are the ones that cause the most trouble.

absence
accept
ACCOMMODATE
achievement
acquainted
addressed
advice
advise
AFFECT—EFFECT
aggravate
all right
allusion

A LOT
amateur
analyze
angle
apology
apparent
appreciate
Arctic
athletic
attendance
believe
benefited
Britain
bureau
calendar
capital
capitol
category
cemetery
changeable
choose
colonel
committee
comparative
compliment
conceive
conscience
contemptible
cooperate
courteous
deceive
desert
dessert
dictionary
difference
dormitories
eighth
embarrass
environment
especially
exaggerate
excellence

existence
existential
fascinate
February
forehead
foreign
fourth
government
grammar
handkerchief
humorous
influence
initiate
intellectual
irrelevant
ITS—IT'S
let's
library
LOOSE—LOSE
mathematics
misspelled
ninth
occasion
occurrence
omitted
pamphlet
parallel
perform
permanence
personnel
persuade
playwright
politician
preferred
prejudice
PRINCIPAL—PRINCIPLE
pronunciation
prophecy—prophesy
psychology
questionnaire
RECEIVE

recommend
resemblance
reservoir
restaurant
rhythm
seize
sense
SEPARATE
sincerely
sophomore
stationery
subtle
syllable
temperament
tendency
THAN—THEN
THEIR—THERE
TO—TOO
truly
until
usually
Wednesday
were—where
whether
writing

Start your own list. Keep track of words you have misspelled on your essays or on early drafts of your papers. Learn these words. There is no excuse for misspelling "separate" twice.

If you have a computer with a spell-check program, use it. But remember, it won't help you if you misspell a name, or write "short comings," or confuse "there" and "their."

EXERCISES

Punctuate the following sentences. Insert commas, semicolons, colons, exclamation marks, question marks, periods, hyphens, and dashes where needed.

1. When the outfielder caught the second hand baseball he saw that the hide was torn
2. Charles Lackey the famous actor died on stage last week
3. He never complained he knew it would do no good

4. The nun asked me if I knew the way to Elm Street
5. During the summer I spent at least eleven thousand dollars on eighteenth century furniture
6. The price and I can't tell you how pleased I am to say it is only $4800.00
7. After six weeks of trying my brother finally learned to play hearts
8. The boy who won first prize a silver cup was our neighbor's son
9. I think *The Iceman Cometh* is the best American play written in this century and I absolutely refuse to teach it to this know nothing class
10. Would you kindly pay this bill by the first of the month
11. The wife got the stereo the television and the Lexus but the husband got to keep the dog
12. They insisted on waiting for Rex had never been there before
13. Then he wrote *Getting There from Here* 1955 a play about Nazi oppression
14. He studied seven year old children with personality problems
15. Our main concerns are the above ground hook ups and feed rates. During the shut down, we will install up to date equipment.

In the following sentences, add apostrophes, quotation marks, italics, and capital letters as needed. Remove them where they are unnecessary.

16. My lawyer asked if I read georges mail. I said never in a million years.
17. My mother loved to read the *Bible,* especially the story of Moses flight from Egypt.
18. It became an idée fix: he was sure he could find a word to rhyme with jeffersonian.
19. Kate said my favorite song is Bette Davis Eyes.
20. They worked hard on it, but the boys buick was still a wreck.
21. I prefer Yeats poem that celebrates Ulysses courage.
22. His first poem winter dreams was published in the Atlantic Monthly.
23. The Professor asked In what year did Coleridge write Christobel?
24. No wonder he gets straight Cs in mathematics. His 7s all look like 1s.
25. The details of the coup d'état were published in last sundays New York Times.
26. The best song in hello dolly is hello dolly.

Correct any errors in abbreviation, numbers, and spelling that you find in the following sentences.

27. The suspect lived at 901 West Blvd. for 6 months. He burglerized a jewelry store, taking stones valued at ten thousand three hundred and fifty dollars. He was indited and convicted, and his new adress is Rockway Prison, Temple City, Mich.

28. 15 percent of the students at the Massachusetts Institute of Technology do not plan to work in the U.S. Most want to get their doctor of philosophy degree, emigrate to Canada, and make seventy-five thousand a year working for the aircraft industry.

29. Your education already has cost me thirty-six hundred dollars. By the time you get you're M.A. in math, I'll be bankrup.

30. Citizens of Washington, District of columbia, loved Pres. Reagan. 10,000 of them attended his speech praising the C.I.A. and it's dedicated Personell.

31. We watched TV from eleven ante meridiem until after midnight. No more than ten % of the shows, however, were worth watching.

32. It's an odd occurrence. Whenever we hire new personell, they expect to recieve top wages.

33. We bought a Nestles Crunch bar and carried it into Toys R Us.

34. So far this month, we have received only one (1) poster.

Final Reminders

"Just say it."

—JAMES COUNCIL

Following the eight rules for good writing should make you an effective writer. You may be further helped by these recommendations.

■ CREDIT YOUR SOURCES

In general writing, you do not need formal scholarly documentation. But often you will want to specify your sources. Don't use footnotes for this; few people read them. Put information about your sources in your text. Any of these forms is acceptable.

> According to Genie Hamner (*Bald Windows Revisited,* 1988), man has endured . . .
> In *Bald Windows Revisited* (1988), Genie Hamner argues . . .
> In her article "Decision Making in Washington Transportation Systems" (*Fortune,* June 1987), Kathleen Kelly describes . . .
> According to *Time* (February 15, 1991), President Bush has . . .

This kind of informal documentation need not be elaborate. But it is important to give your readers enough information so they can refer to the sources you used.

If you need formal documentation, see "The MLA System for Citing Sources" on page 382.

■ USE YOUR SPEAKING VOICE

Try to use your talking voice in your writing. You would never say, "This radio needed repair from the date of purchase"; you'd say, "This radio hasn't worked since I bought it." In talking, you tend to use short sentences, plain words, active voice, and specific details. You don't worry about beginning a sentence with "and" or "but." You don't use words like "shall" or "secondly" or "societal." You rarely say words in a series, and you'd never say, "My reasons were threefold" or "Quiet was the night."

Try to avoid long sentences full of paired or parallel constructions. Look at this example. (Italics and parentheses are added to show the pattern.)

> Children need generous amounts of *affection, guidance,* and *discipline* in order to develop into *intellectually* and *emotionally* mature adults. Children (who feel *rejected* or *unloved*) or (who are given *inconsistent* or *ineffective* discipline) tend to develop *serious* and *long-lasting* psychic disorders, such as *schizophrenia, alcoholism, drug addiction,* and *psychopathic personality.*

This is *written* language; nobody talks like that. Don't write this kind of social-science prose.

Trust your ear. What sounds like good spoken language—at a level suited to your subject and your audience—will be good writing.

Don't get hung up pursuing some hypothetically "correct" form. Don't trouble yourself about a choice like this:

> You will meet situations *where* all answers are wrong.
> You will meet situations *when* all answers are wrong.
> You will meet situations *in which* all answers are wrong.

All three usages are acceptable. Write the sentence the way *you* would say it.

Remember the "twelve garbagemen rule." The importance of simple language was stressed in a document addressed to practicing attorneys. It said, "When you begin your final summation to the jury, imagine that you're talking to 12 garbagemen who just stepped off the truck." That's good advice for anybody.

■ GET HELP FROM FRIENDS

In all likelihood, you will never be asked to write a document that someone else will read and judge immediately. Impromptu themes are sometimes assigned in college classes, but in the outer world you will usually have time for reflection and revision. As part of your revision, have a friend, spouse, teacher, secretary, or colleague read through your essay for clarity and correctness.

Correctness in matters of punctuation, italics, number, idiom, and spelling is important. A misspelled "their" or "it's" can make a well-informed paper seem illiterate. An omitted comma can make an important sentence almost unreadable. A "not" that is typed "now" can cause big trouble.

Proofread your work carefully. Authors report embarrassing examples where "a bead" became "a bear"; "a political ideal" became "a political deal"; and "therapist" became "the rapist." A document from Senator Bill Bradley's office in 1984 assured readers that, under his tax plan, a family with a $15,000-a-year income would pay only $16,000 in federal tax.

Of course, you should resort to a dictionary, an English handbook, or a computer aid when you have difficulties. But serious errors may exist where you don't see a problem. If a piece of writing is important to you, ask a knowledgeable friend to look it over.

■ MAKE IT NEAT

Imagine you're applying for an executive position and are well qualified. Then you come to the interview chewing gum and wearing an old Batman sweatshirt. You're not going to get the job.

Similarly, if you write a first-rate letter of application and send it off in sloppy form (with a bad handwriting, cross-outs, irregular margins, and on paper ripped from a spiral notebook), you won't get the job. If you send a messy manuscript to an editor, forget it. Major publishing houses and magazines now receive so many submissions that they immediately dismiss those that are cluttered or hard to read.

This is a reasonable response. The form in which you send out your material says something important about you and about your attitude toward your reader and your subject matter. Make it look good. There's a lot of truth in the ad: "If it's important, it belongs on Hammermill paper."

■ REMEMBER YOUR AUDIENCE

Keep in mind the kind of audience you are writing for. It makes a difference.

There is a danger in assuming that your reader knows what you know. This can lead you to commit what Edgar Dale calls the "COIK fallacy" and to write casually about Ken Maynard or Riverside Drive or real time because these terms are clear and meaningful to you. They are Clear Only If Known.

Addressing an educated audience, you can use words like "arcane" and "protean." Speaking to Southerners, you might venture "tump" or "catty-wampus." When writing to a specialized group (scholars or athletes or priests), you can refer to Romantic poetry, a trap play, or John 3:16. But don't use such terms with a general audience; they won't understand you. Don't say, "They can look it up." They won't.

A problem arises when you are forced to use an obscure term. Here, along with the word, you should include an explanation of what it means. But you don't want to sound preachy or condescending. ("I suppose I have to explain to you that a 'shard' is a piece of pottery.") In such instances, you must give the explanation in an indirect way. See how necessary clarification is included in these sentences:

> As spokesmen for the Jewish establishment, the *Scribes* and *Pharisees* were immediately hostile to the message of Jesus.
>
> The *trap play* worked perfectly: The linebacker charged through the space we left open and was blocked out of the play.
>
> No one ever understood what motivated Lizzie Borden. She remains an *enigma*.

The burden is always on you to make sure your reader understands your message.

Writing school assignments, you may have to violate many of the rules in this book. Your sociology teacher may assign a term paper and ask for 25 pages of text and dozens of footnotes. Your education professor may ask for a 200-page dissertation full of technical jargon. When teachers want that, give it to them. But remember, in the outside world, academic writing won't work for you. You're always better off keeping things clear, short, and talky.

Remember that some audiences are sensitive in particular areas. Writing to an African-American reader, be careful about using words like "negro" and "black." Don't tell Polish jokes in Milwaukee. Addressing women's groups, try not to say "chair*man*" or "spokes*man*" or to insist that "a surgeon really earns *his* money." Don't address a letter to "Miss Gloria Steinem" or to "Ms. Phyllis Schlafly."

Finally, recognize that some audiences cannot be reasoned with at all. When a zealot begins to talk about abortion or gun control, find a way to change the subject. Say, "Did you see the Dolphins play last Sunday?" Or, "What's your son doing these days?"

▓ REMEMBER YOUR PURPOSE

The motto of one New York advertising agency is "It's not creative unless it sells." There is a lot of truth in that. Keep in mind the purpose of your writing. What is it you are trying to sell?

The eight rules of good writing just given are based on the assumption that you want to communicate information, to make an argument in a clear, forthright manner. But this isn't always the case.

Sometimes it's best to say nothing. Recent history provides examples of individuals who spoke out forthrightly when they shouldn't have. When the Democratic national headquarters at the Watergate was burglarized, Republican officials denied involvement before anyone had accused them of anything. When pro-life and pro-choice delegates clashed at the 1980 Democratic convention, President Carter volunteered a middle-of-the-road statement on abortion. Addressing stockholders of Bendix, Inc., the board chairman announced that the young woman working as Vice President for Strategic Services had won the job on her merits, not because of her personal involvement with him. In each case, silence would have been a more effective argument.

President Reagan learned this lesson well. After a few early (and conflicting) statements about the Iran-Contra affair, he resolutely kept quiet. He avoided reporters' questions and held few press conferences. Only when the congressional committees had finished their investigations did he comment on the outcome.

Any time you are involved in an adversarial situation—that is, when you are responding to police officers, lawyers, newspaper and television reporters, relatives who enjoy lawsuits, an ex-spouse, or an insurance adjustor—don't be too quick to frame an argument, volunteer information, or write clever letters. They may return to haunt you. (Lawyers routinely advise accused clients to say nothing. They repeat the adage, "There are no mutes on Death Row.")

In argument, it is always a mistake to lie. But there are times when truth won't do you much good. Always consider the virtues of silence.

There are also situations where you will want to express yourself indirectly. You might want to spare the sensibilities of your reader ("By the time he was twenty, Dudley had demonstrated a range of sexual abnormalities"). You might want to discredit an adversary ("The initial response to his book seems to be fairly favorable") or to veil a threat ("If you pay this bill promptly, your credit rating will remain excellent"). Such situations are not uncommon.

And sometimes you don't want clarity at all. Suppose, for example, you are obliged—in a school or business situation—to write on a subject you know little about. Now your purpose is to conceal your deficiency. You want to fill up a page, to sound fairly learned, and to avoid any specific assertion that will demonstrate your ignorance.

So you reverse many of the rules in this book. You will add "which" clauses and sprinkle modifiers (like "truly," "more or less," and "on the other hand") to ensure that no sentence has fewer than 30 words. You will write of *quintessential* issues and suggest that *procrustean* tactics are the *ne plus ultra* of folly. (This will obfuscate your message.) You will avoid proper names by using the passive voice ("a decision has been made that" or "word was received that"). You will write of vague entities like "business leaders," "the former," and "fair play." These can be described as "adequate" or "unfortunate"; but if you want to avoid even this minimal level of judgment, you can call them "notable," "meaningful," or "significant." (These words don't mean good or bad or much of anything.)

Write all this in small print (either in cramped handwriting or in 9-point type) and put it in long block paragraphs. The final work will be meaningless and unreadable, but in particular situations—where you can't or don't want to communicate directly—this may be the kind of writing you want.

Most of the time, however, you write to say something specific. You want to persuade your audience that marijuana should not be legalized, that gas rationing is essential, or that Sacco and Vanzetti were guilty. You want to describe your new boat. You want someone to give you a job, to buy mutual funds, or to settle that insurance claim in your favor. In such cases, the eight rules for good writing will help you get the effect you want.

Anything that thwarts the purpose of your writing (misspelling, wordiness, errors of fact, or even direct and meaningful statements) should be avoided. And anything that furthers your cause with a particular audience (even such features as expensive paper, folksy language, neat typing, and footnotes) should probably be used.

Good writing may not always win you the final effect you want—that job, that insurance adjustment, that sale. But it will do all that language can do to achieve that end.

■ BE SMART

Here is an important question: How many of these topics do you need to know about to be a persuasive writer?

alcohol and baldness
Antarctica
biorhythms
the causes of homosexuality
competition in China
creationism in court
Freudian psychology

friendly fire
a googolplex
Halley's comet
Sherlock Holmes
modern cryptography
monkeys and sign language
Duke Snider
St. Croix
State and Main
The Tales of Hoffmann
tax-free bonds
true believers
ufologists
zen tennis

The answer, of course, is all of them. Nothing is irrelevant in persuasion.

Remember that every book you read, every movie you attend, every town you visit, every TV show you see, and every relative and bartender you talk to is giving you material you can use in writing.

The lessons in this text will be useful. But you also have to read a lot of books, talk to all kinds of people, and stay alert if you want to be a first-rate persuader. It's a worthy goal.

Go for it.

Appendixes

Exercises for Review

How valid are these arguments? Identify examples of induction, deduction, expert testimony, semantic argument, analogy, argument in a circle, post hoc, begging the question, ad hominem argument, extension, the either-or fallacy, and statistical manipulation.

1. How can you oppose capital punishment for a convicted murderer and favor it for innocent unborn babies?
2. Of course you favor federal aid to education. You're a teacher. You stand to profit on the deal.
3. "Our cheese is like a good love affair."—Rondele
4. A Tampax poll found that 22 percent of the respondents thought menstrual pain is psychological.
5. Pizza and spaghetti are good for you. According to a summary study published in the *Journal of the National Cancer Institute,* high consumers of tomatoes and tomato products have a substantially decreased risk of numerous cancers.
6. Asking Britain to desert Northern Ireland is like asking the United States to give up Texas.
7. "Seven out of ten Americans cheat on their income tax."—Professor R. Van Dyke Ellington III
8. I never knew an Auburn football player who could read or write beyond the eighth-grade level.
9. Couples who live together before getting married have a higher rate of divorce and separation (within 10 years) than couples who didn't live together before marriage. There's a message in that.
10. It's about time students demanded their rights. A group just filed suit against Southern Methodist University seeking financial damages. They claimed a computer course they took was too hard.
11. A reported study (*New York Times,* Dec. 18, 1985) in Canada claims that consistent moderate beer drinkers, as a group, are healthier than wine drinkers, hard liquor drinkers, or the general population.
12. If you're overweight, you can consider the new diet books. These offer the Wine Diet, the Metabolic Typing Diet, the Alternative Medicine Diet, the Detox Diet, the Food Rotation Diet, the Bone Density Diet, the Quit-Smoking Diet, the Xenical Diet, the Blood Type Diet, the Portion Diet, and the Sleeping Diet.

13. We should not ban laetrile just because it didn't prove effective in laboratory tests. Pretty soon, they'll want to ban holy water.

14. In 1985, Ann Landers polled her female readers. She asked, "Would you be content to be held close and treated tenderly, and forget about 'the act'?" Over 90,000 women wrote in, and nearly three-quarters of them said "Yes." I guess that proves something.

15. "There is no proof that sugar confectionary gives rise to dental cavities."— *Association Internationale des Fabricants de Confiserie*

16. I don't believe drugs, alcohol, and gambling are addicting habits. Pretty soon they'll claim that Billy Cannon had a counterfeiting sickness and Jesse James had a train-robbing sickness.

17. A recent study by a Stanford scholar suggests that abortion reduces crime. After all, unwanted children are the ones most likely to get into trouble.

18. Swimmers and scuba-divers needn't worry. The chance of being attacked by a shark is 1 in 360,000,000.

19. We scientists working on astrological data expect to be criticized. We know that Newton and Einstein were ridiculed in the past.

20. *The Husband* (a novel by Sol Stein): "The dilemma of countervailing demands on the sensual man of good will . . . rich and true . . . modulated with a respectful reserve . . . handled with hardly a false note."— *New York Times*

21. "For every rape that is reported, from 9 to 23 are not."—Southwest Radio Church

22. "When the fish-pond that was a meadow shall be mowed, Sagittarius being in the ascendant, Plagues, famines, death by the military hand, The century approaches renewal." (Prophecy of Nostradamus)

23. Why all the congressional debate about flag-burning and partial-birth abortions? How often do these things happen?

24. If your name is Makay, Malloy, or Murray, beware of drink. According to John Gary, director of the Council for Alcoholism in Glasgow, Scotland, people whose last names begin with the letter "M" may be eight times more prone to alcoholism than others.

25. *Miss MacIntosh, My Darling* by Marguerite Young: "What we behold is a mammoth epic, a massive fable, a picaresque journey, a Faustian quest, and a work of stunning magnitude and beauty . . . some of the richest, most expansive, most original and exhaustively revealing passages of prose that this writer has experienced in a long time."—William Goyen, *New York Times*

26. Read *One in Twenty* by Bryan Magee—an adult, plainly written study of male and female homosexuality.

27. All this effort to register and confiscate handguns will not help us fight crime. Violence rises from the souls of men.
28. It's not safe to walk on the streets of New York City. I'm glad I live in Cleveland.
29. "Ever wonder why kids instinctively go for soft drinks in bottles?"—Glass Container Manufacturers Institute
30. *Miss MacIntosh, My Darling* by Marguerite Young: "In fact, this is an outrageously bad book, written by an author with very little of interest to say and very little skill in saying it . . . wholly unreadable."—*Time*
31. The accident can't be my fault. I have no-fault insurance.
32. "'In John Doe We Trust' is not a good motto."—Ad for Hillsdale College.
33. Why spend millions of dollars sending a space-ship to Mars? We could use that money to improve America's schools.
34. A clever magician can always perform tricks, but a genuine psychic can sometimes produce paranormal effects and sometimes not. Uri Geller produced no effects at all when he appeared on the *Tonight Show.* He is a true psychic.
35. On a typical television poll, an early-evening newscaster poses a yes- or-no question, asking viewers to phone one number to vote "yes" and another to vote "no." Then a late-evening newscaster reports the result—for example, that 72 percent oppose socialized medicine.
36. "You grew it before, you can grow it again."—Rogaine ad.
37. The president of Chick-Fil-A says he won't hire me because I'm a white guy wearing an earring. This is discrimination. He wouldn't dare reject me if I was a woman—or if I was black, Hispanic, or gay.
38. How about a law to compel anybody publicly lobbying against abortion to have a baby, or two or three, or else go to jail. Same thing.
39. "One Out of Two Marriages Has Serious Sex Problems"—*National Enquirer* headline
40. Dial. The most effective deodorant soap you can buy.
41. Do you approve of pornographic and obscene classroom textbooks being used under the guise of sex education? Yes____ No ____
42. I disagree with Abby Van Buren when she says no woman should be forced to have a baby she doesn't want. A lot of people have parents they don't like, but we don't let them go around murdering their fathers and mothers.
43. "Will $1 million be enough to solve your problems for the moment?"—Poll question from an ad offering "Your Golden Astral Number"
44. Athletics teach our young people how to play the game of life.
45. Naval ROTC should be abolished. I'm learning nothing from it.
46. Now conservatives want to execute convicts as young as 16. Why not 14? Why not 12?

47. "I lowered my vibrations to be able to come to Earth and pay off a debt I owed to a girl in a previous lifetime—a karmic debt."—Omnec Onec, a visitor from Venus, speaking at the World UFO Congress held in Tucson in May 1991

48. An Ohio woman is suing because her 65-year-old husband began using Viagra, then left her to enjoy a womanizing social-life. She insists the drug shouldn't be sold without a product-warning like the one on packs of cigarettes.

49. We can't get family counseling from a priest. What does he know of marriage?

50. Homosexuality is no illness. It is a widespread practice, like vegetarianism. The homosexual has a sexual preference for members of the same sex; a vegetarian has an alimentary preference for noncarnivorous foods. In neither case is there any impairment of function or any disease.

51. A pamphlet distributed by the Fellowship Tract League is titled "The Burning Hell." It contains the line "20,000 degrees—and not a drop of water."

52. "You wouldn't sweep dust under the rug—so don't put clean food in a dirty oven!"—Easy-Off Oven Cleaner

53. Gordon's—"Largest selling gin in England, America, the world."

54. To All Citizens and Taxpayers. QUESTION: "Do you favor our city and county governments devoting more of our present tax money to police protection?" Yes____ No ____

55. "A good club soda is like a good woman: it won't quit on you."—Canada Dry advertisement

56. How can you deny the power of the moon's influence? The oceans have tides; women have periods; and emergency rooms are full on moonlit nights.

57. "There now exists an all natural, bio-active weight-loss compound so powerful, so effective, so relentless in its awesome attack on bulgy fatty deposits that it has virtually eliminated the need to diet. News of this super pill from Asia is sweeping the country."—Ad for Fat Burner

58. "The execution of a person possibly in the state of mortal sin and spiritual unreadiness potentially sends that person to eternal damnation and thus constitutes the most egregious violation of the Eighth Amendment's proscription of cruel and unusual punishment and the First Amendment's guarantee of religious liberty."—A legal claim made by the Alabama Representative Resource Center

59. I can't decide which Supreme Cutlery setting to buy. I'm choosing between Ron de Vu, Bamboo, Arctic, Marchese, Colonnade, Ionic, and Snowflake.

60. "Coke is like family. You can never have enough."

61. *Ed Anger's Smoking Poll.*

    Check "yes" if you agree with Ed Anger that Americans ought to be able to smoke anytime, anywhere they please and the wimpy anti-smoking nuts should shut up and take up knitting.

    Check "no" if you think the anti-smoking fruitcakes have a right to impose their will on the rest of the nation and ban smoking in public places—even if it violates the Constitution of this great nation.
    Yes___ No ___

62. A new study interviewed more than 500 men and women who had recently suffered cardiac crises and compared them to over 500 healthy men and women. Out of the sick group, over half said they were nonreligious. But in the healthy group, only one in five were nonreligious. This proves religious men and women suffer significantly fewer heart attacks than people who don't believe in God or go to church regularly.

63. Lawyer Peter Wold said that his client, a Northwest Airline pilot, wasn't drunk while flying a Boeing 727 from Fargo to Minneapolis. The pilot did drink 17½ rum-and-diet-cokes the night before, but he was an alcoholic and had a tolerance for alcohol.

64. "Eighty percent of people who think their mates are cheating are right."—Irwin Blye, New York City private detective

65. Dr. Michael Leitzmann of the Harvard University School of Public Health presented a study in the *Journal of the American Medical Association.* It says that men who drink 2–3 cups of regular coffee a day have a 40 percent lower risk of gallstones than men who don't drink regular coffee. Men who drink 4 or more cups a day have a 45 percent lower risk.

66. Producer Dick Wolf denied that TV programming motivated the kind of violence that occurred in the Columbine High School shootings. He said, "In all the police records I've ever examined, I've never seen a 30-inch television listed as the murder weapon."

67. An article distributed by Jews for the Preservation of Firearms Ownership is titled "DIAL 911 AND DIE!"

68. My cousin Kathy is asking the insurance company to pay for her breast enlargement. She calls it correcting a birth defect.

69. *60 Minutes* reported that two glasses of red wine daily lower your chances of a heart attack. I feel sorry for you if you don't drink red wine.

70. If you think the jails in this state are bad, you should see the jails in Iran and Turkey.

71. "Junk Food Causes Teens to Worship the Devil!"—headline in *Weekly World News* (25 May 1993)

72. "I want to be the type of football player the Lord would be if He played football."—Herschel Walker

73. "The average man makes up his mind in six short seconds whether or not he wants to know a woman better."—Dr. Joyce Brothers

74. *Lost in Yonkers* by Neil Simon. 1991 Pulitzer Prize winner. Winner of the 1991 Tony Award for "Best Play."

75. Feminists are rejoicing at the recent Supreme Court ruling that women cannot be denied access to jobs working with lead batteries simply because this involves serious risk to their reproductive organs. Hooray for civil rights!

76. *Lost in Yonkers* by Neil Simon. "There's not one glimmer of honesty or authenticity in this family melodrama by Neil Simon."—*New Yorker*

77. "The fact remains: every threat to the fabric of this country—from poverty to crime to homelessness—is connected to out-of-wedlock teen pregnancy"—Jonathan Alter, *Newsweek*, Dec. 12, 1994

78. "The risen Jesus Christ, when He came back to earth, the first food He ate was bee pollen. God had Him use bee pollen symbolically, to show that bee pollen should be an integral part of everyone's diet."—TV ad for High Desert Bee Pollen

79. So Pee-wee Herman was caught at an adult theater. I can understand that. What I can't understand is why they sent a dozen cops to raid a showing of *Nancy Nurse*. Don't Sarasota police have anything better to do?

80. Figures given by the Institute for Sex Research, at Indiana University, suggest that sooner or later 35 to 40 percent of American wives are unfaithful.

81. We can't elect a woman as Vice President. My God, what if the President died?

82. "We don't go for fakes. And neither should you."—Ad recommending "genuine G.M. parts"

83. "Some things you can just count on. Like a good friend and the great taste of Maxwell House Coffee."

84. "Thank You for Not Speaking in Tongues"—Placard distributed by the Tobacco Institute

85. A man wrote "Ask Marilyn" with the question: "Can you give me just one good reason why I shouldn't look for an attractive woman to marry, rather than an ordinary one?" The answer: "A good-looking set of china doesn't make the meal taste better."

86. A woman has a right to abort a baby that has invaded her body, just as she has a right to repel an intruder who broke into her home. It's a matter of self-defense.

87. *There Is a Cure for Arthritis*—A book by Paavo O. Airola, N.D.

88. "I think it's time to ask for the other tobacco statistics." How many fatal accidents are caused by smoking? How much violence out

there—shootings, public and domestic—are caused by smoking? How many rapes are caused by smoking?—from the "Sound Off" column, calls made to the *Mobile Press Register*

89. "If God didn't believe in the death penalty, why are the graveyards so full?"—Ed Anger

90. The homosexuals who protest Dr. Laura Schlessigner's radio show are saying they have a right to be gay, but she doesn't have a right to criticize them. Does that make sense?

91. This year, the Southern Baptist convention voted that women could not serve as church pastors. This makes sense. A woman's place is in the cave, sweeping out dirt, and feeding the dinosaur.

92. I believe we should give pay-raises to public-school teachers. But I want a little accountability. The raises should be tied to merit. They should reflect how well students did on statewide standardized exams.

93. What I want to know is who masterminded the plot to impeach Bill Clinton?

94. The best seller, *Purpose Driven Life,* urges readers to make God their best friend and to do deeds "which will bring a smile to His face."

95. Marriage is dangerous for men. Of the women on death row, over one-half are there for killing their husbands. Of the men on death row, less than one-third are there for killing their wives.

96. "Every time the Nile River floods, Americans get married in droves."—headline, *Weekly World News,* May 5, 1992.

97. "What will the universities of America do when they run out of victims groups to coddle and appease? Might they be forced to resume teaching the great works of civilization? Nah."—Mona Charen's column in the *Mobile Register,* May 5, 2002.

98. About the meteor shower Sunday: Why couldn't they have had this at a reasonable hour? I guess it is all right for all these party people who stay up all night anyway, or retired people who don't have anything to do. For most people, this was ridiculous and I think they should do something about it.—from the "Sound Off" column, calls made to the *Mobile Press Register.*

99. "Did you know 8 out of 10 women are wearing the wrong size bra?"—ad for J. C. Penney.

100. "In my opinion, those suicide bombers should be hung."—from the "Sound Off" column, calls made to the *Mobile Press Register.*

101. "Until 1987, jet pilots could carry guns because airliners transported the U. S. mail along with civilians. Is it asking too much for today's passengers to receive the same protection once afforded their postcards?"—Deroy Murdock, columnist with Scripps Howard News Service, July 12, 2002.

102. Don't tell me diets don't work. There are no fat people in prison camps.

Subjects for Argumentative Essays

abortion rights
teenage abstinence
academic writing
Academy Award winners
acid rain
ACT test scores
acupuncture
adoption by unmarried couples
adoption by gay couples
adult children who don't leave
    home
affirmative action
Agent Orange
aging American population
agoraphobia
AIDS as God's punishment
AIDS testing
airbags
airline accidents
alcoholism as a disease
Mohammed Ali
Alice in Wonderland
alimony payments
All My Children
Alzheimer's Disease
animal experiments in research
anorexia
Antichrist
anxiety disorders
aphrodisiacs
arthritis cures
aspirin to prevent heart attacks
astrological signs
athletes' salaries
Atlanta Braves
    required auto insurance

bad teachers
baldness cures
Barbie dolls
Barry Bonds
baseball cards
battered wives
beef as a health threat
bending spoons with mind power
betting on *Monday Night Football*
the Bible as literature
the Big-Bang theory
Bigfoot
bikini bathing suits
bilingual education
biorhythms
birth control devices
birth order
body building
body piercing
bombing abortion clinics
bottled water vs. tap water
professional boxing
brainwashing
breaking up Microsoft
breast enlargement
breast-feeding
bulimia
bungee jumping

cable TV
California earthquakes
Camilla Parker-Bowles
campus speech codes
cancer cures
capital punishment
carbon dating

Catholic schools
cats vs. dogs
Edgar Cayce's powers
celibacy
cell phone issues
censorship
census figures
chain letters
channeling
chemical weapons
chemotherapy choices
the Chernobyl accident
child abuse
child custody laws
childhood obesity
children of divorced parents
chiropractors
Christian Science
Christmas with the family
the CIA
cigarette smoke and the nonsmoker
circumcision
circumstantial evidence
civil rights for men
civil rights for minorities
Bill Clinton as orator
Hillary Rodham Clinton
cloning
coaches' salaries
cocaine as a recreational drug
Coke vs. Pepsi
cold fusion
colorizing black-and-white films
Christopher Columbus, hero
    or villain
communism
competency tests for teachers
computer dating
computer viruses
Confederate flag
consenting adults

conspiracy theories
copyright laws
the core curriculum
corporate casual
correct English
cosmetic surgery
crack
crack babies
Creationism in public schools
credit card debt
Cuba
cultural illiteracy
cyberspace

date rape
the Davidians at Waco
day-care centers
daylight savings time
Dear Abby
death penalty
death penalty for women
declining educational standards
deconstructionist criticism
the defense budget
deficit spending
designated drivers
the designated hitter
designer-label clothes
detainees vs. POW's
dialects
diet drinks
diet plans
dioxin
dirty lyrics
disarmament treaties
discrimination against overweight
    people
divorce laws
Jeane Dixon
DNA testing
docudramas

dog racing
drug-prescription costs
drug-testing
dumbing-down
DVD players

e-bay auctions
e-mail
E prime
Earth Day
Easter Island
Ebonics
ecology
ecumenical Christianity
effects of a full moon
Electoral College
elephants-in-captivity
Elgin Marbles
Elvis today
empty-nest syndrome
endangered species
English teachers
entrapment by police agents
ephedra
escort services
ethnic cleansing
extrasensory perception
euthanasia
evolution
exorcism

faith healing
family values
fashion trends
father–daughter relationships
father–son relationships
fear of public speaking
FEMA
the fetus as a human being
high-fiber diets
fire walking

the First Amendment
flag-burning laws
the flat tax
foreign language requirements
forest fires
four-letter words
Freud
Friday the 13th
Friday the 13th
frozen embryos
fundamentalism
funding private schools
fur coats

gangs
Bill Gates
gay rights
Gaza Strip
Uri Geller
Gender Studies
gene therapy
generic drugs
genetic engineering
ghosts
global warming
glossolalia
good manners
good taste
Al Gore
Graceland
grammar vs. usage
Greenhouse Effect
Alan Greenspan
Guantanamo
Gulf Coast Humanities
    Consortium
gun-control laws
guns in schools

HMOs
Haiti

Halley's comet
handwriting analysis
health-care costs
health-care reform
health-food stores
Heaven and Hell
the Heaven's Gate suicides
heredity vs. environment
modern heroes
high school pregnancies
the Hillside Strangler
John Hinckley
high school proms
Jimmy Hoffa's disappearance
holistic medicine
the homeless
homeschooling
homosexual teachers
homosexual clergy
Hooters restaurants
horror movies
Hurricane Katrina
Saddam Hussein
hyperactive children

illegal aliens
immigration quotas
inflation rate
insanity plea
insecticide manufacturing
insider trading on Wall Street
instant replay
instinct
intelligent design
Internet investing
interracial romance
intuition
IQ test results
Ireland vs. Northern Ireland
Israel
Israeli-Arab peace efforts

J, the Old Testament author
Jack the Ripper
Jesse Jackson
Michael Jackson
Japanese trade competition
Jesus
job security
jogging
junk bonds
junk foods
junk mail
jury selection
"Just a housewife"
"Just say no"
trying juveniles as adults

Erica Kane
killing abortion doctors
Senator Edward Kennedy
the Kennedy assassination
Dr. Jack Kevorkian
Ayatollah Khomeini
killer bees
Martin Luther King Day
Korea
Ku Klux Klan

L.A. Police Department
labor unions
laetrile
landfill locations
LASIK surgery
latchkey children
Latin classes
the Latin Mass
lawsuits against tobacco companies
lawyers
lead poisoning
leash laws
legal insanity
legalized gambling

predatory lenders
John Lennon
Leno vs. Letterman
lesbians
Monica Lewinsky
libel laws
lie-detector tests
life in space
life-support systems
Rush Limbaugh
literature classes
living alone
lobbyists
the Loch Ness monster
state lotteries
Lourdes miracles
love relationships
lucky numbers

Madonna
the Mafia
man as animal
Nelson Mandela
mandatory jail sentences
marijuana laws
marriage adjustments
water on Mars
math scores of U.S. students
medical school quotas
menopause
MIAs and POWs
Microsoft
miniskirts
Miss America pageants
the missing link
Miss Manners
modern painting
modernism in the church
Marilyn Monroe's death
Moonies
personal morality of candidates

mother–daughter relationships
mother–son relationships
movie critics
movie ratings
multiculturalism
Muslims

the effect of names
names of automobiles
national debt
National Endowment for the Arts
National Enquirer
National parks
NATO
natural law
NCAA rules on recruiting
new morality
1984
Nintendo
Noah's Ark
No-Doz
no-fault divorce
no-fault insurance
noise pollution
non–English-speaking Americans
no pass–no play
Nostradamus
National Rifle Association
nuclear power plants
nuclear waste
nudist colonies
numerology

off-track betting
oil prices
oil spills
older women having babies
one-night stands
one-parent families
"Onward, Christian Soldiers"
opera

Operation Iraqi Freedom
Oprah
organ transplants
overachievers
overweight people
ozone depletion

PACs
palm reading
Papal Infallibility
paparazzi
paranoia
parity products
paroles and pardons
patriotism today
People for the American Way
perpetual motion
personal ads
PG-13 movies
phobias
teaching phonics
memorizing pi to 100 places
pit bulls
the placebo effect
plagiarism
Playboy
Playstation III
Pledge of Allegiance
PLO
PMS
Polish jokes
politically correct language
polling systems
pollution levels
poltergeists
polyunsaturates
Pope Benedict XVI
population growth
pornography
pornography on Internet
postal rates

Powerball
prayer in public schools
prenuptial financial agreements
preservation of historic buildings
prisoners' rights
prison systems
private clubs
private schools
modern prophets
prostitution as a victimless crime
Prozac
psychoanalysis
psychokinesis
psychometry
public smoking laws
the public's right to know
public television
Purgatory

quack doctors
quasars
quinoa
admissions quotas
job quotas
medical school quotas

race and capital punishment
racial superiority
racism on campus
ransoming hostages
rap music
readers vs. nonreaders
reality television
recruiting top athletes
rednecks
redshirting freshmen
reincarnation
replacement workers
required courses
retirement age
Book of Revelation

reverse discrimination
right to bear arms
right to die
right-to-work laws
rights of the accused
rights of the victim
Ritalin
Rolex watches—real and imitation
Roman Catholicism
Pete Rose
RU-486, the abortion pill
running as a religious experience
rural vs. urban living

Sacco–Vanzetti
safe sex
salt as a health threat
same–sex marriages
Santa Claus
Satan worship
Terry Schiavo
Scientology
mandatory seat-belt laws
secular humanism
selling college degrees
sex-change operations
sex education
sexist language
sexist language in the Bible
sexual harassment
sexually explicit textbooks
teaching Shakespeare
Shakespeare's plays
shock treatments
shoplifting
the Shroud of Turin
O. J. Simpson
single-sex schools
666
skyjacking
slander and libel

sleeping pills and tranquilizers
smoking and health
smokers' rights
soap operas
social-science classes
Social Security funding
solar power
South Africa
space programs
special prosecutors
speed limits
speed reading
spelling reform
spelt
Star Wars weaponry
statute of limitations
statutory rape
Stealth bombers
steroid use by athletes
Stonehenge
stress and anxiety
striker replacement
student illiteracy
students' rights
sugar vs. substitutes
teenage suicides
sun tanning
Super Bowl games
Supreme Court decisions
Supreme Court nominees
surrogate mothers

tabloid advertisements
tabloid exposés
a talisman
talk therapies
talking animals
tanning salons
tarot cards
tatooing
tax reform

tax relief for private schools
Zachary Taylor's "poisoning"
teacher strikes
technological pirating
telecommuting
telemarketing
telephone company competition
telephone sales
televangelism
television after midnight
television commercials
television ratings
tenure for teachers
term papers for sale
test-tube babies
Three Mile Island
salvaging the *Titanic*
tithing
the tobacco industry
the top 40
toxic wastes
translating the Bible
Trilateral Commission
Trivial Pursuit
true believers
Donald Trump
Ted Turner

UFOs
unemployment compensation
United Nations effectiveness
Universal Product Code
unlisted phone numbers
U.S. savings bonds
utopias

the V chip
vampires
Vatican II
VCRs
vegetarianism

Velikovsky
Jessie Ventura
veterans' rights
Viagra
Vice President Cheney
victimless crimes
video games
Vietnam War
Virgin Mary apparitions
virginity
virtual reality
vitamin supplements
voter fraud

Wal-Mart
Watergate
weapons of mass destruction
wedding extravaganzas
Weekly World News
weight-lifting for women
welfare for unwed mothers
Western Civilization courses
Vanna White
white-collar crime
Whitewater investigation
woman's role
women candidates
"womyn" in "herstory"
Tiger Woods
worker-protection laws
WWF versus WWO

X-rated movies
X-ray treatments

yoga
Yugoslavian turbulence
yuppies

Zionism
zoning laws

Good Words, Bad Words, and Persuasive Words

GOOD WORDS

In the following list, the word on the left may be correct on a particular occasion. Most of the time, however, the word on the right is clearer, more direct, and less clichéd. Write with everyday words.

achieve	do, make
advise	tell
and/or	and, or
approximately	about
attempt	try
benefit	help
commence	start, begin
conclude	end, stop
contribute	give
deem	think
demonstrate	prove, show
depart	leave
desire	want
dialogue with	talk to
disclose	tell, show
discontinue	stop
due to the fact that	because
e.g.	for example
enumerate	count
exhibit	show
expertise	skill, ability
the fact that	(omit)
failed to	didn't
finalize	complete, finish
for a period of	for
the following	these
Gentlemen:	Dear Mr. Clark:
has the ability to	can
herein	here

i.e.	that is
in addition	besides, too
in order to	to
in regard to	about
in the event that	if
in the near future	soon, Wednesday
invaluable	valuable
it is noted that	(omit)
last but not least	last, finally
the latter	(repeat the noun)
locate	find
the majority	most
the month of	(omit)
my intention is	I will
notify	let me know
not later than	by
not only . . . but also	and
numerous	many, two dozen
observe	see
obtain	get
parameters	limits
perform	do
personnel	people; Molly and Ed
possess	own, have
prepared	ready
prioritize	rank
prior to	before
probability	chance
provided that	if
purchase	buy
regarding	about
relative to	about
remainder	rest
remuneration	pay, payment, $50
request	ask
secondly	second
share with	tell, talk to
similar to	like
state	say
state-of-the-art	latest
submit	give, send

sufficient	enough
terminate	end, stop
therefore	so
this point in time	today, now
touch base with	talk to
transmit	send
truly	(omit)
until such time as	until
utilize	use
very	(omit)
viable	practical, workable
whenever	when
whether or not	whether
with reference to	about
with the exception of	except
the writer	I, me

■ BAD WORDS

These words will weaken any argument. They make writing seem vague, illiterate, clichéd, angry, insensitive, and pretentious. Avoid them.

the above	history teaches us
am of the opinion that	idiotic
and . . . was no exception	ignorant
asinine	in lieu of
bastard	in life
bimonthly	in view of the fact that
cognizant	just doesn't get it
crap	keratectomy
datum	let's face it
Dear Sir:	logistical
down through the ages	mesdames
enclosed please find	mode
falso lectio	Mr./Mrs.
first and foremost	N.B.
goddamn	Negro
his or her	nitty-gritty
his hope was that	per

per se
peruse
Polack
quintessential
Sear's
shall
societal
some people
stated
syndrome
thirdly
To Whom It May Concern
truly
viz.

■ PERSUASIVE WORDS

After you have made your best case, you can enhance it by using some of the favorite words of professional persuaders. These ten may be particularly useful.

Claim—This is a word to apply to your adversary. You *say (insist, prove)* vitamin C cures a cold; he *claims* it does not.

Clearly—You can use this to begin any sentence: "Clearly, John Hinckley was framed."

Colonel—People with titles love to hear them. Use them often. Work *Colonel* (or *Mayor* or *Doctor*) into every fourth sentence.

Fair—This, of course, describes your position. Because it cannot be specifically defined, *fair* (like *positive, realistic, just,* and *reasonable*) is a key word in politics and commerce.

Integrity—Write of "personal integrity," "family integrity," "professional integrity," "instructional integrity," etc. The terms mean pretty much what you want them to mean.

Mature—This sounds like a compliment, but you can use the word to suggest your opponent is old and his ideas are obsolete. Other double-edged words are *young, sensitive, free-spirited, witty, experienced,* and *intellectual.*

Notable—This is an important word when you have to evaluate something and don't want to call it either good or bad. *Notable* (like *meaningful* and *significant*) means almost nothing.

Pro—On every issue, you want to be *pro* rather than *anti*. Call yourself "pro-life" or "pro-choice." Describe your opponent as "anti-baby" or "anti-woman."

Relatively—This is a useful qualifying word. You can talk of "a relatively short time" or a "relatively inexpensive product." This can mean anything.

Superficial—Because your opponent's argument cannot treat every conceivable detail involved in the issue, you can always dismiss it as *superficial*. Another useful adjective is *unrealistic*.

Unfortunate—This is the perfect word when you have to say something negative and don't want to assign blame. You can speak of "an unfortunate decision," "an unfortunate incident," or "an unfortunate choice of words."

These persuasive words won't win an argument for you unless you have your facts, authorities, and statistics in order. But they can help.

Writing a Business Letter

Probably the main form in which you will write persuasive prose is the business letter. You'll want to convince someone you deserve a job or a raise. You'll want to make a sale or get a larger insurance adjustment. You'll want to pacify someone who has written an angry letter to you.

Business letters take a fairly standard form.

Read the two letters on the following pages. Both are effective examples of business writing.

Now consider the seven parts of a business letter as illustrated in these examples.

■ THE RETURN ADDRESS

Notice that this is omitted if you write on letterhead stationery. Always use the two-letter U.S. Postal Service abbreviations to indicate the state. (See pages 334–335.) And always include the ZIP Code, in its five- or nine-digit form.

▤ THE DATE

Either of the two forms shown is acceptable. Just be consistent.

■ INSIDE ADDRESS

If your letter is at all important, send it to someone by name.

On pedestrian matters, you can address the "Subscription Office" or "Catalog Department," but never address anyone simply as "Personnel Manager," "Chairman," "Publisher," or "President." If you use your library and your telephone, you can get the name of the person you want to write to.

If you raise the question, you will probably find that friends of yours (either through their jobs or their relatives) have access to a WATS line. This can be immensely useful when you have to write to the personnel manager at Philip Morris, or to Mr./Ms. Leslie Rogers.

◼ THE SALUTATION

Write "Dear Mr. [or *Mrs.* or *Miss* or *Ms.*] Name." This is always followed by a colon. Writing to a friend, you can use "Dear Bill" but this too must be followed by a colon.

Try never to write "Dear Sir," "Dear Madam," "Dear Sir or Madam," or "Gentlemen." These forms, which prevailed some years ago, now seem offensively vague and sexist. If you don't have a name to write to, address a title. You can get by with "Dear Editor" or "Dear Manager." You might try "Dear Red Cross Representative." But it's always best to take the extra time and find a name.

◼ THE BODY OF THE LETTER

Usually a letter has at least three paragraphs, with the first acting as introduction and the last as conclusion.

The first paragraph should be short and should define the issue. Your reader should never have to move into the second paragraph to know what your letter is about. If you are answering someone, it is a good idea to begin, "Thank you for your letter of July 17." Giving the date lets the reader check the appropriate file and refer to the original message. Saying "thank you" sets a positive tone.

Through the body of your letter, use the forms that mark good writing anywhere. Use short sentences, plain words, active voice, and specific detail. Sound like yourself talking. At all costs, avoid "letterese," the clichés of business writing:

am cognizant of
are in receipt of
as per your request
at your earliest convenience
do not hesitate to
enclosed herewith
thanking you in advance
under separate cover
with reference to

Work particularly hard to avoid the words "advise," "acknowledge," "per," and "transmit." They are deadly.

Keep your language plain. Remember, you're not answering a letter. You're answering a person.

862 Callaway Drive
Medford, WI 54101
15 December 2006

Mr. George Blazdon, President
Silver Shadow Pen Company
1515 Vermont Street
New York, NY 10009

Dear Mr. Blazdon:

Last year I was given one of your Silver Shadow pens (Model 364A) for an anniversary present. I love its looks, but I'm having trouble with it. I wonder if you can help me.

After a few months, the point no longer came out when I twisted the pen. I had kept all the original papers and followed the warranty instructions. I sent the pen to your Atlanta office, and they fixed it and returned it.

At the same time, because I can't seem to find refills locally, I sent for half a dozen red-ink refills. You sent them, along with a bill for $18. This seemed pretty steep to me, but I had no choice if I wanted to use the pen, so I paid it.

Now the pen is broken again. When I twist it, the point doesn't come up. I phoned your Atlanta office to see if the pen was under warranty. They said it wasn't, but that they'd be able to fix it for $10.75.

I'm not sure I should have to pay this amount. Either the pen was defective in the first place or repaired poorly in the second place. Should I have to pay for your mistakes?

I'm not a consumer-crank, Mr. Blazdon, but I don't think this situation is fair. What do you advise me to do?

Sincerely,

Thomas Ridgeway

Thomas Ridgeway

SILVER SHADOW PEN COMPANY

1515 Vermont Street
New York, NY 10009

December 21, 2006

Mr. Thomas Ridgeway
862 Callaway Drive
Medford, WI 54101

Dear Mr. Ridgeway:

Thank you for your letter of December 15. I'm pleased you like our Silver Shadow pen, and I'm sorry it's giving you trouble. I hope this information helps you.

Your pen is indeed out of warranty. You have used it for over a year. I'm sure you understand that we cannot offer a lifetime guarantee with our products.

You can purchase refills for your pen at Redman's Office Supplies in Medford or at Quality Stationery Company (3201 West Lane) when you drive into Milwaukee. The refills do cost $3 each, but these are jumbo-cartridges containing 2 1/2 times as much ink as usual ballpoint refills.

May I offer a compromise, Mr. Ridgeway? You don't want to be without your Silver Shadow pen, and we can't afford dissatisfied customers. I suggest you have the pen repaired in Atlanta and pay the $10.75. Thereafter, if the same problem recurs, send it to me and it will be repaired free of charge.

I hope you have a pleasant holiday.

Sincerely,

George Blazdon
President

GB:itm

It is often effective to repeat the name of the person you're writing to. ("I am genuinely sorry, Mr. Metcalf, but there is no possibility we can give you a loan at this time.") Save this for an important sentence.

Never express anger in a business letter. You can feel it, but don't write it.

The concluding paragraph should be short, general, affirmative, and personal. Even if your letter expressed criticism and unhappy truths, finish on as positive a note as you can. ("I'm sorry I have to give you this bad news, Bill. But I know you can handle it.") And even if you've been speaking for your company and using "we" throughout your letter, use an "I" in the final paragraph.

THE COMPLIMENTARY CLOSE

A simple "Sincerely" or "Sincerely yours" is best. If you're writing a governor or an archbishop, use "Respectfully."

THE SIGNATURE

Always type your name beneath your signature. And put your title (if you have one) on the line below that.

If someone else types your letter, the typist indicates the fact by putting the author's initials, then his or her own, on the left margin below the signature.

A final word about the overall appearance of your letter. Keep it on one page if at all possible. Center the writing so that the white space around it seems to frame it. Double-space between paragraphs, and begin a new paragraph often. All this will make your letter more inviting to read.

In general, your business letter will be most effective and persuasive if it is short, informed, natural-sounding, and marked by unrelenting good will.

You can learn a good deal from the following example. It was published in the *ABCA Bulletin* under the title "The World's Worst Business Letter: A Candidate."

PROCANE INSURANCE
5111 Lincoln Avenue
Mobile, Al.

Feb. 22nd. '06

Anarda Bonding Co.
1601 Mirrabel St.
Locksley, Ala.

Attn: Mrs. Sally Hall

RE: Truckstop Ranch
       Mobile, Alab.
       QAP #958-25~8927A

Dear Madam,

Per our telephone conversation this date, please be advised of the fact that we are no longer insurance carrier for the above referenced company. We regret we cannot, pursuant to your request, transmit information in regard to the record of said account in the area of fire-protection viability. Enclosed please find documentation in reference to the referenced account. Be advised that during the month of January and subsequently, the above company and/or its personnel did not honor our requests to forward data describing interface between manpower and fire-protection hardware capability. Again, permit me to remind you that insurance was carried on the subject company only for the period from June 1973 to December 1982. Transition data relative to specific transactions prior to termination date are indeed available. In the event that you can utilize aforementioned documentation (in lieu of requested information), do not hesitate to contact me at your earliest convenience or at any point in time thereafter. Feel free to direct your request to the writer (at the above address), and we shall transmit required data by return mail.

Thanking you in advance, I remain

Very cordially yours,

J.D.R.McMann, Jr.

Thomas D. R. McMann, Jr.
B.S.C.

TDRMc/MH/jp

Making a Speech

Another form in which you may have to make an argument is the platform speech. You may have to make a case to a civic club, a church organization, a union group, or a town meeting. You may want to sell some product or service or idea. You're going to have to stand before an audience and talk.

It is not difficult to make an effective speech if you're willing to give the necessary time to the job.

■ PREPARING THE SPEECH

Most of the suggestions about good writing also apply to effective speaking.

In preparing your speech, you need to choose a subject that lends itself to detail, get specific facts, narrow the topic, organize the material, and express it in an everyday talking voice. But a speech is different from a written essay in several ways.

Here are rules to remember:

1. *Make Your Organization Clear.* Because your audience has no paragraphs to look at, you have to be more specific in announcing the outline of your talk. You might say, "I have three reasons for opposing the construction of a nuclear power station in Arneson," then follow this with markers "first," "second," "third," and "in conclusion." (This would be mechanically offensive in an essay, but it helps a speech.) You can get the same effect with a time reference ("Every day last week, I thought of a new reason to vote for the school tax") or with an extended metaphor ("If the Patman Bill was a used car, you wouldn't buy it"). Your audience should always have a general idea of how far along your speech is and where it's going.

2. *Make Your Introduction Short and Provocative.* Don't dawdle around. Greet the audience. ("Good morning, ladies and gentlemen.") Add a note or two of personal goodwill. ("I'm pleased to be here with you today.") Announce your subject. ("I want to talk to you about our new turbines.") And make it interesting. ("They're giving us strange problems, and they're costing us money.") Then get on with your talk.

   In platform speaking, you have about 30 seconds in which to "catch" your audience. If you don't win them then, you probably won't do it at all.

If you begin saying "In 1895, the Senate of the United States . . . " or "Young people today . . . " you've said all anybody is going to listen to.

Don't begin your speech with a joke unless it is particularly related to your topic. The isolated opening joke is now a cliché. It suggests the speaker has a frivolous attitude toward the audience and the subject. You can, of course, offer any amount of relevant humor as your speech moves on. But don't begin, "Being here today reminds me of the story of the monkey and the artichoke." Spare your audience that.

3. *Refer to the Audience and the Local Scene.* Don't talk *to* an audience, talk *with* an audience.

Address them as "ladies and gentlemen" or "gentlemen" or "friends" or "you" or "we" (meaning you and them together). Speak to them courteously and directly. ("Please follow this now; this is important.") Refer to people in attendance. ("Tom here can tell you what happened.") Never let your talk become so abstract and objective that it loses this "you and me" note.

Refer to what is going on around you. Mention other features of the occasion: the preceding speaker, the orchestra, the meal, the awards ceremony, a special guest, whatever. Use immediate objects as illustrative props. ("It's like this saltshaker; if you don't shake it, nothing comes out.") Mention things everyone is concerned with at the moment (Christmas shopping, unusual weather, inflation, an upcoming election, the Super Bowl, etc.). These things tie you and your audience together.

4. *Don't Let Your Speech Get Boring.* You know how quickly you lose interest in a sermon on "faith" or a graduation speech on "responsibility." When a book becomes dull, you can skim a few paragraphs and get on to the more compelling material. When a speech gets dull, it just drones on, and you begin counting the bricks in the wall.

In preparing your talk, therefore, it is important to narrow your subject to a richly specific topic. Then talk about real things and use proper names. Say "for instance" and "for example" a lot.

Don't give long lists of names, facts, or statistics. These might be acceptable in an essay, but they're deadly in a speech. Put such material on a chart or a handout sheet; then refer to it.

Always edit your speech to make sure you're not saying the same thing over and over.

Unless you are singularly eloquent, don't let your speech go beyond 20 minutes. And shorter is better.

5. *Keep Your Concluding Remarks Brief.* When you've said what you have to say, quit. Never pad out a speech to fill up some artificial time frame.

Have an upbeat final line. Don't trail away with a dull sentence. ("That's pretty much what I have to say about those turbines.") Make it more dramatic: "We *can* make these turbines work, but it won't be easy. We must begin tomorrow morning."

◼ GETTING READY FOR THE EVENT

Besides preparing an effective speech, you can do other things ahead of time to ensure the success of your talk.

1. *Rehearse.* Practice your speech. Give it over and over. Talk to anyone who will listen to you: your spouse, your brother, your golden retriever, anybody. If you plan to use an opaque projector or flip charts or a pointer, practice with these props. You might even have a dress rehearsal. Invite a few friends over, ply them with food and drink, and make them listen to your speech. Pay attention to their response.

2. *Make Yourself Look Good.* In a speech, everything counts. The audience is looking at you and making judgments. While a writer is happily invisible, a speaker has to be concerned about appearance. A man might want to buy a new suit; certainly he should have a haircut and shoeshine. Speakers should never wear clothes or accessories that draw attention away from their message. For an important occasion, they might want to lose 5 or 10 pounds.

   These things may sound trivial. But they're all part of the total impression you make. They are part of the persuasive process.

3. *Arrange the Setting.* Get to the speaking site half an hour early and look over the scene.

   Make necessary arrangements. Check the lighting. Make sure there is a speaker's stand, and adjust it to the right height. See that the microphone works. Get props and audiovisuals ready. Make sure that you have a blackboard (or a flip chart) if you need one and that there is something to write with. Sometimes you can even arrange the chairs so the audience will sit where you want them.

   None of these things happens by itself. Many speaking problems can be avoided if you check things out ahead of time.

◼ DELIVERING THE SPEECH

Finally, the moment arrives. It's time to stand up and give that talk. This counsel should help you.

1. *Stand Facing the Audience.* If you can avoid it, never give a speech or deliver a report sitting down. And when you stand, don't slouch in an effort to look supercasual.

   Face your listeners. Don't make extended references to a blackboard or flip chart and talk with your back to the audience. When pointing to things on a chart, stand directly beside it so you're still facing the audience. Don't make them listen to your profile.

2. *Control Any Nervousness.* The best way to avoid nervousness is to prepare a first-rate speech and rehearse it a lot. If you're confident you can do a good job, you'll have less reason to be nervous.

   Even if you are uncomfortable, don't mention your nervousness to your audience. Unless you are shaking or falling down, they won't know you're nervous. It doesn't show.

3. *Sound Natural.* Don't be intimidated by a formal term like "platform speaking." You've been talking to people all your life. Speaking in public isn't that much different.

   Always sound like one human being talking to another human being. (Don't use "speech" words like "auspicious," "incumbent," and "threefold.") In a formal speech, you'll want to talk somewhat slower than you usually do and, if you don't have a microphone, you'll have to speak somewhat louder. Nevertheless, keep your tone as conversational as the audience, subject, and occasion will allow. Don't use any models. Don't try to sound like Dan Rather or Bill Clinton or Barbara Walters. Sound like yourself.

   Never sound (or look) like you're reading a document to the audience.

4. *Speak from Notes or from a Full Text.* Once you have written your speech and rehearsed it and rehearsed it, you can decide whether you want to bring the full text to the speaking event or whether you want to rely on outlined notes. Both ways have advantages.

   Never memorize your speech; you could black out in the middle of it. Because you want to look like you're "just talking" with the audience, however, you shouldn't keep looking down to notecards or sheets of paper you're holding in your hand.

   If you are comfortable speaking extemporaneously, simply put an outline of your speech on the speaker's stand and resort to that when necessary. This allows you to sound conversational and to talk more directly at your audience. (You can also put an outline of your talk on a chart and have it up front for the audience to look at. The lines on the chart are, in fact, *your* notes.) Not being tied down to the exact words of a written text, you're free to modify your talk so it meets the responses of the audience.

If you need the security of the full text, you must take care that it's written to sound like natural speech and that it doesn't freeze you so you can't change your lines when necessary.

In general, it is better to speak from notes than from a full text.

5. *Use Whatever Gestures Come Naturally.* As you address your audience, don't simply stand motionless, and don't move in any way that feels artificial to you.

Remember you have many props to occupy your hands. You have the speaker's stand, your pockets, a pointer, chalk, your glasses, and so on. Feel free to use these.

And move your feet if you want to. You can step away from the podium, go over to your flip chart, walk toward your audience, whatever. Move any way that seems natural to you.

Be careful of mannerisms that draw attention away from your message. Don't fiddle with a paper clip or with your hair or tie. Don't click your ballpoint pen. Watch out for those collapsible pointers. Almost invariably speakers begin opening and closing them and look like they're playing an accordian.

If you can relax and get involved with what you're saying, whatever gestures come naturally will be fine.

6. *Use Common Sense.* Sometimes all your preparations aren't enough. Before or during your speech, unexpected things happen. Here you have to make common sense adjustments.

If you are one of a series of speakers and those preceding you have all run overtime, what do you do? If you rise at 5:10 P.M. and have a 15-minute speech to deliver, forget it. Say one or two ingratiating things, then sit down. If you discover your audience is more conservative or more hostile than you expected, skip over material they are likely to find offensive.

If you are in the middle of your speech and find you are taking longer than you should, paraphrase a long section into a sentence or two. If you find you're going to end sooner than you expected, don't pad. Let the talk end.

If you misspeak, correct yourself. ("Excuse me, I should have said *Henry* Kissinger.") Then go on.

Watch your audience. You can tell when they are with you and following your argument. You can also tell when they start to shift around in their chairs and the glaze comes over their eyes. If you feel you're losing them, you may want to insert a quick, stimulating line ("Now get this; this is important." "Anyone who doesn't understand this next point is going to lose money."). You may also need to end your speech as soon as possible. An audience always wakes up when it hears, "In conclusion."

If a water glass tips over or your manuscript falls on the floor during your speech, mention the accident ("I'm sorry about that"), then get back to your talk. Don't panic or giggle or make jokes about the event; that just draws attention away from your subject.

These are just a few of the unexpected things that can happen during a speech. When they happen to you, make the necessary adjustments. Use your common sense.

The best way to give a good speech is to have a good speech. When you stand before your audience, all that time you took researching and writing and rehearsing your talk will pay off handsomely.

The MLA System For Citing Sources

When you're writing longer arguments or working from a number of books and articles, you need a formal system to identify your sources. The method recommended by The Modern Language Association of America (MLA) will serve you well. This is an efficient system. With it, you don't have to repeat information or write footnotes.

It is a two-step process. First, you list alphabetically all the works you used. This goes at the end of your paper in a section called "Works Cited." Then, in the text, when you express an author's idea or quote an author, you use a brief parenthetical insert citing the source and the page. That's all there is to it.

There are two MLA publications which offer these documentation guidelines: *MLA Handbook for Writers of Research Papers* (1995) and *MLA Style Manual and Guide to Scholarly Publishing* (1998). The *MLA Handbook* is probably the more likely choice for undergraduate writers, but because the *MLA Style Manual* includes updated guidelines on citing electronic works, we refer to it for our coverage of documenting electronic sources.

■ CITATIONS

The citations refer the reader to the "Works Cited" list at the end of the paper. This gives bibliographic information about the books and articles you used. (It is written in a prescribed form that will be detailed later.) Part of the list could look like this:

Jackson, Thomas P. "Prisoners Alone." *S.A.G. Newsletter* Aug. 1988: 5–8.

"Knowing It All." Editorial. *Nationality* 28 Mar. 1987: 4–5.

Linder, Chuck. *Ghost of the Past*. New York: Regency, 1979.

———. *Haunted City*. New York: Regency, 1981.

Muster, Thomas, and Albert Meyer. *Where Are They Going?* San Antonio: Richland, 1989.

This list allows readers to check your sources.

In the text, you will refer to the authors you listed. Based on the entries given, the citations might look like this:

Few prisoners are ever reformed by incarceration (Jackson 6).

As Thomas Jackson reminds us, few prisoners are reformed by incarceration (6).

Many school systems in the city are approaching bankruptcy ("Knowing" 4).

Ghosts have been described as "inner-outer counterprojections" (Linder, *Haunted* 51).

[This takes a longer citation because the author has more than one title on the "Works Cited" list.]

The cultural literacy of young Californians has been called "bad and/or absent" (Muster and Meyer 141).

Muster and Meyer have called the cultural literacy of young Californians "bad and/or absent" (141).

These are the main citations you will use. Be sure to follow the forms exactly as they are shown here.

■ **WORKS CITED**

This is the MLA form for entries in "Works Cited." Put the list at the end of your paper, and always start it on a new page. Follow the spacing, punctuation, and abbreviations exactly as they are shown here. The list is typed double-spaced and publishers' names are routinely abbreviated.

Books

The general format for books is this: Author. *Title,* Edition. City of Publication: Publisher, year. Below are the main forms you will use.

A Book by a Single Author

Tuchman, Barbara. *The Zimmerman Telegram.* New York: Macmillan, 1958.

[With a book published before 1900, you can omit the name of the publisher and put a comma rather than a colon after the city.]

Dewey, John. *The Study of Ethics: A Syllabus.* Ann Arbor, 1894.

A Book by Multiple Authors

> Hanna, Michael S., and James W. Gibson. *Public Speaking for Personal Success.* Dubuque: Wm. C. Brown, 1987.

[If there are more than three authors or editors, you have a choice. You can name them all, or you can name just the first and add "et al."]

A Book by a Corporate Author

> American Medical Association. *The American Medical Association Family Medical Guide.* Rev. ed. New York: Random, 1987.

An Anthology

> Lawn, Beverly, ed. *Literature: 150 Masterpieces of Fiction, Poetry, and Drama.* New York: St. Martin's, 1991.

A Work in an Anthology

> Chekhov, Anton. "The Kiss." *Themes in World Literature.* Ed. George P. Elliott, et al. Boston: Houghton, 1975. 334–48.

> Mixon, Janet. "The Admission of Women to the Catholic Priesthood." *Read and Write: A Guide to Effective Composition.* Ed. James F. Dorrill and Charles W. Harwell. San Diego: Harcourt, 1987. 319–21.

An Introduction: Preface, Foreword, or Afterword

> Le Carré, John. Introduction. *The Philby Conspiracy.* By Bruce Page, David Leitch, and Phillip Knightley. Garden City: Doubleday, 1968. 1–16.

Material Reprinted from Another Source

> McCown, J. H. "The Truth About Nicaragua." *Catholic Week* 26 Oct. 1984: 2. Rpt. in *The Language of Argument.* Ed. Daniel McDonald. 5th ed. New York: Harper, 1986. 170–71.

A Multivolume Work

> Churchill, Winston S. *A History of the English-Speaking People.* 4 vols. New York: Dodd, 1956–58.

[or]

Churchill, Winston S. *The Age of Revolution.* New York: Dodd, 1957. Vol. 3 of *History of the English-Speaking People.* 4 vols. 1956–58.

An Edition Other Than the First

Alison, Alexander, et al., eds. *Norton Anthology of Poetry.* 3rd ed. New York: Norton, 1983.

Chaucer, Geoffrey. *The Works of Geoffrey Chaucer.* Ed. F. N. Robinson. 2nd ed. Boston: Houghton, 1957.

A Translation

Borges, Jorge Luis, and Adolfo Bioy Casares. *Chronicles of Bustos Domecq.* Trans. Norman Thomas Giovanni. New York: Dutton, 1976.

A Republished Book

Montagu, Ewen. *The Man Who Never Was.* 1953. New York: Bantam, 1964.

[The book was first published in 1953.]

A Pamphlet

Weigle, Charles F. *A Deck of Cards.* Grand Rapids: Zondervan, 1976.

[Treat a pamphlet as if it were a book.]

Articles

This is the general pattern for articles: Author. "Article Title." *Journal Title* Volume Number (Date): pages. The main forms are shown below.

An Article from a Newspaper

Grandy, Fred. "NEA's Job Is to Battle Mediocrity." *USA Today* 22 June 1990: 10A.

[Notice that between the journal title and the date, there is no punctuation and only one space.]

O'Neil, Cindy. "The Curse of Satan's Corner." *Weekly World News* 21 Jan. 1992: 5.

[Except for May, June, and July, all months are written as three-letter abbreviations.]

An Article from a Periodical

Clemente, Vince. "Meeting Mozart." *Negative Capability* 11.1 (1991): 119–24.

[This refers to volume 11 and issue 1 of the magazine.]

Marion, Robert. "The Mystery of Cassandra." *The Saturday Evening Post* Jan.–Feb. 1991: 26+.

[The "26+" means the article began on page 26 and was continued later in the journal.]

Wilson, Gerald L. "An Analysis of Instructional Strategies for Responding to Illegal Selection Interview Questions." *Bulletin of the Association for Business Communication* Sep. 1991: 31–34.

An Article in a Journal with Continuous Pagination Throughout Volume

Davis, Fred E. "Hi-Fi Audio Pseudoscience." *Skeptical Inquirer* 15.3 (1991): 250–54.

[The article appeared in volume 15, issue 3 of the journal.]

Sheridan, Daniel. "Changing Business as Usual: Reader Response in the Classroom." *College English* 53.7 (1991): 804–14.

A Government Publication

Cong. Rec. 7 Feb. 1973: 3831–51.

An Editorial

"Mayor Halfway." Editorial. *New York Times* 5 Jan. 1992: 12E.

An Anonymous Article

"Compromising on Clean Air." *Time* 12 Mar. 1990: 25.

A Letter to an Editor

Bailey, Susan F. Letter. *Chronicle of Higher Education* 27 Nov. 1991: B4.

Sinclair, Robert. "Schools Have Enough Money." Letter. *Mobile Press* 6 Jan. 1991: 7A.

A Review

Braestrup, Peter. Rev. of *Live from Bahgdad: Gathering News at Ground Zero,* by Robert Wiener. *New York Times Book Review* 5 Jan. 1992: 9.

An Interview

Lansbury, Angela. Interview. *Off-Camera: Conversations with the Making of Prime-Time Television.* By Richard Levinson and William Link. New York: Plume-NAL, 1986. 72–86.

Mitchell, Hilary. Telephone Interview. 12 Mar. 1991.

Material from Reference Works

"Apus." *American Heritage Dictionary of the English Language.* 1969 ed.

"Kansas." *World Almanac and Book of Facts.* 1990 ed.

Pochmann, Henry A. "Washington Irving." *Encyclopaedia Britannica.* 1970 ed.

[With less familiar reference works, give full publishing information.]

Crystal, David. "Language vs. Dialect." *Cambridge Encyclopedia of Language.* Cambridge: Cambridge UP, 1987.

"Matthew B. Brady." *Webster's American Biographies.* Ed. Charles Van Doren and Robert McHenry. Springfield: Merriam, 1975.

Documenting Electronic Sources in MLA Style

The following models demonstrate the guidelines for citing electronic sources according to the 1998 *MLA Style Manual and Guide to Scholarly Publishing.* The MLA recommends these general conventions.

PUBLICATION DATES For sources taken from the Internet, include the date the source was posted to the Internet or last updated or revised; give also the date the source was accessed.

UNIFORM RESOURCE LOCATORS Include a full and accurate URL for any source taken from the Internet (with access-mode identifier–*http, ftp, gopher,* or *telnet*). Enclose URLs in angle brackets (<, >). When a URL continues from one line to the next, break it only after a slash. Do not add a hyphen.

PAGE NUMBERING Include page or paragraph numbers given by the source.

When citing electronic sources, follow the formatting conventions illustrated by the following models:

An Online Scholarly Project or Database

> *The Walt Whitman Hypertext Archive.* Eds. Kenneth M. Price and Ed Folsom. 16 Mar. 1998. College of William and Mary. 3 Apr. 1998 <http://jefferson.village.Virginia.EDU/whitman/>.

1. title of project or database
2. name of the editor of project
3. electronic publication information
4. date of access and URL

A Short Work Within a Scholarly Project

> Whitman, Walt. "Crossing Brooklyn Ferry." *The Walt Whitman Hypertext Archive.* Ed. Kenneth M. price and Ed Folsom. 16 Mar. 1998. College of William and Mary. 3 Apr. 1998 <http://jefferson.village.Virginia.EDU/whitman/works/leaves/1891/text/index.html>.

A Personal or Professional Site

> Winter, Mick. *How to Talk New Age.* 6 Apr. 1998 <http://www.well.com/user/mick/newagept.html>.

An Online Book Published Independently

> Smith, Adam. *The Wealth of Nations.* New York: Methuen, 1904. 3 Mar. 1998 <http://www.mk.net/~dt/Bibliomania/NonFiction/Smith/Wealth/index.html>.

1. author's name
2. title of the work
3. name of the editor, compiler or translator
4. date of access and URL

An Online Book Within a Scholarly Project

> Whitman, Walt. *Leaves of Grass.* Philadelphia: McKay, 1891–2. *The Walt Whitman Hypertext Archive.* Ed. Kenneth M. Price and Ed Folsom. 16 Mar. 1998. College of William and Mary. 3 Apr. 1998 <http://jefferson.village. Virginia. EDU/whitman/works/leaves/1891/text/title.html>.

1. author's name
2. title of the work and print publication information
3. name of the editor, compiler or translator (if relevant)
4. electronic publication information
5. date of access and URL

An Article in a Scholarly Journal

> Jackson, Francis L. "Mexican Freedom: The Ideal of the Indigenous State." *Animus* 2. 3 (1997). 4 Apr. 1998 <http://www.mun.ca/animus/1997vol2/jackson2.htm>.

1. author's name
2. title of the work or material in quotation marks
3. name of periodical
4. volume number, issue number, or other identifying number
5. date of publication
6. page numbers or number of paragraphs, pages or other numbered sections (if any)
7. date of access and URL

An Article in a Newspaper or on a Newswire

Unsigned

> "Drug Czar Wants to Sharpen Drug War." *TopNews* 6 Apr. 1998. <http://news.lycos.com/stories/TopNews/19980406_NEWS-DRUGS.asp>.

Signed

Davis, Robert. "Drug may prevent breast cancer." *USA Today* 6 Apr. 1998. 6 Apr. 1998. <http://www.usatoday.com/news/nds14.htm>.

An Article in a Magazine

Pitta, Julie. "Un-Wired?" *Forbes* 20 Apr. 1998. 6 Apr. 1998 <http://www.forbes.com/Forbes/98/0420/ 6108045a.htm>.

A Review

Beer, Francis A. Rev. of *Evolutionary Paradigms in the Social Science. Special Issue, International Studies Quarterly 40, 3 (Sept. 1996). Journal of Memetics 1* (1997). 4 Jan. 1998 <http://www.cpm.mmu.ac.uk/jom-emit/1997/voll/beer–fa.html>.

An Editorial or Letter to the Editor

"The Net Escape Censorship? Ha!" Editorial. *Wired* 3.09. 1 Apr. 1998 <http:// www.wired.com/wired/3.09/ departments/baker.if. html>.

An Abstract

Maia, Ana Couto. "Prospects for United Nations Peacekeeping: Lessons from the congo Experience." *MAI* 36.2 (1998): 400. Abstract. 6 Apr. 1998 <http://wwwlib.umi.com/ dissertations/fullcit?289845>.

A Periodical Source on CD-ROM, Diskette, or Magnetic Tape

Ellis, Richard. "Whale Killing Begins Anew." *Audubon* [GAUD] 94.6 (1992): 20–22. *General Periodicals Ondisc-Magazine Express.* CD-ROM. UMI-Proquest. 1992.

1. author's name
2. publication information for analogous printed source (title and date)
3. title of database
4. publication medium
5. name of vendor
6. date of electronic publication

A Non-Periodical Source on CD-ROM, Diskette, or Magnetic Tape

> Clements, John. "War of 1812." *Chronology of the United States.* CD-ROM. Dallas: Political Research, Inc. 1997.

1. author's, editor's, compiler's or translator's name (if given)
2. part of work being cited
3. title of the publication
4. name of the editor, compiler, or translator (if relevant)
5. publication medium
6. edition, release, or version
7. place of publication
8. name of publisher
9. date of publication

Electronic Mail

> Mendez, Michael R. "Re: Solar power." E-mail to Edgar V. Atamian. 11 Sept. 1996.

> Armstrong, David J. E-mail to the author. 30 Aug. 1996.

An Online Posting

> For online postings or synchronous communications, try to cite a version stored as a Web file, if one exists, as a courtesy to the reader. Label sources as needed (e.g., *Online posting, Online defense of dissertation,* etc. with neither underlining nor quotation marks). Follow the following models as appropriate.

Listserv

> Kosten, A. "Major update of the WWVL Migration and Ethnic Relations." 7 Apr. 1998. Online posting. ERCOMER News. 7 May 1998 <http://www.ercomer.org/archive/ercomer-news/0002.html>.

Usenet

> Dorsey, Michael. "Environmentalism or Racism." 25 Mar. 1998. Online posting. 1 Apr. 1998 <news:alt.org.sierra-club>.

Synchronous Communication

Mendez, Michael R. Online debate "Solar power versus fossil fuel power." 3 Apr. 1998. CollegeTownMOO. 3 Apr. 1998 <telnet:// next.cs.bvc.edu.7777>

Computer Software

Gamma UniType for Windows 1.5 Vers. 1.1 San Diego: Gamma Productions, Inc., 1997.

These examples will get you through most writing situations. If you need a bibliographic entry that is not shown here, refer to *MLA Handbook for Writers of Research Papers* (1995) or *MLA Style Manual and Guide to Scholarly Publishing* (1998). They are probably in your library or at your local bookstore.

Index